Praise for
BEAUTY AND SADNESS:
MAHLER'S 11 SYMPHONIES

The Amazon No. 1 Bestseller

'A beautiful and important book.'

– Marina Mahler

'A book that sends you back to listen again to music you thought you knew, with fresh insight and understanding.'

– Tim Ashley

'This is an important contribution to the Mahler bibliography ... a perceptive, insightful and thought-provoking book. Mahler devotees will find much in its pages to enhance their understanding of these ever-fascinating works. [Vernon] can bring the music to life through vivid and enthusiastic turns of phrase.'

– MusicWeb International

Praise for
DISTURBING THE UNIVERSE: WAGNER'S MUSIKDRAMA
The Amazon No. 1 Bestseller

'A rattling good read. Vivid, colourful ... A valuable addition to any Wagnerian's library – highly recommended.'

– Paul Carey Jones

'A great and necessary addition to the Wagner literature. Clever and clear without being intellectually boring.'

– Matthew Rose

'A sensational tome. A perfect introduction to Wagner's complex world, but also completely engaging for the lifelong Wagner nut.'

– Kenneth Woods, artistic director, Colorado MahlerFest

'Engaging, wry and topical.'

– The Wagner Journal

ada to zembla
THE NOVELS OF VLADIMIR NABOKOV

ada to zembla
THE NOVELS OF VLADIMIR NABOKOV

david vernon

Endellion Press

Ada to Zembla: The Novels of Vladimir Nabokov
Copyright © 2022 David Vernon

The moral rights of the author have been asserted

All rights reserved. No part of this publication may be reproduced, distributed, or transmitted in any form or by any means, including photocopying, recording, or other electronic or mechanical methods, without the prior written permission of the publisher, except in the case of brief quotations embodied in critical reviews and certain other non-commercial uses permitted by copyright law.

First edition November 2022

Cover and interior layout: miblart.com

ISBN:
978-1-7391361-0-9 (hardcover)
978-1-7391361-1-6 (e-book)

Published by
Endellion Press
Edinburgh
Scotland

To

my wife

E quant' io l'abbia in grado, mentre io vivo convien che nella mia lingua si scerna.

Dante: *L'Inferno*, XV: 86–7

CONTENTS

Introduction: The Conjuror & the Craftsman   13
Exile: The Life of Vladimir Nabokov   25

PART ONE: THE RUSSIAN NOVELS

1. *Mary:* Purgatory & Paradise   51
2. *King, Queen, Knave:* Dogs, Dolls, Dachau   59
3. *The Luzhin Defense:* Fatal Patterns   71
4. *The Eye:* A Hell of Mirrors   81
5. *Glory:* Quixotic Voyages   89
6. *Laughter in the Dark:* Seeing Is Deceiving   97
7. *Despair:* Literature as Ecstasy   105
8. *Invitation to a Beheading:* Negating Negation   113
9. *The Gift:* Pushkin Avenue to Gogol Street   123
10. *The Enchanter:* Pregnant with Death   135

PART TWO: THE ENGLISH NOVELS

11. *The Real Life of Sebastian Knight:* Dead Men & Dead Ends   143
12. *Bend Sinister:* The Embassy of Silence   153

13. *Lolita:* Comedy, Catharsis & Cosmic Crime 165
14. *Pnin:* The Faculty of Pain 187
15. *Pale Fire:* The Poet & the King 201
16. *Ada or Ardor:* Letters from an Ambidextrous Universe 225
17. *Transparent Things:* Proofreading the Past 239
18. *Look at the Harlequins!* Invent Reality! 251
19. *The Original of Laura:* Smirk in Progress 261

BEYOND THE NOVELS: MEMOIR, STORIES & OTHER WORKS

20. *Speak, Memory* 269
21. Short Stories 281
22. Poems, Plays, *Eugene Onegin* 293
23. Letters, Chess, Lepidoptery 303

Further Reading 313
Acknowledgements 323

INTRODUCTION
THE CONJUROR & THE CRAFTSMAN

The controlled explosions of Nabokov's novels enthral, excite, amuse and obsess. They can also frustrate, confuse and shock. His works are playgrounds of perfection and dungeons of despair, workshops of invention and laboratories of cruelty. They can appraise the cosmos with a limitless reach before instantly zooming down through the microscope to scrutinize the most exacting detail (of a character, an object, an event, an emotion).

Nabokov's novels tease and play games, generously inviting us to join in, before sealing the exits, confiscating the rule book, and opening a trapdoor. They flaunt patterns and splendour, only to invert or corrupt the design for the sake of the sport. They assert ambiguity with a certainty of spirit and seductive security, luring us into the magnificent maze, agitating our values, stirring our conscience, the writing mixing intensity with languid relaxation.

Like the work of his compatriot Stravinsky, the colours and surface ironies of Nabokov's output enhance rather than hide the profound dark emotions at work, pain and play combining to mesmerizing and often devastating effect. Master of verbal amusement and textual entertainment, Nabokov chooses subject matter that is about as serious as it can get: sexual abuse, genocide, revolution, totalitarianism, exile, poverty, insanity, adultery, torture, murder and suicide. But, in Nabokov, the art of comedy encircles and ensnares that of tragedy, showing – like in *Ulysses* or *The Winter's Tale* – the decisive triumph of the one over the other.

To read Nabokov is to experience sensual pleasure, ambling in the pastures of his prose (but with a rapidly eclipsing sun on our faces). Then there is cerebral joy, as we nod our appreciation of his well-stocked mind and lively library. We need to find energy, too, for the rigour, malice and complexity of his literary activities: the balance and flexibility of his intellectual gymnastics, the dazzle and coordination of his aesthetic acrobatics, and the precision and reach of his ethical exercises. Nabokov's pyrotechnics in prose ignite his combustible texts, but he is also on hand with bucket and hose lest things get out of control. Firefighter and arsonist, teammate and opponent, player and referee, judge and accused, Nabokov, as a creator should, takes on every role, conjuring up possibility and crafting his art.

The very complication of this virtuosity – its intricacy, its density – has tended to exclude many readers from fully enjoying its wonders. This book seeks to be, then, without oversimplification or trivialization, a sort of starter kit, a stargazer's manual, a map or travel guide to the landscapes, towns and beauty spots Nabokov lays before us. It is written with the hope that tourists will return, even stay and put down roots, visitors becoming inhabitants. Just as we don't usually read travel guides from cover to cover but turn to the page we need, each chapter of this book forms a self-contained essay on one of the novels or other aspects of Nabokov's literary (and non-literary) life. The inclusion of a short biography also allows some features of Nabokov's extraordinary life to contextualize and, to a degree, illuminate his work.

Our world likes to binge and splurge, but it also likes to consume its art and entertainment in bite-sized portions. This book hopes to marry a little of both aspects. Individual chapters on each novel allow readers to digest Nabokov in a more manageable way, while also engaging with all of what he wrote, gorging on the entirety of his output, from the *hors d'oeuvre Mary* to the postprandial liqueur *Laura*.

Each essay does not seek to be comprehensive or all-embracing, though they are wide-ranging and reach far into the ideas and techniques their subjects stimulate. Nabokov's work invites scrutiny in relation to a vast range of disciplines, isms and ologies – painting, cinema, synaesthesia, ethics, metaphysics, entomology, etymology, cryptology, theology, philology, feminism, communism and totalitarianism, to name only a few. In many cases, excellent full-length studies on these topics already exist. All great art tempts and requires continual (re)interpretation, fresh points of intersection in an almost infinite nexus of possibility, and this book can naturally only begin to sift these immense sands.

In addition, this book wants to maintain the strangeness, the ambiguity, of Nabokov's works. Complete elucidation undermines the experience of reading literature, endangering its mystery and wonder. Nabokov is a writer of such depth and intricacy that some explanation is often necessary; yet he is also an artist of immense suggestion, evocation and equivocality, and we need to be cautious about offering either assured clarification or bland supervision.

What should be clear is the remarkable consistency of Nabokov's writing, and this book proclaims the significant brilliance and assurance of each of his works, from the early novels written in émigré Berlin to the last marvels of Montreux. Rarely has a writer been so markedly themselves as soon as they have picked up a pen. Even if they are not all masterpieces (whatever that term really means), every one of Nabokov's novels deserves a place not just in this book but on your bookshelf and inside your head. It is hoped that the reader, in consulting this guidebook, will make new discoveries after initial visits to the landmarks: the famous novels are places of interest for a reason, but they are far from all there is to see.

For Nabokov has an extraordinary dependability. Even his early works have a distinctive style, a particular and peculiar voice, and an impressive structure, as well as a noticeable attachment to his great themes of consciousness, coincidence, memory, pain, perspective, deception, truth, time and loss. Yet, over the course of his career, we observe no dreary rehashing: the quality and variety remain as the themes are revisited, reworked in inimitable new creations, stealthily enhancing both what has gone before and what is still to come.

Midway through his life, in 1940, Nabokov – the principal writer of the post-Revolution émigré communities – switched Europe for America and Russian for English. Fluent since a small boy in the latter, this was the key to his and his family's future, allowing him to lecture on literature as well as pursue a second writing career (in addition to developing and consolidating a more professional interest in lepidoptery, his beloved butterflies). The relentless creation of the staggering pieces of literature that Nabokov composed in his new language –

Lolita, *Pnin*, *Pale Fire*, *Ada* – has, through its appearance of ease, paradoxically tended to undermine some of this achievement. To forge a new literary identity within an entirely new cultural atmosphere, as well as obtain a new readership as an unknown immigrant author of obscure Russian poems, plays and novels, was an immense task.

The scandalous success of *Lolita* (1955) obviously helped: it provided not merely financial security and possibility – the chance to resign from teaching and return to a now peaceful Europe – but fuelled curiosity from the book-buying public into his previous literary life. Translations followed, and Nabokov's bibliography began to expand from both ends: new English works were created, while the old Russian ones appeared in English for the first time.

At the centre of this risky but ultimately triumphant switch, Nabokov wrote his autobiography, *Speak, Memory* (1951; revised 1966). Mainly concerned with his idyllic Russian upbringing but also touching on the thrills and privations of his émigré life, it is a meticulous masterpiece of the genre and as much a work of art as any of his novels or stories. Nabokov's massive (and tremendously entertaining) four-volume annotated edition (1964) of his homeland's most celebrated poem – Pushkin's seminal, foundational *Eugene Onegin* (1833) – also helped confirm the importance of Russian reinspections during this later period of his life.

This threefold process of literary rebirth, rediscovery and self-examination re-liberated Nabokov to conceive even more versions of his self, which he poured into his brilliant later work (*Transparent Things*, *Look at the Harlequins!* and the unfinished *Original of Laura*), with their remarkable sardonic considerations of personality and biography. More comprehensively, translating his Russian works into English freed Nabokov to regulate his own legacy and balance the two halves of his career.

By revisiting both his own life and his earlier novels, Nabokov ensured an evenness and validity to his entire work: a consistent body of literary achievement, now in a uniform language, but full of enough subjects, references, jokes, shifts, hints and games that meant the Russian side to his life was not only not forgotten, but indispensable to a complete and proper understanding of his literary world. He had accomplished the impossible: he had united, not merely connected, the torn fragments of his life, sewing them together, if not seamlessly, then more exquisitely than any purer fabric. Indeed, these splits and tears in Nabokov's life helped forge his themes and designs: his quest for symmetry, precision and parody; his understanding of fractured identity and wretched loss.

This book will address and explore some of the most persistent Nabokovian motifs – in particular exile, patterns, and the 'otherworld'. The last of these is an imperfect translation of the Russian *potustoronnost*, the quality associated with the 'beyond', with the transcendent, uncertain border between life and death, existence and non-existence. The textures, plots and meanings of Nabokov's work are immersed in this idea, yielding an optimism which bonds love and lucidity while offering understanding, reconciliation and possibility. He takes our experience of living in a complex, often frightening world without answers and fashions responses to this predicament.

Nabokov tended to reject traditional religion, especially its institutional aspects (and even the more accessible sacred imagery and poetics) to investigate space, time and eschatological questions in his own way, his hopes not clouded or burdened by conventional spiritual teachings or the bogus promises of salvation heralded by those claiming to be God's representatives on earth. Yet scholarship's inclination to exaggerate Nabokov's disinterest in religion has often obscured or excluded important theological readings of his works, as well as crucial spiritual and philosophical concerns, which are linked to both his patterns and his principles.

In Nabokov, metaphysics is inseparable from ethics and aesthetics; indeed, as these essays show, these form a specific continuum of Nabokovian principles rather than three distinct categories, each mutually illuminating the others. This makes the aesthetic designs of his art (which have generally been seen as his defining trait) inescapably bound to his moral challenges and ambiguities as well as his otherworldly gestures and intuitions.

We see this in Nabokov's plots and wider structures, as well as in detailed motifs he employs, such as recurring objects and entities: the flowers of *The Real Life of Sebastian Knight* (1941), the puddles in *Bend Sinister* (1947), and the squirrels of *Pnin* (1957). (The former two we will leave readers to discover for themselves; the latter, we will find, populate *Pnin* as sly rodent envoys from a possible hereafter and as subtle moral indicators.) Nabokov's patterns embody, mirror and inform the hope for (rather than belief in) some form of transcendent, timeless, non-material existence – not one associated with a god or celestial figure, but rather a realm of being.

Patterns are beautiful, ordered, regular, predictable, but they also invite misgiving and scepticism. Is there something sinister in their perfection? Does their symmetry conceal something? Their very flawlessness invites chaos via its own destruction. Uniformity can turn monotonous, hypnotic, disturbing. Nabokov's patterns – his signature structures, devices, characters, perspectives, alliteration, rhythm and syntax – encourage these qualms and questions, forcing us to interrogate and negotiate his meanings and the complex ethics involved.

This synthesis of concerns exists even (and especially) at the level of punctuation: Nabokov is, notoriously, the master of parentheses, a literary tool which patterns and plagues his texts. Each pair contains a confined explosion, linguistic and moral energy held in a trap of power and precision. Take the most famous: *Lolita*'s '(picnic, lightning)', which Humbert uses to laconically inform the reader of the manner of his mother's death. On only the novel's second page (not including John Ray Jr's crucial, hilarious false foreword), the rhythm, sonic mirroring, spectacular casualness and striking unconcern are together performing a range of interlocked ethical, aesthetic and metaphysical duties. They warn us to Humbert's linguistic power and moral laxity, as well as to the way the dead can regain, if not their life, then their legitimacy, their integrity, their ultimate victory over their callous narrator (something Lolita herself will eventually claim by the novel's close).

Nabokov's parentheses form patterns across his work, their strength and economy a pure and distilled form of his comic but deadly serious art: '(picnic, lightning)' is almost a perfect concentration of *Lolita*'s verbal exuberance and moral complexity in hyper-intense form. Parentheses are his style, sophistication, tomfoolery, difficulty and dexterity – as well as his ethical veracity – at its most refined.

For all the superb fun of Nabokov's use of language and patterns, they are no mere superficial stunt: they are there to enrich the gravity and scope of his art. They are the conscious means to both enter and escape the vortex of his exquisite ethical tornadoes. Correspondingly, across Nabokov's work, characters themselves often have an inkling of their own fictional existence, a textual self-consciousness that can guarantee their sanity (as well as take it away). Their self-awareness is no mere game either (though it is often a delight), but is an integral part of Nabokov's moral and otherworldly patterns, as the author invites his characters to transcend the bonds of their fictive prisons.

Exile is a crucial theme in Nabokov, and not merely the forced or voluntary separation from one's homeland, even if this is a persistent feature of his work, one understandable from a writer compelled to move on again and again in his life. Rather, exiles of all kinds proliferate. Characters within his tales, even parts of the novels themselves, are alienated from each other, isolated or divided. Identities and texts are split and expelled, displaced and destroyed, coerced into psychological camps, their right of return unclear. Nabokov's muster of psychological and textual refugees seek shelter and representation in imagined jurisdictions of sanctuary. To enter these havens, some employ not so much false passports or forged visas as entirely illusory personalities, ones known not even to themselves but only to their creator, who is both the chuckling, cynical immigration officer and the benevolent embrace of the charitable committee.

Unlike Nabokov, or his heroes and heroines, we might not ourselves have suffered the adversity of political oppression or a perilously fragmented identity. But all of us experience anguish, anger, confusion, loss and loneliness, and Nabokov is there, in the tone and texture of his art: to explore, to empathize and to understand. Grief and isolation skulk and linger – dangerous, destructive – simultaneously eroding and enhancing confidence, waiting to terrorize, bewitch and bewilder. His works show how these states can persecute and manipulate us, playing mind games, deforming normality, blurring frames or perimeters.

Yet if boundaries in Nabokov – psychological, cultural, geographic, linguistic – are often zones of anxiety and trepidation, they are also precincts for anticipation and opportunity, to be traversed with amusement, even indulgence. We have seen the quiet optimism of the otherworld theme, but Nabokov also suffuses through his creations infinite intersections with past – and future – textual collaborators. Much of his art is an art of parody, automatically making him highly intertextual, dialoguing with other authors and their work. Though this is often to mock (Dostoevsky is a habitual target of Nabokov's rapier wit), it is more frequently to rejoice in the pleasure of connection and the charm of discovery, as well as the elucidation of meaning such interactions can promote.

Pushkin and Shakespeare, for Nabokov the respective forefathers of the two languages in which he wrote, permeate his texts. Sometimes they do so quite straightforwardly: Hermann's dark Pushkin perversions in *Despair* (1934) are overt, as this pathological narcissist seeks to flaunt his familiarity with the Russian poet. Significant parts of *The Gift* (1938) directly engage with and develop Pushkin's achievements. Typically, however, these connections are subtler, a little sly, and often combine directness with evasion, such as the way Kinbote both observes and overlooks the networks of Shakespeare's *Timon of Athens* in *Pale Fire* (1962). Timid or unversed readers need not be put off by such intertextual games.

They are part of the stuff and substance of Nabokov's writing, an aspect of its fun, but failing to grasp them (which no one can hope to do all the time) does not hinder enjoyment of the works' pleasures.

These references, taken along with Nabokov's scientist's eye for observation and minutiae, as well as his conjuror's knack for tricks and surprises, are all accomplished aspects of his painstaking attention to detail. At the other extreme, but closely connected with these features, is his craft, the art of his compositional administration, the delight and dexterity of his organization. Here, long-term plot lines meet and join local features, producing his intricacy of patterns and cross-connections amid uncompromising multidimensional labyrinths.

Correspondingly, this book strives to portray all Nabokov's works as a box set of highly individual but interrelated works that tackle similar themes in diverse ways, restless and dynamic, exploring and re-exploring. Because of their incessant (and often very necessary) rereadability, as well as the interconnection between the works themselves, Nabokov's novels and stories are an endless source of intellectual, sensual and emotional activity, taking us to sights, people and places we never imagined.

Yet Nabokov can, too often, seem the sneering, mocking magician, full of portentousness and conceit, so sure in his genius that he can get away with almost anything. Certainly he is mischievous, scandalous, dangerous. But he is also genial, jolly and just. He cares about us both as readers and human beings, attendant travellers in literature and fellow sufferers in life.

Nabokov is like an ideal walking companion. He has excellent stories to tell, is almost absurdly well read and well informed, but he understands, too, how to listen:

he is empathetic, serious, concerned. Occasionally a little crotchety and fastidious – he insists on the best boots and the finest wet-weather gear – he is also tolerant and carefree, methodically planning the day but happy to wander or get slightly lost as part of the fun. In sun or squall he is energetic, scrambling on bluffs and peaks but delighted to slow down and pause, reflect on a bench, admire a view.

From time to time, he'll surprise you with a hidden bar of chocolate or tot of whisky, make you roar with his impression of a mutual friend, or gasp through a conjuring sleight of hand. He is generous, convivial and kind: he knows the best places to eat and sleep ('just a little further, over that hill') and is quite likely to offer to pay for the wine. But he'll have you up at six, for there are butterflies to catch, marvels to behold, on the outrageous adventure of his art.

EXILE
THE LIFE OF VLADIMIR NABOKOV

> ... to sigh for somber Russia,
> where I suffered, where I loved,
> where I buried my heart.
>
> – Pushkin, *Eugene Onegin*
> (trans. Vladimir Nabokov)

Russia

Vladimir Nabokov (1899–1977) was born into an ancient noble family with astounding riches, both material and cultural. His lawyer-statesman father's library contained over five thousand volumes, and not just legal or political texts, but vast sections of Russian, English and French literature, swaths of fiction, verse and drama in the languages that would come to dominate and invigorate his son's existence. When his later life was consumed with the work of writing, teaching and translating, Nabokov would pinpoint the importance of his early life's saturation in his father's well-stocked throng of books. From the great and hallowed Russians Pushkin, Tolstoy and Turgenev to the exotic and dangerous Frenchmen Flaubert, Verlaine and Rimbaud; from Shakespeare and the English Romantic poets to *fin de siècle* science fiction; from American horror to Victorian Gothic; together with picture books on insects and the usual children's crop of the *Arabian Nights*, Jules Verne, Lewis Carroll, Robert Louis Stevenson and Arthur Conan Doyle – the young Nabokov devoured them all. He did so voraciously, sitting on the floor of the library's long wood-panelled room in the family's gigantic Saint Petersburg townhouse or in his bedroom out at the Nabokovs' estate, Vyra – the family's favourite summer home among their many manors.

Vladimir's mother would read him bedtime stories, fairy and folk tales which he would later weave into his own works, assimilating the characters, plots or themes as well as the very experience of reading them (seen especially in *Glory*). Elsewhere, we can see the young Nabokov in a sailor costume, perched on an adoring uncle's knee, a book of butterflies on his lap and a look of stern fascination on his face. His visual imagination would become a vital aspect of his own verbal creativity. Not only the enchanting world of lepidoptery (which later became a part-time professional occupation) but also garish toys and games (especially the duelling black-and-white designs of the chessboard), house decorations and ornaments, his mother's jewels, then paintings excited and fascinated his young mind.

Art would become an enduring fixation. Later, he would train for a time to become a painter, even sharing Marc Chagall's tutor in Paris. Over a hundred paintings inhabit his fiction, dexterously woven into the narratives and displaying a masterly understanding of optical and chromatic techniques. (*Ada*'s themes of imitation and resemblance are frequently conjured by repeated reference to art and artists; Hieronymus Bosch in particular stalks and haunts the novel.) As a child, Nabokov began to see the world around him in colours, images, patterns and particulars, which would illuminate, shade and energize that same world when his prose came to recreate it in art. That Nabokov had synaesthesia – the neurological trait which mixes or merges the senses – from a young age can surprise no one who spends even a short time with his work, for the intermingling of colours, sounds, letters, words and ideas is a constant disturbance and delight in his writing.

His father was an opera fanatic, as his own son would one day be (the latter even taking to the stage professionally), but Nabokov never really tolerated what he perceived as the easy seductive power of music. Perhaps unfairly, but understandably, given the enormousness of his other concerns, Nabokov never seemed to grasp or be interested in the deeper complexities and intellectual potential of music, not least in his own century, though some of his stories and a novel (*The Luzhin Defense*, 1929) would explore some of the wider cultural and artistic aspects of musical talent and technique.

A string of English- and French-speaking governesses, as well as the ease of switching between languages at home (both Nabokov's parents, Vladimir and Elena, were fluent in English and French), meant that Nabokov and his younger siblings spoke these supposedly alien languages as well as, even better than, their own; Russian tutors followed later. This provision of a multilingual milieu was no self-satisfied showing off; it was a perfectly ordinary way for a Russian family of the Nabokovs' class and education to interact at home. More vitally, it opened the young Vladimir's mind to the shifting possibilities and variations of language, the way some had puzzling genders or perplexing characteristics, the way you could pun or parody them against each other. The estates, books and domestic staff might soon be taken away in the Revolution, but language could not be repossessed and would see Nabokov through not only his Russian émigré exile in Berlin and Paris, but America too.

Nabokov's parents indulged and developed their eldest child's talents and interests as well as his emotional and intellectual security, possibly at the expense of the well-being of their other children. At home, the bedtime stories, the toys and games, might be the stuff of most childhoods, and there is a certain normality to Nabokov's upbringing which allows him to communicate with us, especially in *Speak, Memory*, despite the distances of time, space and capital between his background and our own. His father was often away, a busy public figure occasionally in prison for his anti-government activities, but he, like so many doting dads, passed on his own passions to his offspring, as well as his sense of humour and strong capacity for work. The seven-year-old Vladimir inherited the hunting and hoarding of butterflies – and the patient scientific art of their categorization – directly from his father and, as we have seen, it was from his father's library that Nabokov first encountered the literature that would inspire and enrich his own life and work.

At school, an excellent and egalitarian establishment, Vladimir's progress was varied and not exceptional, and it was here he began to encounter some of the pain of the outside world not experienced via his father's bookshelves. His school reports remark on him as a moral child, good at sports, but often working with 'style but no substance' on what the boy perceived as dull subjects, or otherwise 'unnecessarily exhibiting' his multilingual skills in essays or the classroom. And it probably didn't help that he let himself be chauffeur-dispensed to school in one of the family luxury cars. By the end of his school career, during World War I, Nabokov was obsessed with the writing of poetry celebrating Russia, family and love – some of which began to be published in prominent journals, despite the understandably unoriginal clichés of his verse – and was also embarking on a passionate affair, playing truant for trysts. Yet all this adolescent normality was soon to swiftly change, the Revolution entirely dislocating his future life.

Combine Nabokov's childhood/adolescent literary excesses and extravagances with his formidable imagination, loving parents, affectionate uncles, thoughtful governesses, and the general aura of immense material and intellectual affluence, and it is easy to see why his upbringing left such a profound, mysterious and multilayered impression on him. It also clarifies why its immediate and total loss was so devastating, and why it was a province he would both constantly re-explore and flee from in his fiction. It would be easy, too, to mock his precociousness, sneer at the family's spoiling of their children, even nod or laugh at the justice of the eventual confiscation of their properties in the Revolution.

But the young Nabokov did not choose this life for himself; he was born into it, as all of us are into our own particular situations and circumstances. He enjoyed it, revelled in it – which of us wouldn't? – then suffered the desolation of its (perhaps legitimate) seizure almost the moment he became an adult. Whatever the very urgent, appropriate arguments over enormous and inherited wealth, we can be thankful for both the cultured, liberal attitudes of this particular privileged family and the way in which one of their members was able to transform (directly and indirectly) the memory and meaning of its richness and splendour into some of the most beautiful, challenging and poignant literature of the twentieth century.

Moreover, it would be a gross oversimplification to see the Russian Revolution in general, or Nabokov's early life in particular, as simply Reds versus Whites, Bolsheviks against Monarchists. In between were – of course – many political hues, not least the republican-liberal attitude adopted by Nabokov's father, then by Nabokov himself. Neither was the Revolutionary drama of the early part of the Russian, especially Petersburg, century merely a vibrant historical scenery for the young Nabokov's luminous, cloud-free upbringing: it was a theatrical performance played out in his own home and on the streets outside.

Nabokov's work rarely addresses politics frankly or straightforwardly, but across his art, and perhaps most directly in *Invitation to a Beheading* (1936) and *Bend Sinister* (1947), the motivations and repercussions of certain forms of political thinking and behaviour are exposed, discussed and dissected, subtly but with an overwhelming power. Nabokov never campaigned for or candidly committed to the liberal causes his father fought for, though they are artfully present throughout his work, the son's literary ambitions shrewdly continuing those of his politician father.

The 1905 Revolution had ended Nabokov's father's parliamentary career; he committed himself instead to journalism and nascent forms of criminology. The February Revolution of 1917 compelled him to return to politics and assume a place in the provisional government, which lasted only a few months until the Bolshevik coup of October. Fearing for their lives, the family were obliged to escape down to Crimea.

Here Nabokov *père* was eventually made minister of justice in the regional government, with Nabokov *fils* pursuing his obsessions with poetry, love and butterflies until the Red advance south in the spring of 1919 forced them all into complete exile. Under astonishingly dramatic circumstances – their departing boat was strafed by Bolshevik bullets as father and son played chess on deck – the family fled initially to Istanbul, then Athens, and finally London. That curious, dangerous deckside game of chess seems the perfect image for what Nabokov was to achieve from now on, after he had seen Russia for the last time: slightly reckless, perhaps rather mischievous, certainly defiant and brave. Order amid and out of chaos.

Europe (I)

A few months later, in October 1919, the twenty-year-old Nabokov enrolled as a zoology student at Trinity College, Cambridge. His family was based nearby in London, from where his father, fond of the English capital, attempted to coordinate renewed political activity in exile. Internal factional disputes, however, compelled him and the family to move to Berlin, where he edited a liberal émigré paper. Back in the fenland of eastern England, his eldest son, too, made changes, switching his degree from the study of the animal kingdom to modern languages, specifically French and Russian. Nabokov's younger brother Sergey, nine months his junior and studying unhappily at Oxford, also joined Vladimir in Cambridge, though the siblings had never been close.

Nabokov had had a lucky escape. His father had always intended him to attend an Oxbridge university, and here he was doing just that, with only that most middle class of modern scholastic digressions – the gap year – added on. Nabokov's eighteen months of love and butterflies in Crimea was not so wildly different from the contemporary student experience. Neither he nor his father or brother had been killed or conscripted, and for the imaginative, adventurous young man it was perhaps all part of the colourful exuberance of youth. But the amputation of Russia from his life pained him deeply: many of his school friends were dead, as was the upbringing he cherished so much.

Quaint as Cambridge was (and he mostly enjoyed its work and opportunities for sport), the time was darkened by traumas fresh in his mind. He felt isolated by his differences and losses, even if he understood many of his peers had experienced similar or worse ordeals in the war. We see glimpses of this period in *Speak, Memory*, but Nabokov's emotional state at this time is perhaps best captured in *Glory* (1932). His fifth novel, *Glory* follows much of his own early life, particularly that in London and Cambridge, before culminating in a high-spirited, foolhardy and surreal bid for repatriation and a daring return to Russia. Its hero's fantasies seem to represent the feelings of the lonely, displaced young Nabokov, who now dreamed of becoming a Russian writer, thereby forever recapturing and sustaining the stolen land of his childhood.

He was writing more and more, getting poems published and crafting his early stories, even as he prepared to graduate, but fate and history had yet another bleak hand to deal. His university vacations had typically been spent with the family in Germany or undertaking various sportive/lepidoptery pursuits in France or Switzerland (as well as working one summer as a farmhand). He arrived in Berlin, as usual, for the Easter holidays on 18 March 1922. Ten days later his father was 'accidentally' assassinated, killed as he intervened to protect his friend and fellow activist Pavel Milyukov from Monarchist extremists. Nabokov himself answered the family telephone to receive the news, and the gigantic diary entry he made of this, the most tragic day of his long life, is a harrowing document. His father's death dominates *Speak, Memory* as a ruptured wound that never heals, but was nevertheless also a centripetal force that intensified and focused his mind, concentrating his approach to life and art.

For the family, it meant further fragmentation. Nabokov's mother went to live with her daughters and youngest son on a pension in Prague, seeing her favourite child only intermittently until her death in 1939; Sergey went to live in Paris, working as an educationalist and occasional poet until dying in a Nazi concentration camp at the very end of the Second World War, in January 1945. Vladimir, after burying his father in Berlin's Orthodox Cemetery on 1 April, went back to Cambridge to sit his final exams before returning to Berlin in the summer of 1922, where he would live for the next fourteen years, until further turmoil forced him to move on once more.

Nabokov never reconciled himself to either Berlin or the German language, finding both largely tedious, monotonous and depressing – and he had a persistent fear of contaminating the purity of his Russian by speaking the Teutonic tongue (though his German was always better than he maintained). The Berlin years were not helped, either, by unrelenting, grinding poverty, his meagre writing income supplemented by teaching languages or giving boxing and tennis lessons. Despite and perhaps because of this, he formed an important, if occasionally detached, part of the émigré literary world, an enclave within an enclave of the sizeable Russian population (although their numbers began to diminish rapidly after the mid-1920s). Whatever its shortcomings, Berlin helped both shape and inaugurate Nabokov's ultimately glittering literary career, even if he quite reasonably never acknowledged the debt.

This was the Berlin of Brecht and Weill, cinema and spies, cafés and cabaret – of which the émigré community had its own particular variety. Nabokov himself wrote occasional comic sketches for the night haunts, had even joined a clandestine anti-Bolshevik group, and his Russian novels are full of secrets, defections, and riddles and revelations, as well as the glitz and glamour of the silver screen: its possibilities, fantasies and delusions. He also had room for the zany farces of Laurel and Hardy, Charlie Chaplin and the Marx Brothers, all firm favourites he would refashion into his own distinct black parodies on the page, marrying comedy and tragedy, clowning and drowning.

Isolated from his family in this peculiar community of fellow exiles, his life carried on. He continued writing, publishing poems, Russian stories, and translations at a steady rate (issuing them under the pen name 'Sirin' to distinguish himself from his famous father) before launching his career as a novelist with *Mary* in 1926. Indeed, his entire Russian output of nine novels was written or begun in the German capital. Many are set there, and they are perhaps the most striking portrayals of 1920s and '30s émigré Berlin we have: its strangeness, dreariness, defiance and desolate joys; its misfits and eccentrics, loners and lovers.

Nabokov's own romantic life had persisted with the customary post-pubescent fits and starts, even an engagement, before, in May 1923, he met Véra Evseevna Slonim, the highly cultured, patient, intelligent and extraordinary woman who was to become his lover, wife, editor, lifelong companion, and mother to his son, as well as the first (and arguably finest) reader of his books. No one could replace his beloved papa, but Véra – as well as a number of benevolent, helpful figures in the émigré publishing world – ensured he was never alone again.

By the mid-1930s, Germany's initially precarious and then appalling political situation compelled the Nabokovs to flee to Paris, then America. They had lingered longer in Berlin than most émigrés, but Nabokov was finding increasing success and recognition there as a writer, as well as domestic stability and happiness, for all the essential penury of his existence. He also, of course, encountered envy of his accomplishments and a conservative reaction against his literary innovations, both of which he addressed in the book that was to be the triumphant climax of his Russian career: *The Gift* (1938), begun in Berlin but finished in France. By now, however, not only was the environment of this, to Vladimir, unlovable city even more toxic, but Véra (and their boy Dmitri) were Jewish, meaning flight was the only option. (Nabokov's compassionate discussion of Jewish people, history and causes in his work remains a somewhat overlooked aspect of Nabokov studies, including, alas, by this book, though we will see its importance in works like *King, Queen, Knave*, *Bend Sinister* and *Pnin*. Fortunately, much contemporary scholarship is beginning to redress the balance.)

During the last months in Berlin and then from January 1937 in Paris, Nabokov wrote frantic letters seeking author bursaries or else employment at British or American universities: anything to help his family. This was something he would do for the next three years with escalating desperation and need. He continued to write, under appalling conditions in their tiny apartment. Unable to secure a two-room flat in Paris, Nabokov withdrew to the bathroom to write his first novel in English, his fingers numb from the cold and hours of work, on a desk he devised out of a suitcase positioned over the bidet. As he wrote, Hitler was subjugating the continent and his mother lay dying in a by now unreachable Prague. He tried to involve himself in the Parisian cultural scene, receiving support from a fellow writer (the swiftly ageing, near-blind James Joyce) as well as financial aid from compatriot and long-term Sirin fan Sergei Rachmaninov, the Russian composer already exiled in America since the Revolution. But Nabokov could not stay.

In the autumn of 1939, as the war began, he finally received news of a possible academic appointment in America, and the following May, only weeks before the Nazis arrived in Paris, Vladimir, Véra and Dmitri set sail for the United States, the six-year-old boy clutching a stuffed toy rabbit – just visible in his passport photo – which he would keep for his entire life. Nabokov himself had little with him and no guarantee of a job on the other side of the Atlantic. But he had what mattered: a new family, a bag of lecture notes, a novel written in English and ready for publication, and the fermenting, embryonic material for the masterpieces that would make his name known around the world.

America

Given his fluency in the language virtually since he was able to talk, and the galactic linguistic proficiency of his English-language novels, many assumptions and misconceptions have been offered regarding Nabokov's transition to English. Chief among these seems to be that it was somehow either easy or a fascinating experiment he wholeheartedly embraced, a chance for a new audience and fresh challenge. The truth is that further abandoning his Russian identity disturbed him greatly. Not only had he forsaken a flourishing (and, with novels like *Despair* and *The Gift*, truly outstanding) career as a Russian novelist, in which he had captivated a small but very astute reading public, but Russian was both his mother tongue and a finely tuned instrument for his imagination. It was like being asked to throw away his Stradivarius for any old fiddle, trade in his Rolls-Royce for a Toyota. He could play on it, he could drive it to the shops, but it wasn't the beloved piece of wood he had polished and refined to speak, weep, sing and sigh; the cherished old family car, with its memories and secrets, smells and compartments.

Nabokov and his little family arrived in the New World in the late spring of 1940. Vladimir was forty-one, his wife a couple of years younger, their boy six. They were refugees, Nabokov himself for at least the fourth time in his life. Human arrogance and hatred had forced them to fly to the all-inclusive arms of Lady Liberty. But here was no immediate paradise. He quickly established some friendships, including an enduring one with the novelist and critic Edmund Wilson, but he spent most of the next year trying to confirm an academic position before finally, in May 1941, being offered a temporary post teaching comparative literature at Wellesley, a private women's college in Massachusetts.

Yet this was no nirvana either: he was a total alien on an obscure American campus where students were seldom interested despite their animated appearance. Colleagues were generally kind, sympathetic to his status, but he experienced terrible culture shock as both a Russian and a European. America in the 1940s was far more different from Europe than the Americanization of the globe in the second half of the twentieth century might have us believe.

As ever, Nabokov turned adversity into art. As the poverty and alienation of Berlin had helped forge his Russian works, the newness and estrangement of America would help shape some of the richest characters in his English-language novels, especially those in his great trilogy set in academic America: *Lolita* (1955), *Pnin* (1957) and *Pale Fire* (1962). *Lolita*'s haughty monster (and poetic pervert) Humbert Humbert has an English mother and exotic hybrid father; Timofey Pnin, pedantic professor late of tsarist Russia, is proud but pained, lost and eternally confused on campus; *Pale Fire*'s Charles Kinbote, an apparently insane, awkward exiled 'king', is presented in constant and mortifying parallel with the cosy, all-American poet John Shade. Humbert, Pnin and Kinbote make us laugh, but they make us weep more. In an age of easy travel, instant communication, globalization and (relative) peace, we perhaps forget the true horror of exile across vast distances and with no hope of return.

Yet Nabokov triumphed. The originality of his characters, the sheer quality of his prose and his creative imagination unshackled him from the tribulations and restrictions of exile. He embraced his new language and culture in the twenty or so years he spent in America, honing his English to a degree that equalled, even surpassed, the quality of his Russian. He also had the advantage of the outsider. Where familiarity might blunt a native speaker's acuity, Nabokov could flex, exploit and tease with the enormous toy box of the English language, always in complete control of his playthings and curios. He perfected the ornate abnormality that is the stamp of so much of his very particular – charmingly and alarmingly peculiar – language. With age and experience, too, came an even finer aptitude for the art of conceiving, then constructing, a novel or story, perfecting his patterns and the astonishingly intricate architecture of his fictional creations.

By 1943, Nabokov was permitted to teach Russian literature at Wellesley, giving him some of himself back. He was made professor the following year. In 1948, the same position was offered at the prestigious Ivy League Cornell in Ithaca, New York. Many aspects of his university lectures have become famous (the *Metamorphosis* diagrams; the *Ulysses* maps), and a large number of them have been published, offering Nabokov's appetizing observations on, among others, Dostoevsky, Tolstoy, Chekhov, Austen, Dickens, Flaubert, Kafka, Joyce and Proust. At times delectably crotchety, agonizingly pedantic, or just plain rude, Nabokov is a splendidly engaging literary critic. But, for all the fun, he is also immeasurably insightful. He brings his poet and novelist's vision to the great canon of Western literature, opening his students' (and our) imaginations to Stephen's and Bloom's journeys around Dublin or the way moonlight and silence function in *À la recherche du temps perdu*. The published texts are as Nabokov delivered them: no extemporizing larks at the lectern for him. Although their style is not, naturally, of the same quality they might have had had he worked them up into essays, they nevertheless showcase some superb prose and an endlessly fascinated, witty and resourceful mind, discerning of literary construction and design, obsessed with detail, enjoying flair and panache, frowning at falsity. His lectures on European fiction became wildly popular, and he engaged his students of literature in the same way his own fiction absorbs us. The great novels were not to be pondered as bags of ideas or libraries of concepts, but as houses of wonder and forests of enchantment.

From his lectures, as well as the interviews collected in *Strong Opinions*, we can locate a variety of the writer's own literary preferences, some of which we will share; with others we will likely be a little slighted by the haughty Nabokovian snub. Among the more famous names, Shakespeare's 'verbal poetic texture [was] the greatest the world has ever known', though he preferred Beckett's prose (especially the *Trilogy*) to his 'wretched' plays. Cervantes and Hemingway were 'crude' and 'juvenile', while Flaubert, Robbe-Grillet and Sterne were great favourites. D. H. Lawrence, García Lorca, Balzac, Faulkner, Mann, Camus and Sartre were second-, even third-rate; Ezra Pound a 'venerable fraud' and Bertolt Brecht 'a nonentity'. Boris Pasternak was a fine poet but a poor novelist, while John Galsworthy, Maxim Gorky and Theodore Dreiser were a trio of 'formidable mediocrities'. Karl Marx he loathed, Jane Austen he considered 'great', while John Milton was a 'genius'. Lewis Carroll was 'the greatest children's story writer of all time', while Nathaniel Hawthorne, Herman Melville, John Updike and Jorge

Luis Borges were particular favourites: Borges a man of 'infinite talent', Updike 'one of the finest artists of recent years'.[1] For Nabokov, the three finest prose works of the twentieth century were *Ulysses*, *The Metamorphosis* and Bely's *Petersburg*, with the 'first half' of Proust fourth. *Anna Karenina* was the 'supreme masterpiece' of nineteenth-century literature, with *The Death of Ivan Ilyich* a close second.

On campus, Nabokov was known for his flamboyant multicoloured shirts and ties mixed with Old World tweeds. There was also a certain amount of the absent-minded professor in him, though he never approached a version of his own Pnin. He once went to the wrong classroom and began reading his lecture. Eventually realizing his error, he told the bemused assembly of undergraduates: 'You have just seen the Coming Attraction for Literature 325. If you are interested, you may register next fall.'

Nabokov spent nearly two decades teaching in America and was meticulous in planning and delivering his classes, but when *Lolita*'s success in the late 1950s allowed him to stop, he stopped. He continued to pursue and categorize butterflies, the passion having led him in the 1940s to work as a research fellow in zoology, organizing Harvard University's butterfly collection. No mere hobby, this was a serious, taxing and technical scientific pursuit, but one that brought him immense pleasure: Nabokov more than once claimed he often wished he had simply pursued lepidoptery and not the writing of novels. His achievements in the former were considerable and are being increasingly recognized both by lepidopterists and

---

1 Of Melville, Nabokov would like to have 'filmed him at breakfast, feeding a sardine to his cat', while it would have been a joy to film Shakespeare playing the king's ghost in *Hamlet* ...

by the collectors of his fiction. In the 1940s and '50s, lecturing had provided Nabokov with an income and occasion to revisit the old literary classics, some of which he hadn't read since the days sitting on the floor of his father's library. But lepidoptery gave him an intellectual rigour that he felt he could never get from his teaching, as well as the opportunity to discover the wider America, away from the tiresome internal machinations of East Coast academia.

Since arriving in the United States, his own writing had continued, if slightly reduced in volume, given time needed for lecturing and lepidoptery. Along with a short biography of a mighty predecessor, *Nikolai Gogol* (1944), he wrote his two finest English-language stories, 'Signs and Symbols' (1948) and 'The Vane Sisters' (1951), and the first version of his autobiography, *Speak, Memory* (published in America in 1951 as *Conclusive Evidence*). His first and second English-language novels, *The Real Life of Sebastian Knight* (1941) and *Bend Sinister* (1947), had appeared as he taught, attracting modest attention. Both works have been by and large overlooked even by Nabokovians but hold a special place in many readers' hearts. By the 1950s, Nabokov had begun both his mammoth four-volume literal translation of, and commentary on, *Eugene Onegin*, as well as the two novels that made him famous: *Lolita* (1955) and *Pnin* (1957). *Pnin* was first published serially, before *Lolita*, and made Nabokov's name quite well known in literary America, though the ultimately colossal *succès de scandale* of *Lolita* tends to eclipse this.

Lolita was methodically prepared, with a huge amount of research needed for what Nabokov always claimed was the hardest of his novels to write, the subject matter being so alien to him – though he also claimed the book a favourite to create, the demanding cultural legwork marrying well with his gifted imagination. He researched everything from the height and weight of young girls to the fads and fashions of post-war America, studying advertising, pop culture and contemporary teen fiction, as well as the darker elements of sexual perversion and abnormality the novel's hazardous subject demanded. The celebrated motels and other highway accoutrements of the novel were scrutinized in person for fictional utilization as Vladimir and Véra themselves criss-crossed the USA on summer butterfly-hunting trips, their emotional and intellectual harmony as far from Humbert and Lolita's dissonance as it would be possible to get.

By the end of the 1950s, the book which Nabokov had kept literally under lock and key for fear of dismissal or incarceration had made its author both rich and famous – as well as something of a cult personality on the Ithaca campus. As it turned out, however, these linked bonuses that derived from the sensation of *Lolita* – fame and fortune – allowed Nabokov not only to leave his teaching post at Cornell and return to Europe, but to set out on the comprehensive publication of his Russian work in English, closing the circle of his life's immense work. He had grown to love America, after the early period of confusion and isolation, but he longed to see Europe again, even if he knew Russia would never be possible: the Soviet Union he refused to ever set foot in.

Lolita stands as a testimony to the America of the late 1940s and early '50s, the garish, incongruous, ugly and alluring culture that would come to dominate the world in the decades after *Lolita*'s publication, as well as the hopes, dreams, failures, paradises and punishments of a country that continues to fascinate and repel a beguiled planet. For Nabokov, America had not only given him the recognition he rightly felt his due but had turned out to be his true second home, behind only the Russia of his childhood. He had become an American citizen and watched his little boy grow up there – playing sports, dating girls, driving cars. He adored its vast landscapes and friendly, warm-hearted people. He comprehended its dark side too: he had written about it. He knew America contained fools, crooks, degenerates and philistines. But there was no overarching evil of the sort he had encountered in Revolutionary Russia or Nazi Germany.

He took a leave of absence from Cornell, in reality never going back, and set sail for Europe in September 1959, where he was reunited with his surviving siblings. He returned briefly to California the following year to work on a screenplay for *Lolita*, writing a vast draft which the amused director, Stanley Kubrick, largely rejected. Nabokov was still credited with the film, and indeed he was nominated for an Academy Award, competing against *Lawrence of Arabia*, but both lost out to Horton Foote's *To Kill a Mockingbird*. He attended glitzy Hollywood parties – once asking John Wayne what he did for a living – but this wasn't Nabokov's world. He still had work to do.

Europe (II)

By the autumn of 1961, Vladimir and Véra were comfortably installed in their suite of rooms on the sixth floor of the Montreux Palace, a luxury hotel in the grand old style on the shores of Lake Geneva. For Nabokov, now past sixty, it was a return to not just Europe but the wealth and extravagance he had experienced as a child. Swiss hotels, he once remarked, also had excellent postal services – no mere quip in an age before even the fax, never mind email, the internet or videoconferencing. He needed to keep in touch with his publishers, especially in America, for this was not a genteel retirement but a period of intense activity. Tremendously complex new English-language novels – *Pale Fire* (1962) and *Ada* (1969) – were being composed; his gargantuan *Eugene Onegin* (1964) project was finally coming to publication; his early Russian novels were being either supervised into translation or translated by Nabokov himself; lepidoptery work continued, Montreux being ideally situated for extended collecting trips to the Alps, Corsica or Sicily.

His boy Dmitri, now in his late twenties and early thirties, was developing not only his ludicrously diverse talents as a mountaineer, racing driver and opera singer, but also his close working relationship with his father. Never pressured but only delighted, he translated many of his father's works, including the stories and several of the novels, as well as Nabokov's early plays, which had been largely forgotten but are now finding a small readership (if not yet many audiences). Nabokov was immensely proud of his boy's singing and climbing achievements, but working with him on his own writing meant a great deal to him, and his paternal pride can be observed amid the often rebarbative or mischievously misleading forewords he gave to the English translations of his Russian novels.

The grandeur and setting of his hotel allowed him to time-travel, feeling in the staff the domestic retainers of his childhood, as well as experience the wealth of literary talent that had been drawn to the lakes and mountains. And in the Montreux Palace, guests could feel as if they were living in an old photograph. The Swiss allowed Nabokov to be a private citizen as well, partly through their reserved manner but also because of their cosmopolitan composition. The Russian American blended in easily with the international assortment Switzerland has always attracted. Here, too, he found a locus for the final stage of his career as a novelist.

When Neil Armstrong and Buzz Aldrin stepped onto the lunar surface in July 1969, Vladimir and Véra had had a small television set (temporarily) installed for the occasion. Nabokov watched, spellbound by the astronauts' 'gentle little minuet' on the moon, with the ecstasy of a child, astonished. A couple of months before, his largest and perhaps most ambitious novel, *Ada*, had come out, a vast alternate history speculating on and playing with the rich textures of space-time, and *Time* magazine had even placed him on their front cover. Science fiction had never really appealed to him, apart from some H. G. Wells he read as a boy, though one of his final stories ('Lance', 1952) deals with some of the practical and philosophical problems, as well as the romance, of cosmic travel, having been written as the space age was beginning to rocket into global consciousness.

Profound questions of time and space and the potential of any future survival after death, however, were abiding, lifelong concerns, and his late fiction took them on too. His short, devastatingly morose novel *Transparent Things* (1972) is a magnificent essay on the raptures and ruptures of space-time; *Look at the Harlequins!* (1974) a parodic biography but also a study of generational time, variant levels of reality, and the impish ambiguities of being. His last, unfinished, novel, *The Original of Laura* (finally published by a hesitant Dmitri in 2009), shows

Nabokov again preparing to investigate how identity is unravelled and fragmented by the strangeness of what lies beyond death.

By the 1970s, his health was failing, in no small part due to overwork: he had taken on, amid everything else, the French translation of *Ada*. Two significant and intriguing projects, in addition to *Laura*, were to remain unfulfilled: a scientific study of butterflies in art and the compilation of a complete catalogue of European butterflies. He continued to spend summers scaling up crags and skipping across creeks to catch the subjects for these books, but he was also spending more and more time in hospital, writing hardly at all. He died on 2 July 1977 in Lausanne, of bronchial congestion after a fluid build-up in his lungs.

Nabokov's ashes were interred on 8 July in Cimetière de Clarens, under the shadow of a château, and with only his wife and son in attendance: privacy to the end. His tomb, where Véra joined him in 1991, is a vast grey-blue slab of marble and, along with his name and dates, simply says 'ECRIVAIN': writer. It is all that is needed. The last phase of his life had ended with some measure of the opulence and harmony with which it had begun, the intermediate losses, ordeals and pain never forgotten but eventually at least memorialized and partially consecrated through love and art.

PART ONE

THE RUSSIAN NOVELS

1

Mary
PURGATORY & PARADISE

First novels, like first loves, can be memorable, flawless and enduring. They can also be unremarkable, perfunctory and dull. Or simply surpassed by the ones that follow, undertaken later with more experience, caution or wisdom. Nabokov's first novel, *Mary* (*Mašen'ka*, 1926), presents the protagonist's attempt to rediscover his first love, the eponymous Mary, and with her recapture not only a lost love but a remote past, a vanished country and – perhaps – a mythical idea, Mother Russia.

Following his affluent, enchanting, pre-Revolution upbringing in Saint Petersburg and academic studies in Cambridge, in the summer of 1922 Nabokov joined his family in Berlin, the centre of the Russian emigration, where he would stay for fourteen indifferent years (and nine novels) before Hitler and his 'jack-booted baboons' rose to power, compelling Nabokov's apathy to be replaced by abhorrence, and a new series of exiles could begin.

In Berlin, Russian newspapers, journals, bookshops and publishing houses (with their lofty, esoteric names: 'Orion', 'Logos', 'Cosmos') flourished, and for all his determined intellectual autonomy, Nabokov occupied himself with a range of polemical confrontations across a broad spectrum of literary and cultural trends, both local and international, recent and distant. His main concerns, however, were those that would enrapture *Mary*: the freedom of youth; nostalgia for his childhood, adolescence, and homeland; the agony of exile and the feverish possibilities of time and memory.

All Nabokov's Russian novels (along with numerous poems, plays, and short stories) were written during the Berlin years, and as such they confuse bids to contextualize him geographically or culturally, just as his English novels – written in France, America and Switzerland – would confound convenient labels of period, place or peoples. Nabokov's works, like so much modernism from Franz Kafka to James Joyce to T. S. Eliot, muddle and mystify one's sense of belonging: multidimensional visions, identities, concepts are constructed, extended, then collapsed or reconfigured. Like Joyce's, Nabokov's existence was characterized by its transitory, tenuous and often farcical nature. But these constantly shifting perspectives, with their anguishes and annoyances, would feed into the layers of his art, stimulating the ultimate victory of his imagination.

If Nabokov's love for English was erotic and, to some extent, vain, a love affair he could not give up, his affection for the Russian language was fraternal, familial and affectionate – and this feeds into his fiction. The self-contained cosmos of émigré Berlin, and the wider diaspora, is fiercely, durably portrayed by Nabokov in his Russian works: its energies and lethargies, its tragedy and its comedy. Ganin (*Mary*, 1926), Luzhin (*The Luzhin Defense*, 1929), Smurov (*The Eye*, 1930), Martin (*Glory*, 1932) and Fyodor Godunov-Cherdyntsev (*The Gift*, 1938), as well as many others in the short stories, are a diverse gathering of characters populating exiled communities, trying to comprehend their own identities and shifting, uncertain place in the world.

Exiles literal and metaphorical will come to dominate Nabokov's art, for this sense of separation, of not belonging, will shadow all his future English works as well. To mention just three of the most famous: Humbert (*Lolita*, 1955), Pnin (*Pnin*, 1957) and Kinbote (*Pale Fire*, 1962) are all exiled, ejected beings, something that structures not only their novels but their minds, too, in ever-fluctuating degrees of degradation and disintegration. Lolita herself becomes an exile, a wandering and enslaved nomad, within her own country, while John Shade's poem 'Pale Fire' is abducted from its authentic American origins and exiled into Kinbote's fantastical 'distant northern land' of Zembla.

Outsiders, of course, can also have vantage points inaccessible to locals: the spectator sees more of the game. Despite, or possibly because of, his antipathy for Berlin, Nabokov has given us perhaps the most meticulous, vivid and engaging literary picture of the city between the wars. The shabby pensions, bourgeois villas, drab apartments, parks, gardens, cafés, light, skies and streets are richly, radiantly communicated to us. Nabokov's perspective on '20s and '30s Berlin and the wretched burlesque of the Weimar Republic also allowed him to glimpse a future invisible to the natives, as we will see in *King, Queen, Knave* (1928) and *Despair* (1934). Compact, fragile *Mary*, however, is perhaps Nabokov's most perfect balance of the particular and peculiar Russian German context that branded the first decades of his adult life.

Whatever the richness of the literary and intellectual scene in Berlin in the early 1920s, it was not, of course, why most Russian refugees were there. Berlin was merely a cheap big city, relatively accessible from Russia. It afforded a home not only for aristocrats, civil servants and statesmen (like Nabokov's own father, before his assassination in March 1922) but a place to work for scientists, journalists, artists, tailors, taxi drivers, factory hands, film extras (a job *Mary*'s hero himself movingly takes) and any number of casual labourers, waiters, caretakers and doorkeepers. By the middle of the decade, however, many had begun to leave, heading either back to Russia or farther west, to France and beyond. It is at just this point that *Mary* is set.

The novel is straightforward in its basic apparatus. April 1924: we follow a week in the life of several Russian émigrés joined together by luck (or fate) in a dreary Charlottenburg pension, a dwelling-business itself fashioned comically out of personal tragedy and topographically trapped between the noisy railway tracks of the *Stadtbahn* that crossed the city, perhaps emblematically, from east to west.

Appropriately then, *Mary* opens in purgatory, with the protagonist, Ganin, stuck in the boarding house's broken-down elevator, and this lift-based limbo naturally signifies the wider linguistic, cultural and physical perdition which so many Russians found themselves in following the Revolution. And, indeed, Ganin is not alone in the lift: detained in the dark with him is one of his neighbours, loquacious, slightly self-satisfied Alfyorov, who wants to pass the time with a numerical guessing game, something morose, self-absorbed, often inconsiderate Ganin declines, preferring to dwell on his present predicament, as he will throughout the novel, until he is able to free himself from the past and imagine a future.

This first chapter of Nabokov's first novel is already a masterclass of his storytelling art, catching our attention and sneaking important information (whether for the purposes of the plot or broader, symbolic allusions) across to us in the blackness. Personality and mood are almost instantly conveyed. This opening is alert to narrative conventions and the means by which we might disturb them. It is wittily inventive and adroitly economic in its exposition: we travel a long way in that stationary mechanical box, and the deft way in which Nabokov will undermine expectation by the novel's close is already in evidence. It is a subtle, exciting and slightly mysterious beginning: the writer is acutely aware of what his readers (and his characters) can know at any given point in the unfurling tale. He teases us, allowing us to relish the pleasures of patience, deduction and prediction.

Freedom from the elevator does not get Ganin far, however: the pension, Berlin (and, perhaps, corporeal existence itself) remain forms of purgatorial prison from which he cannot escape. The proximity of others is a constant source of irritation and dejection to him: his comfortable upper-class upbringing has been reduced to thin walls and annoying, well-intentioned neighbours of every status and culture. Wanting privacy, he spends most of the week roaming both metropolis and memory, away from gossip, mismatched furniture, singing lodgers, and the perpetual noise, smoke and vibrations of nearby trains and into the liquid infinity of his own past.

Ganin is not immediately likeable: he is sullen and selfish, dreamy in the wrong way – distracted, unable to utilize his rich and precious internal life to illuminate the world around him, potentially then redeeming or even transforming the constant banality he loathes so much. His story corresponds to much of that described in Nabokov's autobiography *Speak, Memory*, but he is not Nabokov (nor is the nebulous narrator, which seems to be a sort of council or committee). His solipsism anticipates the equally restless, frustrated and distrait Martin Edelweiss in *Glory*. And, crucially, like Martin, Ganin is not a writer or intellectual: something is missing from them both, something essential, something they both seem to be reaching for in their respective novels' final pages. Both are burdened by visions and reminiscences that have no outlet, no convenient conduit to channel these furious thoughts into poetry, painting or music. And yet, perhaps, both Martin and Ganin should be considered artists, as the creators and custodians of dreams and memories.

In the week which we spend with him, Ganin constructs a near-perfect recollection of a part of his past, in particular utilizing composite memories of the senses to rebuild, revivify, specific moments of his bygone existence. The smell of a Berlin garage evokes in Ganin's mind an adolescent bicycle, the amorous encounters it allowed him to undertake, their associated sensations and any details concerned he desires to re-experience – an olfactory-psychological hotline Nabokov asserted independently of Proust and his madeleines (*À la recherche du temps perdu* had not yet been published in full). Ganin's procedure is a poetic one, just as much as his mission is. Preserving, selecting, merging, recombining – all are part of the artistic process of memory which Ganin excels at. In *Mary*, Nabokov (and his protagonist) turn memory into an art, and consciousness into a blissful, aesthetic dexterity. But Ganin comes to understand, too, we hope, that if the present is a purgatory, then paradise is to be found not just in the reality of the past but also by a commitment to the future.

The degree to which we might want to read Mary herself (intentionally kept out of most of this essay so as not to blemish for first-time readers the delicacy with which Nabokov engages her) as immaculately symbolic of Mother Russia is restricted, however. The scope of this constraint seems to depend to an extent on how far we want her to instead be a personalized image, from Nabokov or Ganin's pasts, full of the flawed irrationality both of remembrance and relationships – imperfections which then allow her to soar uninhibited in *all* our imaginations as envoy to our own lost loves, lost lives, each irredeemably disturbed by the flux and caprice of time.

In *Mary*, the weird and wonderful world of the Russian émigrés in 1920s Berlin is beautifully, painfully, hilariously drawn, with delightful details (whether ecstatic or repugnant) of rooms, objects, conditions and mannerisms. The physical body and the physical city groan, gasp, screech on every page. But this first novel is a celebration of time, not space (the individual rooms of the pension are identified by affixing torn calendar pages to their doors). *Mary* is full of the tempting, tantalizing taste and texture of the past, delighting in its sensory, sensual seductiveness. It offers us the dread, the stagnation, the revulsion of the present, its unpleasant fixity, while the past floats free.

If *Mary*, understandably, does not fabricate the vertiginous destabilizations to narrative, form and structure that would characterize Nabokov's later work (where such rudiments are spoofed, transmogrified, capsized or simply obliterated), the embryonic novelist is nonetheless creative in finding original and unusual disruptions to the conventional rules of the novel. *Mary*, like our adolescent loves, is often forgotten, eclipsed by the later masterpieces – *The Gift, Pale Fire, Ada* – and it might be easy to dismiss the book as slight, insignificant, a youthful nostalgic indulgence or a lurid hymn to a nonexistent past. Perhaps it is all those things, but we should be wary of saying so. It is Nabokov's tender, throbbing point of departure: a compelling tale, told with great wit, elegance and economy, presenting a gallery of endearing characters, surveying in vibrant prose ideas that will come to dominate his entire oeuvre.

2

King, Queen, Knave
DOGS, DOLLS, DACHAU

GREGORY: Is there any other point to which you would wish to draw my attention?
HOLMES: To the curious incident of the dog in the night-time.
GREGORY: The dog did nothing in the night-time.
HOLMES: That was the curious incident.

There are many dogs in literature. Those that immediately bound to mind might be poor Argos, Odysseus's noble, neglected hound; Dora's cosseted lapdog Jip in *David Copperfield*; Bull's-eye, Bill Sikes's vicious bull terrier from *Oliver Twist*; or dear Crab, the 'sourest-natured dog that lives' in *The Two Gentlemen of Verona*. But perhaps the most famous, especially to twenty-first century readers, following the immense success of Mark Haddon's 2003 novel *The Curious Incident of the Dog in the Night-Time*, is the significantly silent hound in the Sherlock Holmes story 'The Adventure of Silver Blaze' (1892).

In Arthur Conan Doyle's story, the dog's muteness indicates to the great detective that not a stranger but someone it knew well stole the eponymous racehorse around which the story's scenario revolves, allowing him to clear up the case. It is a memorable and original negative plotting: the dog does something which, it transpires, is nothing.

In *King, Queen, Knave* (*Korol', dama, valet*, 1928), the protagonists have an Alsatian dog, Tom, who reappears, with ceaseless, bouncing, annoying energy, apparently meaninglessly throughout the novel – until, that is, his structural and thematic exit. He constantly demands, as dogs do, to play the (rationally pointless) game of fetching his slimy old tennis ball, a staged, monotonous and futile amusement no one wants to join in with. Like the dog of the curious incident, it is the fact that Tom does nothing that is intriguing and draws our attention to him, a 'true inference which invariably suggests others', as Holmes remarks of his own canine curio. It is Tom's partaking in an ostensibly fruitless, unproductive game that stealthily stresses many of this book's concerns with repetition, replication, automation, unthinking behaviour, and an insipid sense of world-weariness – an ennui which begins straightaway in the novel's first two sentences with a surreally bored, contemptuous station clock.

After his intense and romantic debut *Mary* (1926), saturated in the 'human humidity' of the Russian émigré Berlin he knew so well, for his next novel Nabokov preserved the city but changed the cast: the principals are all Germans. In the foreword to the English translation, Nabokov rather defensively insisted – incorrectly – that at the time of writing the original Russian *King, Queen, Knave* he had no German language, friends or books, and that the novel might have easily been set in Romania or Holland, but that his acquaintance with the 'map and weather' of Berlin made his mind up. As we will see, however, not only do the topography and meteorological conditions of the German capital colour and influence the narrative, but certain revisions made to the English version attach the novel to a German setting, German people – and German history.

Like his first, Nabokov's second novel opens in a confined space: not a broken-down elevator this time, but a train compartment. The latter's movement reflects the novel's departure from the former: here, orientation is not to the past, as in *Mary's* wistful, lyrical reminiscences, but to a fleshly, materialistic (seemingly fixed) future. The characters of *King, Queen, Knave* have scant memories and stare, calamitously, only to what is ahead of them, to what they desire.

On the train (proceeding along its dependable, pre-laid, predetermined track) sits nervous Franz Bubendorf, a provincial young man travelling to Berlin after being given employment by an uncle he has never met. This relative – department store owner Kurt Dreyer – and his beautiful, snobbish, philistine wife Martha, are, unbeknownst to Franz, the other two anonymous occupants of the stuffy, claustrophobic booth. The trio furtively watch and ignore each other, not knowing, of course, that they are the king, queen and knave from the title of the novel they inhabit, and are heading inexorably towards Berlin, interaction, duplicity and disaster.

This inaugural chapter on the train radiantly conveys to us the sharply defined personality traits of the three main characters. Fully, almost alarmingly conscious, they are altogether rounded protagonists, transcending their playing-card symbols. Although Nabokov's delineation of them is rich and meticulous, they are nonetheless an unimaginative troika in their inclinations: predominantly crude, perfunctory creatures of whim and kitsch, echoed in the many dummies, puppets and figurines that emblematically populate the novel.

Egocentric businessman Dreyer is undoubtedly the most sophisticated of the three, sharing with his author interests in books, tennis and English, but (unlike Nabokov) using each for cruel, material or manipulative ends, not their inherent joy or diversion. Martha is resolute but shallow, controlling and calculating, keen to blend 'bank and bed' by maintaining her marriage but procuring a lover – as it turns out, from among her husband's own workforce.

Petit bourgeois naive knave Franz, up from the sticks for the first time, is a hostage to physical experience and pleasure, impatient and impulsive with every sort of sensory delight Berlin can offer him: lights, sounds, bodies. But his is no easy awareness. Throughout Nabokov, the senses fail to make sense (as John Ray Jr puns in *Lolita*'s mock foreword): thoughts, feelings, perceptions, sensations (and meanings) confuse, conceal, interrogate and distort, only occasionally illuminating and elucidating.

Significantly, on his first day in town, a Sunday, the jack in the pack accidently steps on his glasses, rendering him partially blind until the shops open on Monday morning – eliciting an empathetic response from Nabokov on the plight of the impecunious: 'Complicated but familiar poverty (that cannot afford spare sets of expensive articles) now resulted in primitive panic.' He is disoriented, bewildered and in considerable discomfort, and bland Franz, lacking imagination, does not appreciate how delightful his temporarily befallen world is. Rowdy, disobedient, fertile, liberated from its customary 'official compartments and cells', this transitory sphere is engulfed in streaming radiance. Outlines did not exist, colours had no substance. Like a woman's wispy dress that has slipped off its hanger, the city shimmered and fell in fantastic folds, not held up by anything, a discarnate iridescence limply suspended in the azure autumnal air.

It is on this day – unseeing – that he falls for Martha, during their Sunday lunchtime tête-à-tête in the Dreyers' 'small but expensive garden', a genuine adoration that is quickly replaced by lust when he can see again (just as his fidgety loins itched in erotic fantasy after observing her as a stranger on the train).

On its bright, brutish material surface, *King, Queen, Knave* consciously toys with the worn-out, trivial 'novel of adultery' – its intrigues, its debaucheries, its liberties, its limitations – but infuses it with a subtle terror, situating and originating the banality of evil amid bourgeois playthings (dogs, balls, dolls, lovers) and contemporary mechanisms (employment, commerce, enterprise, accommodation). These categories, however, will become mixed, interchangeable: sexual fun becomes a chore, an enslavement, a mechanized form of labour; work a source of creativity, expansion and amusement. Robots organic and inorganic are created and destroyed, invented and withdrawn, in a novel that sees characters apparently determined to behave only as physical, spiritless creatures, full of greed and nasty little habits.

King, Queen, Knave is not satisfied with merely parodying (or possibly reinterpreting) its literary genre or poking playful fun at characters as potentially thin as the playing cards superficially representing them. The novel's title may suggest a conventional love triangle, and indeed this is essentially what we get. But Nabokov has a mischievous, and sometimes downright malicious, tone of haughty disdain for his characters – something he will go on to richly develop in later works. This derision is not just an assault but a protection, a resistance, too: it permits an objectivity that can allow us to paradoxically care for persons that might otherwise be unworthy of our kindly considerations.

It can also create a space for teasing pleasures between writer and reader: characters partake of indecorous competition with the novelist regarding plot and fate; the author himself cameos as a character or two; characters themselves then become paranoid, suspicious of an authorial presence in 'their' world. As readers we can enjoy the mischief and the dizziness this brings us; yet we can relish these tricks (and their consequent meanings regarding metaphor, metafiction and metaphysics) only if we have the confidence and insight to know a game is being played. They are serious jokes, but jokes nonetheless, and we shouldn't feel insecure that we – along with the novel's characters – are the target of the pranks and gags too. Nabokov is a 'clever' writer, ingenious and cunning, dexterous and flippant, and we should entrust ourselves to his assurances, as well as his sports and secrets.

The English translation of *King, Queen, Knave* came about forty years after its initial Russian version, in 1968. Nabokov used this opportunity not just to change the language but to sneakily update or recontextualize his work, both in the sense of the German/world history that had occurred in the interim and regarding his own development and maturity as an inventor of fictional universes. Thus, we somewhat lose the place of *King, Queen, Knave* within the Russian literary tradition and context – heir to Pushkin, Gogol and Andrei Bely, as well as Dostoevsky, whatever Nabokov's reservations about him – and refind the work with added puns, wordplay, ethereality, and self-conscious metafictional insinuations that would come to define so much of Nabokov's later writing.

Translation always implies loss, as well as a degree of cruelty, and if the rich Russian subtexts and dialogues of the original *King, Queen, Knave* (Dostoevsky rescored in the manner of Gogol) are at worst eliminated and at best downplayed by the complex, giddy games of the later English Nabokov, it does allow for more unity of style and theme across his output, not least in auto-references. At the Baltic resort where king, queen and knave vacation in the novel's final chapters, a certain character named Porokhovshchikov in the Russian original (alluding both to a character in Dostoevsky's *Crime and Punishment* and to Pushkin's short story 'The Coffin Maker') becomes Blavdak Vinomori (complete with wife and butterfly net) in the English translation – an authorial anagram perhaps without the weirdness and wit of *Lolita*'s Vivian Darkbloom, but one that does create some fascinating questions concerning fictional control, as well as the evolution and obliteration of artifice and trickery.

King, Queen, Knave also features another, earlier, and more Hitchcockian Nabokov walk-on part in the 'fellow-skier and teacher of English' who photographs self-satisfied Dreyer on the slopes of his alpine holiday midway through the book. He is suspiciously named Vivian Badlook, and we feel we know what's up here and immediately run through the letters trying to make up 'Vladimir Nabokov', only to discover we're missing an 'm' and an 'r' – which are then instantly gifted to us by the inclusion in the text of the abbreviated honorific, 'Mr'.

Nabokov was captivated by new ways of understanding word and image, and this fascinating section of the novel also allows us to see some of the cinematic techniques, motifs and ideas Nabokov explores and utilizes in *King, Queen, Knave* and across his fiction. His first hero, Ganin (*Mary*, 1926), works as a movie extra. The heroines of *Laughter in the Dark* (1932) and *Lolita* (1955) are both frustrated in their aspirations to silver screen celebrity. The eponymous Ada will obtain some modest movie success in her novel (1969), though with devastating consequences. The English version of *King, Queen, Knave* inserts a series of references to a cinema being built near Franz's apartment, something with important implications for the novel's own construction, progress and final interplay between fiction and reality.

Like James Joyce (who, indeed, opened – with moderate success – Dublin's first cinema) and other modernists, Nabokov was fascinated by the possibilities of film for narrative: *King, Queen, Knave* (1928/68), like its revolutionary predecessor *Ulysses* (1922), makes use of a range of filmic methods: cutaways, montage, multiple viewpoints, aerial shots, flashbacks, close-ups, cross-cutting, dissolving, tracking, zooming, as well as a clear blurring of the distinction between inner and outer reality, conscious and unconscious.

In *King, Queen, Knave*, Martha, given unexpected space to continue her affair with Franz at leisure, receives a holiday snapshot in the post from her husband, and we peer over her shoulder to look at it: there he is, complacent 'smiling Dreyer, in a Scandinavian ski suit'. We also see in the picture 'the photographer's [Nabokov's!] narrow-shouldered shadow', and immediately the narrative jump-cuts to the snowy scene itself, and suddenly we're on vacation with the king and learn what he's been up to.

Nabokov is enlarging his literary resources: the conventional control of his fiction is being expanded, advanced, cross-bred with other art forms. Characters, events and realities are intruded upon, overturned, reversed or simply viewed from elsewhere. Certainties, demeanours, orientations are shifted, repeated, mistreated and generally interfered with.

In keeping with these cinematic designs and techniques, the revised English-language *King, Queen, Knave* also becomes a work that eloquently flashes backwards and forwards, reflecting on and foreseeing Nazism and the Holocaust, subjects Nabokov touches on obliquely but powerfully in many of his works: the exquisite, haunting short story 'Signs and Symbols' (1948) references relatives put to death by 'the Germans'; the eponymous Pnin (1957) has to supress memories of a girlfriend who perished at Buchenwald; in *Lolita* (1955) Humbert Humbert's complex powers of reminiscence and divination allow, even encourage, reader rumination on the strange absence of the Second World War in a novel set mainly during the mid to late 1940s (appropriately, Humbert spends the war itself in a psychiatric institution).

In *King, Queen, Knave* and elsewhere, Nabokov has narrative enclaves: stories partially, sometimes entirely, concealed within the outward, supposedly main, narrative as systematic allegories and evocations. The external, superficial story becomes translucent, allowing us to glimpse the formidable depths and agonies lying behind; the 'hidden' story becomes, more often than not, the decisive one, imperceptibly governing our reading of the rest of the narrative – occupying, lingering, marking.

The English *King, Queen, Knave* turns out to be a reworked anticipatory warning of the robotic routines and smug conformist attitudes that would develop into some of the conditions animating 1930s fascism and its subsequent revulsions. The knave's development becomes representative and emblematic of many young Germans through the interwar years: coarse habits, base gratification of animal cravings; indoctrination, deadening; obedient, absolute and automatic respect to authority and activity. Like the programmed mannequins of the novel's department store, Franz and great swaths of the population become slaves to procedure, timetables, workplace hierarchy, social ladders, allocated leisure time: routines and restrictions that would be exploited by Nazi propaganda and then put to use via systematic mass murder.

King, Queen, Knave explores the systems involved when we devalue love – clearing up why Franz is so perturbed by the authorial presence of the (essentially) faithful, blissfully happy 'Nabokovs' (Mr and Mrs Vinomori) on the Baltic coast at the novel's close: they represent and inhabit everything he is not – a devaluation that will become devastating for whole peoples in the years to come, when love and tenderness are substituted by lust and envy.

Midway through the novel, an innocuous, almost throwaway remark (inserted in the English-language edition) makes the reader shudder as the whole gruesome, brutal horror of the Holocaust is flashed before our eyes, extending far beyond the novel's own time frame. The 'very old and very sick' knave will have become 'guilty of worse sins than avunculicide' (i.e., 'uncle murder' – the crime Hamlet is afraid of committing).

The rare, faintly comic, word 'avunculicide' connects us verbally to 'genocide', but the power comes in the very brevity and obscurity of the aside, indicating fleetingly that Franz will survive the novel and commit atrocities. It allows us to dread and suspect that the 'roaring laughter' and 'frenzy of young mirth' we encounter in the book's last line will curdle into something far more appalling than the sordid machinations of bourgeois infidelity and the bumping off of a love rival.

Yet this information is not given at the novel's end, but exhibited just briefly with an almost semi-transparent elusiveness halfway through the text, making the character exist far more hauntingly, hideously, in attentive imaginations when we close the book. The futile, automatic repetitions of Tom the dog's ball games, mirrored in the careless, inconsiderate human behaviour around him, have morphed far beyond the novel's time frame into their logical and ultimate horror, their determined endpoint: the unthinking mechanical repetitions of the Nazi murder machine.

3

The Luzhin Defense
FATAL PATTERNS

In the spring of 1919, amid the confusion of the Russian Civil War, several ministers and their families were evacuated from Sevastopol in Crimea on board the 'incredibly dirty' Greek vessel the *Nadezhda*, with an incongruous cargo of dried fruit. There had been numerous protracted attempts to leave the seaport owing to financial disagreements between the commanding French forces and the district administration, and it was only after the attacking Bolshevik soldiers reached the heights surrounding the city that the boat was finally granted consent to leave. The Red Army's artillery were firing across the bay as the *Nadezhda* zigzagged out of the harbour, machine guns spraying the waters of the Black Sea, but up on deck, Minister of Justice for the Crimean Regional Government Vladimir Dmitrievich Nabokov (1870–1922) and his son, ambitious poet Vladimir Vladimirovich Nabokov (1899–1977), pulled out their chess set and began a new game. It was shortly before eleven o'clock on the evening of 15 April 1919. Vladimir Nabokov, *fils*, would never see Russia again.

Nabokov's third novel, *The Luzhin Defense* (*Zashchita Luzhina*), published a decade later in 1929, tells the story of a Russian émigré prodigy who uses chess as a means of escape from the harsh realities of this world, initially as an alternative to playing with other children. But as he gets older, little Luzhin takes it too far: he mistakes his game for his life and goes mad.

For Nabokov, chess was no mere trivial (albeit very complex) game or pastime, contrary to the opinion expressed by several characters in the novel, including Luzhin's future mother-in-law. This echoes the writer's own life: Nabokov himself chose an 'absurd' and 'idle' profession (judgements Nabokov would himself occasionally lament, before seeing – with Pushkin – idleness as the poet's benediction and prerogative).

Chess was High Art, making *The Luzhin Defense*'s protagonist one of the few true artists (or, at least, an avatar of the artist) in Nabokov's oeuvre, populated as it is with wandering bands of crazy aspirants and imitators. Nabokov was himself a great composer of chess puzzles and problems, and in his autobiography, *Speak, Memory* (1951; 1966), elucidates that 'inspiration of a quasi-musical, quasi-poetical, or to be quite exact, poetico-mathematical type [which] attends the process of thinking up a chess composition.'

In 1924 Nabokov had published 'Three Chess Sonnets', wittily maintaining the affinity between poetry and chess, not least with their stringent rules of configuration. *The Luzhin Defense* shares not only some of the poems' subjects and thematic concerns, but also the structure of the sonnet: the novel is divided into fourteen chapters, with the first eight reflecting the familiar octet of eight lines, followed by the six chapters of the sestet, a sonnet's final six lines. It is at the turn between these two uneven halves that (as a sonnet often turns on its ninth line: the 'volta') Luzhin experiences his greatest crisis of lucidity. *The Luzhin Defense* also has an apparent kernel in Nabokov's 1927 poem 'The Chess Knight', in which a scruffy grandmaster sits in a bar, intoxicatingly seeing its patterned floor as a chessboard and himself as a chess piece, just as Luzhin will come to see himself as a chess king confronting checkmate.

In his foreword to the English edition of the novel, Nabokov (as so often, playfully) mentions an American publisher who wanted to substitute music for chess and make Luzhin 'a demented violinist'. We can assume this is a Nabokovian joke, teasing the reader while simultaneously hinting at something deeper, since, as with poetry and chess, a connection between chess and music comprises a fundamental theme of *The Luzhin Defense* – and is, in fact, one of the key elements illuminating the veiled meaning of the novel. Musical references proliferate (Luzhin's grandfather, crucially, is a composer; Luzhin's father dreams of his son as a concert pianist), and the novel's central episode – the great chess match between Luzhin and maverick Italian grandmaster Turati – overflows with musical terms, from the 'muted violins' of their discreet opening moves to the '*agitato*' of its climax.

Two other subjects, important in terms of both plot and theme, as well as in the complicated relationship the book has with metaphor, are childhood and love. The novel's first eight chapters (its 'octet') describe Luzhin's relatively ordered life, like the regular eight columns or rows on a chessboard, and are divided into two 'quatrains': first (1–4) his upbringing, then (5–8) his curious liaison with an unnamed woman he will later marry. These concerns, along with those of poetry and music, colour the black-and-white chessboard of Luzhin's life, expanding it beyond the systems and boundaries of the board to zones where he has no control, with devastating consequences.

These themes of chess, music and eros are interlinked early on in both the novel and Luzhin's life: a violinist has a sexually suggestive phone call immediately before describing the wonders of chess to the boy; in addition, the rules of the game are explained by his father's mistress, and it is at her apartment, with another of her lovers, that Luzhin learns to play. Later, the odd (often platonic) courtship with the female muse he will wed begins in chess fashion 'with a series of quiet moves'. Unfortunately, she, or the corporeal non-spirit (i.e., non-chess or even pre-chess) world she represents, will also be the unwitting instigator of his insanity.

But perhaps we allow Luzhin to mature (or, rather, get bigger) too quickly, for the childhood Nabokov conjures for him is one of the most heartfelt and authentic in all his work, comparable even to that of his own described in *Speak, Memory*. Luzhin shares much of his creator's own past, though they are very far from being identical. For all its luxury of suggestion and pungently evoked points of comparison, it is also a perversion of the author's own luminous youth. The secure haven of Nabokov's own family life, the precious and assured love of his parents, is converted into an uncertain nightmare for vulnerable Luzhin, full of fear and frustration (his mother is depressive, his father a philandering writer of mawkish stories for children). Yet this combination of pleasure and pain is part of the success of its evocation.

From the novel's opening, we are placed immediately in the anxious, puzzled world of a child, feeling, as he feels, the strangeness of change and the proximity of reality. Then we tiptoe imperceptibly but unmistakeably to his parents' bedroom, allured by a brace of images that are both eccentric and absolutely everyday. And we are only two sentences in. Nabokov compliments us on our abilities, too: we are flung into the story, but Nabokov respects that we have the imagination to at once feel a part of Luzhin's world. Flattered, we don't even notice that the grandmaster of storytelling is forcing us to raise our game in order to keep up with him. In only the third paragraph, we suddenly – and fleetingly – leap forward twenty years to experience a vast rearward peek at the past, allowing us to absorb Luzhin's childhood even as we are ourselves learning about it, threatening our concept of time just as Luzhin's is threatened.

The beginning of the novel mixes suppleness with translucence, luminosity with curiosity. We might have many questions (which will endure throughout *The Luzhin Defense*), but so confident are Nabokov's powers of prose that we take up and share that confidence, assuming that all will become clear in time. Yet the mystery propagated by the novel's first sentence is resolved only by its last line. Between them there exists an uninterrupted confrontation between the adult and the child, the past and the future, contentment and desolation, life and chess. During Luzhin's crisis, these contending sides warp and pervert each other, the rich repetitions of the one being twisted and distorted by the other, compelling a need to call a halt to this game of 'dark and pale squares'.

Luzhin's childhood is so richly drawn, with such precise particulars, that it instantly revitalizes our own memories of growing up:

A ten-year-old boy knows his knees well, in detail – the itchy swelling that had been scrabbled till it bled, the white traces of fingernails on the suntanned skin, and all those scratches which are the appended signatures of sand grains, pebbles and sharp twigs.

As well as the injuries and abrasions customary to any childhood, Luzhin experiences the deeper but still shared trepidations of starting a new school, the malice of his classmates, the interruptions to familiar routines. To cope, he constructs his defences, like other children do, but shows a distinctive aptitude for patterns and strategy that will come to define his abilities as a chess genius: deterring, resisting, repelling become stratagems as important as offensive incursions and counterattacks. We at once feel both the ordinariness and the uniqueness of Luzhin, making him both very close and far apart from our own (likely) experiences. When he eventually – aged eleven – discovers chess, however, we lose touch with him to some extent, his dexterity with the game affording him prompt liberation from his strangely uneven, asymmetrical childhood.

This apparent deliverance into the abstract, heady world of chess brings its own problems and opportunities, of course. The text without warning jumps forward sixteen years from Luzhin's first tournament to his preparations for the crucial match against Turati, the game that will form the centre of the novel and prompt Luzhin's mental collapse. We also see his relationship with the delightful, kind-hearted woman he will marry – someone able to decipher his social awkwardness and bungling conversation. She adores him. This Luzhin, the maladroit mastermind, remains as entirely believable in Nabokov's portrayal as the child has been. He is beguilingly alive and real to us:

> Luzhin looked at his hand, splaying the fingers and then closing them up again. The nails, tawny with nicotine, had ragged cuticles around them; fat little furrows ran across the finger joints, and a few hairs grew lower down. He placed his hand on the table next to her hand, milky-pale and soft to look at, with short, neatly trimmed nails.

'He placed his hand on the table next to her hand' – the addictive abstractions of chess now have a rival: love's tendernesses. *The Luzhin Defense* charts the war waged between the two in the virtuoso's sensitive mind. Dare we wish for him to have the modest contentment of love, knowing that this destabilizes, even annihilates, the ability of his art to prevail?

Luzhin himself asks this question and, naturally, devises a strategic defence to solve it, with shattering repercussions. The passages of the novel where Luzhin's wife tries to awaken her husband to life's ordinary joys, away from either the conceptual burdens of chess or his attempts to reconcile the game with love, are filled with affection and goodness, standing as some of Nabokov's most poignant and profoundly compassionate writing on human devotion and the decent, selfless care one person can have for another.

Throughout Nabokov's work we see figures isolated from the transformative power of love: the mutually supportive love within marriage which reflects and recaptures the sanctuary and bliss of childhood (an elicitation the rapture of art, or the magic of lepidoptery, also allow). The Nabokovs' own marriage, after some initial slip-ups, was one of ecstatically conventional monogamy – contra those who have wanted to see Vladimir as a perverted lunatic, unable to conceive that the creator of *Lolita* had an imagination.

For Luzhin, his love for his wife recalls his feelings of childhood, the two often merging in his mind, with disruptive consequences as the book plunges towards the revelation of the last lines and the sadness that has been Luzhin's life, mitigated by the periods of ordinary happiness with his wife. In *The Luzhin Defense*, if we as readers ignore the human/love component – and concentrate only on the chess patterns – we re-enact the protagonist's own mistake.

The connections between Mrs Luzhin's love (she is never named in the novel) and that of his father and grandfather also hint at some of the book's meanings surrounding the mysteries and magic of the hereafter, the 'beyondness' of existence and its delicate, elusive communications to this world, which govern so much of Nabokov's work. The novel seems, through its diaphanous texture, to subtly suggest that Luzhin's deceased grandfather has led his grandson to chess, and that Luzhin's dead father has led his son to the woman that will love him and offer him an escape.

On the anniversary of his grandfather's death, an expert violinist gives a memorial concert of some of the grandfather's virtuosic but often empty music; during the interval the violinist enthuses about the musical qualities of chess, and the young Luzhin is entranced, trembling with excitement to learn. Much later, just as Luzhin meets his future wife, the narrative shifts back to

Luzhin's father's own life and the novella he tries to write just before his death to memorialize, ornament, his son's chess career. This intrusion is again gently indicative of the intricate connection between the departed and those remaining.

At first, chess is Luzhin's fortress, a stronghold of defence and protection. As he grows up it becomes his prison, holding him against his will, before eventually turning into his torture chamber. Luzhin's wife's warmth and benevolence – her love – seem to be a flight from this abyss. But the tension between love/childhood and their antithesis, chess, eventually destabilizes Luzhin further. The wizard violinist-composer grandfather seems to repeat and repeat, as only a dazzling musician can, the melodic theme of childhood, variations suddenly twisting their way into Luzhin's discovery of chess, developing accompaniments and embellishments that send Luzhin's tenuous separation of love/childhood and chess into an irretrievable freefall.

We should be wary of reading *The Luzhin Defense* allegorically: the correspondences between chess moves or chess problems should be read in a general way, loose analogies that shade the text. As readers, we cannot constrain the complex patterns of the life depicted in the novel into those of a game of chess, however much it may be tempting to (like Luzhin) do so. Novels, like human lives and human imagination, are substantially more complex than the limited infinity of chess.

Nabokov's art, like science, cherishes the prospect of new worlds other than our own. The minutiae, the intricacies, the textures of thought and feeling that he immortalizes – all entice us into the exhilarating discovery of novel realms, each revisit encouraging us to confront new problems, disclose new wonders, advocate new meanings as we dive and redive deeper into his art.

If time is a prison, memory might seem to hold the key to an escape. But memory is fallible, unsound, unreliable. Art, however, can grant that getaway: every detail, every triviality, is assured protection from the destructive powers of time and extinction. But this art cannot be that of sentimental stories, sterile showpieces for the violin, or perhaps even the perfect abstractions of chess. It must be a fertile and authentic art that connects us to the possibilities beyond our own confined reality into an ultimate eschatological aesthetic or pattern and other modes of existence.

4

The Eye

A HELL OF MIRRORS

In Jean-Paul Sartre's 1944 play *No Exit*, three people trapped in a room – Hell – confess their sins and, perhaps inevitably, end up in a peculiar *ménage à trois*. Their imprisonment is more than physical, however: they are stuck with the judgements of their infernal cellmates. '*L'enfer, c'est les autres*', says one of them. 'Hell is other people'. Hell is the interminable vigilant pejorative gaze of others. And the appearance of the Other, as Sartre also said in *Being and Nothingness* (1943), forces us into the position of passing judgement on ourselves as an object, for it is as an object that we appear to the Other. When we think about ourselves, we use the knowledge of us which other people already have, subjecting ourselves to their interpretation of us – with foreseeable pessimism and self-destruction.

One way of avoiding other people, and their vexing judgement, is to convince yourself that you're dead and can pass invisibly, invulnerably, among those who previously persecuted you. Or can you? Nabokov's fourth and shortest novel, *The Eye* (*Sogliadatai*, 1930), explores just such nightmares of the self.

Like many of his generation, Nabokov was disposed to commandeer the plots, characters and methods of his great nineteenth-century predecessors before sabotaging them, upturning them, incorporating them within modernist configurations in order to generate fresh connotations. *The Eye* takes up Dostoevsky's 'The Dream of a Ridiculous Man' (1877), with its relatively straightforward exploration of hallucination and humiliation, and fashions a traumatic, frightening world of immense insight where our ghost-narrator wants to persuade us all, himself included, that he really is dead. Reflecting riddles flash and replicate in a hysteria of paranoid pain, signalling everything and nothing in this disturbing, concentrated, and very cleverly executed psychological mystery story.

A nameless first-person narrator, 'I' (a lugubriously self-conscious young Russian émigré in Berlin), is beaten up by a jealous husband whose promiscuous wife has seduced our storyteller. Demeaned and disgraced (his two tutees – a comic and ominous doubling – have witnessed the thrashing), he shoots himself. Believing himself to have died, he nevertheless continues his existence, sustained – he supposes – by his residual imagination, his excess intellectual energy. His hospital, new acquaintances, new employment, a new apartment – all come from his perceived psychological impetus. No one can abuse or embarrass him now: he is untouchable by the slights of his species.

His new life affords him much pleasure. He takes to visiting his new neighbours, an émigré family, and is especially delighted by the beautiful Vanya as well as a new friend of the family, Smurov (meaning 'shadowy' or 'murky'), a quiet young man of innermost passion and self-assurance who seems to make wildly incongruous impressions upon everyone. The narrator, 'I', decides to entertain himself by collecting these diverse impressions of Smurov reflected by the others so that he might discover the authentic Smurov. He searches more and more obsessively for the true Smurov, not just seeking out people's opinions but gathering more tangible evidence: intercepting post, ransacking rooms …

Numerous mistakes, uncertainties, doublings, and eye-opening discoveries ensue before this diabolically engineered metaphysical detective story is able to reach a conclusion. It is brilliantly concentrated, and, just as with another psychological thriller, *Macbeth* (1606), we feel that if it were any longer, it would implode under the mass of its own accumulated liminality. Yet, for all this density, scenes are not rushed or lightly sketched. The affair, the beating, the humiliation, the shooting: all are given sufficient space to build in the reader's mind so that we wholly enter into and experience the narrator's world. Other characters are fully drawn and convincingly realized as well – crucially, since we need to discover how they reflect or distort our self-absorbed narrator's sense of his own identity.

Nabokov's technical accomplishment in keeping separate the different characters, personalities, identities (the constant battle between the subjective/objective), while also maintaining the narrative, is considerable. A range of speculative approaches to person, perspective, voice, consciousness and focus seem to collide and coalesce, so that the character and position of the storyteller in relation to the narrative becomes precariously distorted, grinding one reality against another. Narrative perspective is here a hell of mirrors. And *The Eye*'s mirrors (actual/figurative/linguistic) are endlessly tweaked and fine-tuned by Nabokov in order to craft the necessary illusions, blurs and mergers.

The narrator 'I', with his neurotic fantasies and paranoid delusions, might be judged the prototype for a whole band of self-possessed protagonists to come. Insane, failed or would-be artists populate – infest – the Nabokovian cosmos, their egos romping and raging across their narratives, inflicting their illusory world on us. Hermann Hermann (*Despair*, 1934), Humbert Humbert (*Lolita*, 1955), Charles Kinbote (*Pale Fire*, 1962) and Vadim Vadimovich (*Look at the Harlequins!*, 1974) will all come to disrupt and overthrow, through the will of their own egocentricity, the structures of their tales, sending the function of plot and character out into wildly eccentric orbits. In many ways, none of them do so as purely as the 'I' of *The Eye*.

Significantly, each of these characters has a 'doubled' name: a split, augmented or folded personality. Hermann Hermann and Humbert Humbert speak for themselves. Vadim Vadimovich not only has a double name but is a parody or doppelganger of (Vladimir Vladimirovich) Nabokov. In *Pale Fire*, Charles Kinbote is also suggested to be Professor Botkin, a name that puns on 'bodkin', the dagger in Hamlet's 'To be or not to be' soliloquy. Hamlet is a character we might see as self-regarding, but who is also, unlike Nabokov's oddballs, both an authentic creative artist and entirely sane. Like *The Eye*, *Hamlet* is a distorting mirror of dualities and deformation, containing an unbounded, compulsive stream of multilevel doublings and duplications. (To consider only those of characterization, there are two Hamlets, two kings, two ambassadors, two abused women, two avenging sons, two comically indistinguishable friends: Rosencrantz and Guildenstern.)

Hamlet is also a voyeuristic, ghoulish play about spying: characters constantly watch, eavesdrop, snoop, just as *The*

Eye's narrator does in his increasingly uncontrollable quest for 'truth'. It will come as no surprise that the original Russian title of Nabokov's novel, *Sogliadatai*, means 'spy' or 'secret observer'. But despite all the mind-bending angles of its mysterious narrative, *The Eye* is, at heart, a compassionate book, inspecting closely not only the selfish, destructive aberrations of narcissism but also the plight of drifting, destabilized immigrants in a foreign land trying to establish their own identity inside a strange and suspicious city. The existence of sinister Soviet spies in Berlin, the hectic centre of the Weimar Republic, fuels émigré paranoia, as we see comically reflected through *The Eye*'s agitated bookseller Weinstock, with his panic about agents dispatched from 'over there'.

The Eye is also a stark, curiously kind-hearted, examination of the very real wretchedness of mental illness and rational disintegration. 'I' examines himself to such an extent that he becomes an alien, a stranger to himself, which carries with it a degree of immunization and self-protection, an escape from the person he is that he scrutinizes so intensely. The extent to which his egotism has stretched into a severe disorder stimulates our concern for him, however deluded and irritating he can be, as he dissolves and rematerializes amid the vanishing havoc of his mind. Early on in the book, as he prepares to kill himself, he muses generally on 'presuicidal occupations' – and the passage grows lyrically into one of Nabokov's most tender, disturbing and perceptive statements on the fragility and terror of human existence:

> a man who has decided upon self-destruction is far removed from mundane affairs, and to sit down and write his will would be, at that moment,

an act just as absurd as winding up one's watch, since, together with the man, the whole world is destroyed; the last letter is instantly reduced to dust and, with it, all the postmen; and like smoke, vanishes the estate bequeathed to a nonexistent progeny.

That 'postmen' is immensely powerful, and a breathtaking example of Nabokov's brilliance. Its suddenness and astonishing reality jolt the reader before propelling them into the terrible vacuum and finality of infinite nothingness obligated by self-extermination. We're given an image ('the postmen') we don't expect: with suicide, we normally think of the victim, or the loved ones left behind to grieve, never the officially sanctioned functionaries of public facilities and services. But they are all annihilated.

Then, immediately before 'I' pulls the trigger, there is a moment of ideal softness, as – just for a moment – the confusion seems to cease, before subtly restarting:

> I unbuttoned my shirt ... and located my heart between the ribs. It was throbbing like a small animal you want to carry to a safe place, a fledgling or field mouse to which you cannot explain that there is nothing to fear, that, on the contrary, you are acting for its own good. But it was so much alive, my heart.

Like many Nabokovian protagonists, the narrator of *The Eye* tries to turn pain into art. In the same way that Ganin in *Mary* aims at (and perhaps succeeds in) becoming an artist of memory, 'I' attempts, unwittingly, to become an artist of the imagination. Yet the more he negotiates and interrogates the world he has invented, the more he is drawn to experience it, feel it, destroying the fiction of his own formation. The authentic artist – Nabokov – is asserted over the counterfeit creator, 'I'. But there can be no doubting the vitality of *The Eye*'s narrator, fluttering in multiple dimensions: a butterfly imagination, disgusted with existence but defying its limitations. He is very much alive.

5

Glory
QUIXOTIC VOYAGES

Alfred Hitchcock's 1941 psychological thriller *Suspicion* involves a man who might be trying to murder his wife. As the story unfolds, her apprehensions and misgivings, like ours, begin to mount. At the film's climax, her husband takes a glass of milk upstairs to their bedroom. It shines with a strange radiance: the director had placed a light bulb *inside* the glass to focus all our attention there, and its luminosity is peculiar, cryptic, uncanny, somehow both drawing attention to itself and trying to conceal something. Is the drink spiked? Is it murder time? We're suspicious but captivated, spellbound but wary. The weirdness and doubt, together with an audience's likely knowledge of Hitchcockian games, mix to make our experience of the scene thrilling and unsettling.

Nabokov's fifth novel, *Glory* (*Podvig*, 1932) is a curiously beautiful tale, its eerie brightness and sinuous intensity so deceptively simple that many have underestimated the work, including – perhaps – the protagonist himself. But, like *Suspicion*'s glowing glass of milk, this incandescence seems to be paradoxically hiding something. Its lyrical ambience and superficial straightforwardness must be a cover: this is a Nabokov novel, after all. The author himself, in the introduction to his English edition, had stressed the 'thrill and glamour' of the book. Yet, as so often in Nabokov's forewords, this intentionally and misleadingly conceals the deeper concern. The 'thrill and glamour' of *Glory*, the beauty of its mask, disguises a metaphysical disquiet and a multiplicity of dark meanings.

Another part of the foreword hints at this: 'The fun of *Glory* ... is to be sought in the echoing and linking of minor events, in back-and-forth switches' – here we begin to excavate the characteristically Nabokovian implanting of buried links within the strata of the narrative. These secreted associations (the 'inside' of the text) are subtly relocated to the narrative reality (the 'outside') so that we feel the interior is enigmatically manipulating the narrative within which they are submerged. The hierarchically lower elements, the 'core' of a novel, push themselves higher, trying to weaken the boundary with the 'crust' of the exterior narrative.

Crucially, in *Glory*, this all occurs beneath the surface, screening the assimilation of inner/outer narratives, playing down the metaphysics by emphasizing the protagonist's worldly concerns with adventure, sex, sport and physical labour, before culminating in a test of his convictions beyond language and therefore the novel itself.

The plot, as we've intimated, can be easily summarized. Martin Edelweiss, unremarkable and sane, emigrates from Russia after the Revolution, visits Greece and Switzerland, attends Cambridge, becomes a tennis instructor in Berlin, then (perhaps) works as a farmhand in the south of France before planning a dangerous mission across the prohibited Russian border. Although there is much richness in the communication of all these narrative events, the exuberant enjoyment and veiled import of *Glory* is, as Nabokov suggested, in the reverberation and connection of seemingly negligible or inconsequential occurrences forward and back across – and beyond – the novel. The major events and their inhabitants, then, need to be reasonably realistic and uncomplicated so that the minor events, and their magical conveyances, can be enchantingly detected.

If Martin is, to others, unexceptional, inside he burns with romance and adventure, but fatefully lacks the talent to communicate this in language to the outside world, an external realm vibrantly and exotically transmitted to us via frequently shifting surroundings and superbly painted characters (especially Martin's friend, the unperturbable Darwin, and Martin's love interest, unpredictable Sonia). *Glory* has quick changes of scene and episode: nearly fifty chapters in a book of under 175 pages containing a sizeable cast. The time frame is necessarily great and wants for organization, deliberately matching the untidy, jumbled nature of life. Narrative trails are interrupted, partial, winding. The end of the novel never occurs: it simply evaporates into both fictive, fairy-tale fulfilment and the deftly interconnected pathways of the preceding text.

What then are some of these mysterious, meandering narrative conduits, routes physical and emblematic, which help structure and elucidate *Glory*? They begin – characteristically – outside the novel itself, at the end of Nabokov's capricious foreword and immediately before we enter the text proper, with the sly, subconscious authorial misdirection that 'nothing much happens at the very end – just a bird perching on a wicket in the grayness of a wet day.'

(It is perhaps appropriate that this foreword, written in 1971 for a book originally composed in 1932, should begin to exert some control over its text. In between, *Lolita* (1955) has a comically well-meaning and calculatingly disorienting false foreword from the clownishly doubling 'John Ray Jr.', which many readers skip, assuming it to be a publisher's defensive insertion rather than a crucial element to the novel's ethical snares. In *Pale Fire* (1962), the foreword is aesthetically and structurally integral, now unmissable and impossible to inadvertently skip, sublimated entirely into the four-part fabric of the novel.)

The ending of *Glory*, in the Swiss woods near Martin's mother's house, links back to the beginning through the transferral of recurrent textual and textural motifs of mothers, forest paths, dreaming. Since his Russian childhood, Martin has been a quixotic voyager in time and space, especially to those places distant, prohibited or unreachable. Here, multiple embedded layers of fiction are imparted to us within the structure and texture of the book, as implanted stories implant stories of their own. As an infant, he is read a fairy tale about

> a picture with a path in the woods, right above the bed of a little boy, who, one fine night, just as he was, nightshirt and all, went from his bed into the picture, onto the path that disappeared into the woods.

Martin anxiously hopes his mother will not notice and remove the similar picture that hangs over his own crib, preventing him from exploring the paths in the forest it contains during an adventurous 'nocturnal journey' – one clearly foreshadowing his own grown-up mission back into Russia. Indeed, Martin himself (we are directly told) later wonders

> if one night he had not actually hopped from bed to picture, and if this had not been the beginning of the journey, full of joy and anguish, into which his whole life had turned. He seemed to remember the chilly touch of the ground, the green twilight of the forest, the bends of the trail (which the hump of a great root crossed here and there), the tree trunks flashing by as he ran past them barefoot, and the strange dark air, teeming with possibilities.

Uncanny imaginings, ambiguous expeditions, illicit excursions, crisscrossing paths: these are the key strands that weave the delicate texture of *Glory*, entwining the text and by this means divulging the novel's deeper significance.

These symbolic, fictive and literal trails snake and reappear through the whole narrative forest, sometimes palpable, often intangible, with the frontiers distorted between the buried 'inner' stories and the novel's 'outer' reality, the surface level of Martin's biography, which will gain meaning only in his final journey. To pick only a handful of examples: when he leaves Russia, on the cusp of adulthood and exile, he sees 'the "Turkish Trail" spreading'; in Switzerland, the road is 'brightly lit' and has 'many turns', while Martin also manoeuvres home 'along a dark forest road.' Then, as Martin approaches his bold, not to say reckless, quest to cross the Russian border, he is sent directions to go 'all the way through the wood – it's a very dense wood'.

Martin has tracked a forest trail all the way through the various tiers of reality in his narrative, in dreams and stories, fairy tales and fantasies, yet it is only here that he jumps into the picture that once hung above his infant bed, actuality solidifying the airy imaginings and realizing Martin's childhood desire.

At the very end of the novel, after Martin has enacted his 'glory', his 'exploit' (to take the most literal translation of the original Russian title *Podvig*), the setting of his deed is transferred (the dream hijacking reality) to his friend Darwin visiting Martin's mother's house in the Swiss forest:

> An hour elapsed. Darwin emerged from the brown depths of the melancholy garden ... and started back along the path through the woods. ... The air was dingy, here and there tree roots traversed the trail, black fir needles now and then brushed against his shoulder, the dark path passed between the tree trunks in picturesque and mysterious windings.

Self-referential and repeated images of forest trails thus switch back and forth, patterning and configuring the narrative from beginning to end. Others, such as water and dreams, are scattered and interlinked throughout, as are those of letters and Martin's mother. Midway through the novel, at Cambridge, Martin writes to her, imagining the postman delivering the very letter he is writing:

> Suddenly, in his mind, he saw the mailman walking across the snow; the snow crunched slightly, and blue footprints remained on it. He described it

thus: 'My letter will be brought by the mailman. It is raining here.' He thought it over and crossed out the mailman, leaving only the rain.

Here the narrative suddenly makes one of Nabokov's switches, in this case to the casual vision of Mrs Edelweiss's later anguish reading his correspondences, lamenting outside *Glory*'s time frame in an 'abstraction of the future' the reader can only, at this point, guess at. The snow, the footprints: all link up to Darwin's visit to Martin's mother in the 'wet gray snow', traversing the ground Martin first imagines, then writes, then gets rid of, in his maternal missive.

This also tells us Martin is no artist: he cannot perceive or communicate experience before it has happened, before it has been 'posted'. There is a clear autobiographical component to *Glory*: Martin shares many of the experiences and settings (Crimea, Cambridge, Berlin) of his author's early adulthood, but – critically – lacks Nabokov's creative gifts. Yet Martin's *podvig*, his exploit, is comparable to art, since it has no apparent purpose that his society can appreciate, while in fact offering fulfilment and anticipation. Moreover, when devising his daring mission across the Russian border, Martin crafts an invented world, 'Zoorland', a parodic, frightening domain with compulsory equality, an ersatz Communist state.

But Zoorland is not merely a mockery of the USSR. It is also a space of aesthetic transcendence, a realization of the esoteric tremble that has pervaded the texture of the text through stealthy traversals and interweavings. Martin, ensnared in his narrative, cannot formulate this otherworldly enigma in words. His readers, however, can distinguish it as the transcendent, timeless, beneficent realm of art – Nabokov's art – so that *Glory* discloses how Nabokov could not become an artist until he had genuinely lived his life, experienced it, sanctioning him to enter a new mode of existence, as Martin does when vanishing into the forest.

Martin's absence haunts the end of *Glory*, but only if we do not also grasp his fulfilment, which Nabokov calls 'the fugal theme of [Martin's] destiny', therein. The sense of pointlessness is an intentional effect of the novel, but we need to transcend it to fully appreciate the full wonder of this elusive, exceptional book.

6
Laughter in the Dark
SEEING IS DECEIVING

A camera eye looks down on an old woman gathering herbs on a steep hillside. Below, she sees a pair of cyclists in orange jerseys and a speeding blue car, converging at a sharp bend on the clifftop road. Suddenly, the perspective shifts skyward to a pilot in a small plane flying high above the scene, before moving out still farther to survey the mountains of Provence, and then finally across the entire 'cheek of the earth from Gibraltar to Stockholm'. This rapid zoom-out shot immediately zooms in, now on Berlin, where a woman stands on a balcony, feeling an inexplicable anxiety. Abruptly we sweep back to the south of France, gliding again over the aircraft and down to rest on the old woman harvesting herbs on a rocky slope.

Are we in a television advert? For bicycles or holidays? Or is this the trailer for a thrilling high-octane movie with a Europe-wide plot, car chases, glamorous men and women? But who is the elderly lady, and what are her aromatic plants for? Cooking? Curing? Conjuring?

It turns out, of course, that we are in Nabokov's sixth novel, *Laughter in the Dark* (*Kamera obskura*,[2] 1932), an entire book written, its author claimed, 'as if it were a film'.[3] Techniques, points of view, images, motifs, as well as plot and character exploit the world of the cinema in this painful – and often very funny – vision of failure, conceit and carelessness. (*Laughter in the Dark* began its life in Russian before being translated into English first by Winifred Roy in 1936, then by Nabokov himself just two years later, in 1938, the author making key changes to the novel, though retaining the essential outlines of the main plot. This essay focuses on Nabokov's 1938 translation.)

The herb gatherer witnesses an event with life-changing implications for those involved. But the effortlessly managed perspectives described above are more than a virtuosic exhibition of narrative fluidity: this mesmeric page-long chapter combines numerous viewpoints and locations in order to suggest multidimensional insights available from wider outlooks. This will, in turn, have implications ironic and metaphysical for a (as its title suggests) darkly comic novel that now rapidly shifts into an even more maliciously hilarious mode with a vicious climax.

If all this seems, in the idiom of contemporary film reviews, to have needed a 'spoiler alert', we only need to go to the novel's opening, which employs the language of

---

2 *Laughter in the Dark*'s title has a tortuous history. The novel was serialized as *Camera Obscura* in the Russian émigré journal *Sovremennye zapiski* in 1932–33. In 1933, it appeared in book form as *Kamera obskura*. The English translation by Winifred Roy appeared in 1936 with the title *Camera Obscura*; another English translation, by Nabokov himself, appeared in 1938, with the now familiar title *Laughter in the Dark*.

3 The Russian first edition has its cover stylized as a strip of film, the title and author name endlessly repeated.

another form of narrative convention, the fairy tale, and which proleptically anticipates the calamitous events that are to unfold:

> Once upon a time there lived in Berlin, Germany, a man called Albinus. He was rich, respectable, happy; one day he abandoned his wife for the sake of a youthful mistress; he loved; was not loved; and his life ended in disaster.

The half-rhyme of the traditionally expected 'happily ever after' with its replacement 'disaster' is the first of many wicked, spiteful jokes the novel has in store – from narrator and protagonists alike.

Our immediate reaction on being told the tale in these few short lines ('What's the point in reading on?') is instantly leapt upon by the quintessentially Nabokovian narrator, who informs us of the 'profit and pleasure' of texture, of *detail*. In Nabokov generally, and *Laughter in the Dark* in particular, it is within these twisted twins – texture and detail – that much of the meaning, and perhaps most of the enjoyment, is to be discovered: the particulars, the minutiae and the niceties; the images, the rhythms and the cadences knitted into the story. Specifically, in *Laughter in the Dark*, these details take the form of deliberate distractions from subjects that should summon our emotional reaction. Our sympathy for the protagonist is regulated, even restricted, with significant implications for the novel's wider import, as we shall see.

The allure of the remote, the isolated, the unreachable, is something which troubles Nabokov's texts. Countries, lands, people, states of being, ideas or ideals are inaccessible to many of his protagonists: Nabokov's early novels tend to home in on inept, amateurish characters consumed by the quest of ostensibly inconsequential goals (with the partial exception of Luzhin). Later protagonists retain the desire to access the inaccessible but have creative imaginations and wish to exhibit their invention and originality via the medium of life. Hermann Hermann (*Despair*, 1934) thinks himself a master of lawbreaking and the play of life, pointlessly capturing a false double of his own remote and rotten fancy; Humbert Humbert (*Lolita*, 1955) tries to retrieve his own past and lost first love, via his despicable crimes with his underage stepdaughter, to attain 'aesthetic bliss'.

In *Laughter in the Dark*, prosperous art critic and collector Albinus tries to acquire unreachable Beauty via his affair (and later obsession with) coarse, conniving cinema usherette (and aspirant film star) Margot. She revives an earlier affair with devious artist Rex, and they engineer, occasionally with his own assistance, Albinus's downfall. Like many of Nabokov's earlier protagonists, Albinus is 'not a particularly gifted man' and moreover he is 'a liar, a coward and a fool' – Margot's angry summation, an assessment approved by the nodding narrator as condensing him 'rather neatly'.

If Albinus is last in the line of talentless early Nabokovian heroes, Rex is perhaps first in the procession of gifted later Nabokovian villains. He is a 'very fine' artist, not only in paint and pencils but also in his instinctive malice and sadism – initially, as a child, with animals; then with Albinus, aided and abetted by Margot. Albinus is self-immersed and self-deceived, seeking women as pretty possessions akin to his *objets d'art*; but Rex downright enjoys the exhibition of pain and suffering, gleefully and nastily *crafting* distress. Along with his youthful torture of birds and beasts, this 'dangerous man' also paints fakes, ridiculing the connection between cruelty and credulity, less for material reward than the agreeable cynicism it brings him. Rex is not content to be an artist inspired by life, he must create art in his life as well – and the scenes where he persecutes Albinus, delivering no physical pain but simply mocking a man ruined and helpless, are among the most chilling in twentieth-century literature.

Yet herein lies a problem: our compassion for Albinus is curbed. In part this is our feeling of poetic justice – he is an arrogant adulterer who gets what is coming to him. But there is much more to it than this, for it is here that the Nabokovian details come remarkably and disturbingly into play.

Our narrator is a slippery, sardonic creature, consequently deflecting our consideration towards the particulars of the protagonist's universe. These details are not mere curios, aesthetic knick-knacks like the ones Albinus collects, but fundamental features of the narrative. The textures and details do not just communicate the ambience or emotion of any given scene but dominate it, overshadow it, puzzlingly alleviating the adjacent pain as we – like the character – fixate on them. But the pain has already been associated with the image – tinges and traces which then bequeath the narrative referential, troubling power.

To take only one example: when Albinus's wife discovers his affair with Margot and leaves him, he notices the upturned corner of a rug in their flat. Representative of his now disordered life, it will take on a haunting, repeated presence. But it also disconcertingly distracts us from the real emotional mayhem Albinus has created in the furniture of his life that has caused the fixtures and fittings of his apartment to become displaced.

The key turning point of the story (which directly heralds Albinus's maltreatment by Rex) was highlighted at the beginning of this essay, and it generates an immense physical distance from the event which is to be so emotionally and painfully significant for Albinus, by cinematically zooming out across the globe away from the incident. Comedy, gravity and wonder mix to make us complicit in his fate. Our sympathies have been reduced, diminished, depleted by the icy ironies and devilish details of the third-person narrator. We have become accustomed to his sufferings, even incriminated in them. Like the frames of a film's still images, or those protective, decorative ones that contain paintings, we have become 'framed' in the delinquencies of the narrative frames Nabokov's novel has constructed.

Written and revised in Europe in the 1930s, as tyrannical regimes (in Germany, Italy and Russia) flourished amid a combination of the populations' callousness and vindictive indifference, *Laughter in the Dark* experiments (from without and within) with our own ideas of kindness and cruelty. It also explores cupidity and crudity, duplicity and depravity, collusion and collaboration. It exhibits human suffering and yet – with a shrug – declines to secure our sympathy. It tours the borders of comedy and tragedy, visiting in a jaunty bright shirt the hilarity (and the heartbreak) of not seeing where you're going.

The antics and mirth of *Laughter in the Dark* are vindictive, prophetic, responsive, intentionally disquieting: Albinus little by little loses everything he has ever cherished, the lot cataclysmically disappearing from his life. For a joke at other people's expense to work, there needs to be a suppression of sympathy – a potentially menacing restraint which might, if not itself checked, get out of control, just as the Nazis own (often cartoonish) propaganda worked by gradually undermining further sympathies for already oppressed sections of society.

At the beginning of the novel, Albinus's first encounters with seventeen-year-old Margot take place at the Berlin picture palace where she works, tidily utilizing the cinematic/pictorial/optical/illusionary motifs which colour, shadow and ironize *Laughter in the Dark*. These cinema meetings demonstrate the protagonist's shallow relationship with art, the self-delusions which prevent him from 'seeing the bigger picture', visually and morally, in his life. The movies he half-watches when trying to ensnare Margot give allusions, cautions even, as to his future life and how it will be disturbed, then broken. Blinded by his own lust and sense of self-worth, he overlooks the projected admonitions of the silver screen.

As readers, we have already been alerted by the prolepsis of the novel's opening to be aware of and attentive to any warning signs in Albinus's life. He himself has no such referentiality. As Albinus sits in the dark, flirting and ignoring the flickering premonitions, we are – perhaps even on our first reading – already laughing ...

7

Despair
LITERATURE AS ECSTASY

The idea of the 'perfect crime' is one that has long fascinated the lawlessly minded: a crime that is not only undetectable and unsolvable but ingenious, almost artistic in its conception and execution. Here the talent and skill of the miscreant outshine the duties and competencies of the investigating authorities, the former's ability to evade scrutiny or reprisal helping establish the flawlessness of the felony. These combined elements of both the creative and the confrontational have naturally made the 'perfect crime' a popular subject for detective fiction and films. The ability of the villain to outsmart and outwit their law enforcement counterparts, or the inherent deviousness of the plan itself, lends itself to exciting drama as we enjoy the fiendishness of the plot, the cleverness of the criminal or the frustrations of the investigation.

A great irony of 'perfect' crimes in books and movies, of course, is that they are rarely ever perfect: some flaw unravels the scrupulous work. And, more often than not, this defect resides not in the illicit masterpiece itself but in its perpetrator's vanity. The criminal-artist simply can't resist letting the world know about their brilliance.

In order to succeed, perfect crimes need to pay attention to, and account for, all the details, big or small. Fail to do this, and your downfall is likely to be swift and total. Hermann Hermann, the supercilious, deluded villain of Nabokov's seventh novel *Despair* (*Otchayanie*,[4] 1934), flops for just this reason. He neglects one rather conspicuous detail: if you're going to murder your doppelganger in order to claim the life insurance money, that lookalike should, at the very least, look like you. Hermann thinks himself an artist creating the perfect crime; but crime, for Nabokov, always includes its own imperfection – namely, the impossible desire to control anything and everything.

Like *The Eye* (1930), *Despair* is both a spoof of Dostoevskian delinquency and a burlesque detective story. Nabokov had a problematic rapport with his Russian predecessor: he frequently ridiculed him in a deliberately outrageous manner, but many of his works enter into a riveting recreational gambol with Dostoevsky's themes, style and subjects. Nabokov also had an unsurprisingly multifaceted, even equivocal, relationship with detective fiction. He abhorred its being largely conventional, badly written, and the 'very negation' of his utmost literary concern: style, 'an artist's peculiar nature'. Yet Nabokov was enticed by the genre of detective fiction as a potential metaphysical-epistemological conundrum for *discovering* style: the hints, signs and symbols of fiction returning us to the scene of the aesthetic crime, revealing the fundamental elements or features of an author's personality.

Narrator and protagonist Hermann Hermann is the Russian German owner of a Berlin chocolate factory who,

---

4 The sound of the Russian title is 'a far more sonorous howl' than the English, said Nabokov.

on a business trip to Prague, by chance meets a vagrant whose physiognomies seem entirely identical to his own. Hermann realizes the blessing of this opportunity to substitute the victim for the murderer. He takes out a huge insurance policy, fools the beggar into swapping clothes, murders him, and departs for France, where his faithful wife will soon reunite with him, bringing the indemnity plunder (the 'royalties' for his artistic work) and a life of cosy luxury under a new identity.

While Hermann is ensconced in a Pyrenean parish, biding his time, the problems start to stack up – namely, that the authorities have discovered the tramp's body and are puzzled that Hermann thought he could hoodwink both them and the insurance company simply by clothing an essentially random corpse in his own attire. Frustrated by the crass fiasco of the police, press and public's inability to grasp the artistic splendour of his crime, Hermann resorts to another medium – literature – to record his masterpiece.

Nabokov's novel is a murder mystery, and some of the key, conventional twists and clues of the genre arrive, as one might expect, only towards the book's end – surprising even its narrator, who is forced to reread his own story to discover the fatal flaws in his masterpiece that he hadn't noticed at the first time of telling. Because, of course, there are multiple texts here, and the interplay between competing narratives is one of Nabokov's most characteristic, enthralling (and occasionally exasperating) games.

The novel *Despair* by Vladimir Nabokov contains an incomplete story – also called 'Despair' – penned by its protagonist Hermann Hermann, as well as a fragment of his diary, located in the last chapter, and into which the 'tale degenerates'. Hermann's manuscript 'Despair' is the inner text, Nabokov's novel *Despair* the outer one, and the relationship between the two is troubled by the fact that they are indistinguishable – unlike Hermann and his 'twin' victim. Hermann thinks he is a master inventor-villain, in complete control of both his *magnum opus* and his destiny, whereas his own pen is actually commanded and commandeered by the hand of his creator. Nabokov uses Hermann's own text against him to expose his manifest inadequacies – as a criminal, as an artist, as a husband.

It is a technique Nabokov had used before, especially in *The Eye*, and that he would bring to even greater levels of power and sublimity in *Lolita* (1955), *Pale Fire* (1962) and *Ada* (1969). Eloquent, vigilant narrator-heroes seem totally unaware of proceedings and meanings entirely contrary to those which they articulate. It is Nabokov's immense skill which allows these novels not only to convey (to attentive readers) the subtle codes, furtive connections and devilish details which elude their protagonists, but to – simultaneously – convince us of these same characters' brilliance.

If there is detective work required by the reader in their deciphering of the various texts of *Despair*, hunting for the necessary clues, we can also see some links to detective fiction in more disconcerting ways than the purely mechanical or methodological. There is the fact that murder mysteries all tend, like *Despair*, to be two stories (at least) in one: the story of the crime and the story of the investigation. Yet it is rarely so clear-cut. Akira Kurosawa's fabled 1950 crime thriller *Rashōmon*[5] is structured on this very ambiguity, with its famous plot device that involves various characters offering subjective,

---

5 Based on Ryūnosuke Akutagawa's 1915 short story of the same name.

alternative, self-serving, and contradictory versions of the same incident. Detective fiction plays on the tenuous relationship between the story of the crime (ostensibly 'what really took place') and the inquiry ('how we have come to know about it').

The genre is also necessarily about absence: a body, and the life which inhabited it, haunts the texts of murder mysteries. No matter how gimcrack the prose or clichéd the plotting, the sad reality of death stalks all these tales. Moreover, this human life, as well as the crime which removed it and the story of this crime, necessarily exist apart and at a distance from their book's second, main and investigative story. That is to say, the story of the crime is as dead on arrival as its corpse.

Many of Nabokov's novels arrive with death and are built around it. One ponders how many readers get past the first few pages of *Lolita*, the 'false foreword' by John Ray Jr, without realizing that Lolita herself is dead, as are her mother, father, many of her friends – and, indeed, her own tormentor-narrator-protagonist Humbert Humbert, absent from his own wretched, obsessive tale. The author of the poem 'Pale Fire', which forms the basis of *Pale Fire*, is recently departed. *The Real Life of Sebastian Knight* (1941) – as both Nabokov's novel and the title of the narrator's biography of his dead half-brother – requires its subject to be deceased from the outset. The narrator of *The Eye* seems to exist in various forms of post-mortem reality.

In all these novels, as well as *Despair*, a 'detective' (existing in fluctuating, unstable, often contradictory forms) seeks to determine, via a series of clues, the 'real truth' (two untrustworthy words) about the focus of their inquiry. What is discovered, however, is that the inquiry itself is merely a projection or self-promotion of the investigator, and this presentation is likewise volatile and prone to error. Here exists the complex reciprocal and hostile interaction between various texts lying within Nabokov novels, overlapping or existing inside each other, like Russian dolls.

Hermann Hermann is so astounded by his own virtuosity (as are we, for he is a dazzling, if ill-disciplined and frenzied, writer) that he cannot see the snags and humdrum clichés of his own scheme: life insurance fraud is commonplace and always heavily investigated. Perhaps more troublingly, he is clearly unable to see the lack of resemblance between himself and his prey, upon which the 'genius' of his ruse relies. The glaring obviosity of this 'false double' alerts us to the state of this compulsively unpredictable character's mental health. What he seems to see in the scruffy tramp is perhaps the doppelganger of his own desolation, his own despair, a physical manifestation of his misery and self-hatred. Accordingly, murdering the beggar is actually suicide, but out of joint: a treacherous dislocation confirming his own alienation and despondency (with his work, with his wife), even if it is also a repulsive, brutal act of self-interest and self-aggrandizement.

Hermann's tale, and Nabokov's novel, abounds with a mixture of sly and explicit references to Dostoevsky: both authors mock 'old Dusty', and both 'Despair' and *Despair* contain unyielding, if perhaps not always fruitful, mockeries of the earlier Russian's work, its doublings, its sentimentalities. If *Despair* seems to lack Dostoevsky's great insights into the criminal mind, his intense penetrations that lay bare the psychology of misbehaviour, it is perhaps necessary to understand that Hermann Hermann is no ordinary miscreant with a customary motivation for murder, the insurance scam and his self-disgust notwithstanding.

Hermann is stimulated by art, by becoming an artist. It is this that allows us to recognize the true value and purpose of Nabokov's Dostoevskian insults and imitations: in Dostoevsky, identity theft is a psychological enticement to riches or revenge. For Hermann, it is predominantly an imaginative game, one that he plays poorly and loses, not understanding or wanting to adhere to the wider rules of the cosmos. For Nabokov, identity theft takes the form of parody and is a game with Russian literature, its inheritance and influence.

The true genius, the authentic artist, of *Despair* is not Hermann Hermann but Vladimir Vladimirovich (that is, Nabokov), as the honest author himself shrewdly establishes in his novel's text. In the Russian original, a painting is described as '*malinovoi* siren'*iu v* nabokoi *vaze*', literally translated as 'raspberry-coloured lilacs in a leaning vase' but subtly communicating, too, both Nabokov's Russian pseudonym, 'Sirin', which he used for his earlier works, and his actual family name.

Hermann conducts a war with his creator – and is heavily defeated, punished in hell without parole for his hubristic, narcissistic crimes. But for all his misdemeanours, his ruthlessness, callousness, egotistical despair and abnormality, Hermann is still a resilient, unsinkable scream of delight. His literary self-assurance makes for a jubilant creation. He runs riot in sureness, conviction, perception and parodic glee. He might be vain and enchanted by the mesmerizing peculiarities of his own personality, but he transmits all this to us in such dazzling digressions and quixotic quirks that we not only overlook his failures, we seem to encourage them, becoming precariously complicit in Hermann Hermann's own strange, solipsistic world and his repellent crimes (something his heinous heir Humbert

Humbert will do with us even more perilously, and on an even grander scale, in *Lolita*).

Nabokov's works always invite us to the transcendental, to an otherworldly beyond, to inventiveness, kind-heartedness, inquisitiveness. Here our being can enter a state not just of bliss but of altered consciousness, standing outside ourselves (the literal meaning of 'ecstasy'), beyond bodily injuries or temporal boundaries. *Despair* dangerously ensnares us in Hermann's ecstatic mind, but in so doing – by asking us to envisage the sorrow he both is and instigates – Nabokov prompts us to extricate ourselves, breaking free from Hermann's delectable, unsettled domain and into one of compassion and curiosity: the gifts of integrity and liberty.

8

Invitation to a Beheading
NEGATING NEGATION

Prison dramas tend to fall into two categories: those concerned with prison life and those focusing on prison escape. The latter are inclined to be thrillers, the former a fertile assortment of comedy and tragedy, the two genres often playing off against each together. What they all tend to share is a sense of realism: prison is no picnic. In them we experience the grim truths of prison existence – the regret, the injustice, the loneliness, the despondency, as well as the humour and clowning horror. Nevertheless, the nature of incarceration has ripe opportunities for surrealism, fantasy and dream, effortlessly developing out of either the farce or the misfortune. Hope, guilt or boredom can all spawn violently inventive and stressful hallucinations, incubi of psychosis and despair.

Early in the summer of 1934, Vladimir Nabokov broke off work on *The Gift* (1938) to write, in a furious fortnight, the first draft for one of his greatest masterpieces: an unnerving poetic nightmare of identity and mental labyrinths, *Invitation to a Beheading* (*Priglashenie na kazn'*,

1936). Its essential plot is straightforward. In the first sentence, citizen Cincinnatus C. is quietly condemned to death for an obscure crime. He spends nineteen days in a citadel, held in solitary confinement, never knowing the date of his execution. He frequently attempts – and fails – to escape. On the final page of the novel, he is decapitated.

A hero with an initialled surname; prosecution for an enigmatic crime by an all-powerful authority: many readers will sense an echo of Joseph K. in Franz Kafka's *The Trial* (*Der Prozeß*, 1925), and Nabokov's novel, on such a summary, does seem to share many of the topics and motifs of the Bohemian writer's work. However, Nabokov denied having read Kafka's book – and this seems very plausible, since the émigré claimed he spoke no German (he was terrified of it contaminating his treasured Russian) and, in the early 1930s, Kafka's name and literary importance were only just starting to circulate beyond a German-speaking readership. (Nevertheless, more recent biographical research has shown Nabokov's German was considerably better than he would admit.)

More significantly than any bogus notion of influence or inspiration, Nabokov's *Invitation* is a very different work to Kafka's *Trial*, whatever their superficial similarities, and we should be wary of easy exaggeration or narrow models of correlation. Kafka's superb unfinished novel portrays a gloomy, overbearing world, thick with psychoanalysis, religio-socio-political meanings and historical-critical backgrounds. Nabokov's is – for all the forbidding menace of the title – a much brighter fictional cosmos, teeming with punning repartee and anagrammatic badinage, reversals and replications, enlargements and shrinkages (in both time and space). *Invitation to a Beheading*, and especially its ending, occupies a world closer to that of Lewis Carroll's delectable, irrational, nonsensical *Alice's Adventures in Wonderland* (1865), a work Nabokov had himself translated into Russian a decade earlier, in 1923, and which was a key stimulus in his early career.

Across his works, and within *Invitation to a Beheading* in particular, Nabokov self-confidently rejoices in paradox as opportunity, illogicality as potential: for diversion, discovery, delight. In the future he would emphatically study Kafka, and his pleasure in *The Metamorphosis* (*Der Verwandlung*, 1915), which he later taught extensively, primarily resides in his joy in physical, biological, linguistic or artistic transformation as a natural marvel promising development and beauty (Nabokov was, after all, a part-time professional lepidopterist as well as a writer).

In *Invitation*, Nabokov seems not so much to bear a resemblance to Kafka, but to go beyond him, transcend him – in not qualitative but aesthetic terms. Cincinnatus inhabits a topsy-turvy fictive jurisdiction that is both dystopian and anti-dystopian, certain and indeterminate, sombre and mischievous. Strangely, almost improbably, named, 'Cincinnatus C.' is opaque, obscure in a liquid, lucid world – and this seems to be the crime for which he has been convicted.

Everyone else is in familiar, mutual understanding and agreement with one another; Cincinnatus wonders, quizzes, deliberates where others contentedly consent and conform. He is exceptional, an individual, and consequently a danger to the artificial, undistinguished, histrionic presences around him – character-creatures with slippery, interchangeable traits that switch, invert or evaporate at will. The set is cardboard, badly daubed in cheap paint. All is shoddy fabrication, tawdry mendacity.

A spider, nourished daily with insects by a warder, dwells in the prisoner's cell – but turns out to be made of fabric and metal coils. A furious tempest outside the castle is actually just an enactment, a false spectacle put on by the authorities for their institution's inmate.

Two deceitful prospects of escape entice Cincinnatus: Emmie, the prison governor's lissom and elegant daughter, bounces a ball aimlessly against a wall and draws the prisoner a picture of her escorting him to freedom; but she begins to ridicule him, becoming a brutal figure of deviant temptation and caricature, mocking Cincinnatus's disabled stepson and corpulent stepdaughter. At the same time, the jaded jailbird intermittently hears noises, which give hope of a tunnel being excavated beneath his cell, but it comes horribly to light that the governor and Cincinnatus's own executioner have in fact been burrowing away as a joke to taunt and tantalize their captive. Movement between rooms and spaces are amorphous and formlessly fluid, luring and prevaricating. In time, the cell becomes the governor's office, then the city, then Cincinnatus's own front door, which opens back into his cell.

We have all experienced such distortions and misapprehensions in dreams and nightmares: people, proceedings, environments warp and evolve, acquiring mutability and a vicious sense of determinism. We eventually wake up and try to either ignore or interpret our nocturnal phantasms. No such choice exists for Cincinnatus, who – quite reasonably – responds with escalating consternation to the terrifying, outlandish situations he finds himself in, and to the lurid spectral beings, with their kind-hearted offers to help pass the time (distributing photos, performing card tricks, playing games of chess).

Written in Berlin the year after Hitler assumed the chancellorship, *Invitation to a Beheading* seems initially to summon political readings, indirectly signifying the context of its creation – the rise of Goebbels as minister of propaganda – as well as anticipating the mock trials of Stalin's USSR. Nabokov had, in his own life, more than enough experience of fanatical politics to understand its pitiless effects. Bolsheviks had deprived him of his birthplace; Russian royalists assassinated his beloved father; a Nazi concentration camp would swallow his brother.

On the whole, two key elements inform Nabokov's politics: first, the liberal democratic movement that Nabokov cherished, to which his father had been deeply committed and which had been destroyed by Bolshevism; second, the affirmation of a profound personal independence, which Marxism (ostensibly) weakened through its stress on collective instead of individual values. Both these components are evident in *Invitation to a Beheading* and across his work, but Nabokov was not – for all his gifts – a political prophet or agitator, nor would he claim or want to be one, and his novel is not a narrowly political product. Indeed, quite how the cloistered, introverted protagonist of *Invitation* might hope to demolish a totalitarian state is a mystery and should silence any overtly political interpretation. Subtler forms of oppression lurk behind Cincinnatus's prison bars and avow Nabokov's appeal for individual liberty in a variety of forms.

Nabokov claimed the novel was set in Russia in the year 3000 AD, as a portentous, insubstantial management administrate a provincial city, where swan-shaped rechargeable carts supply the streets with transportation and the docile citizenry compliantly tolerate the unremarkable, with individual thought outlawed. In this submissive atmosphere, Cincinnatus struggles to conceal his apparently engrained inclination to observation, contemplation, imagination.

Invitation seems, then, not to be condemning communism, fascism, Leninism, Nazism or any political system – religious or radical, left or right, past or present – as such. Rather, Nabokov is attacking the attitude of perfunctory conventionality, of tamely toeing the line, that is possible under any circumstances or conditions (be they political, social, verbal, aesthetic). Here, any idiosyncrasy or individualism, anything unfamiliar or unusual, must be immediately obliterated. Socio-psychological mechanisms of tradition and embarrassment tend to accomplish this fairly automatically, culture and custom instinctively upholding uniformity and conformity.

The spurious dishonesty of this cohesion, with its additional potential for manipulation and corruption, is something Nabokov surveys and dissects throughout his work, and can be considered via the untranslatable Russian word *poshlost* (or, in Nabokov's punning transcription, *poshlust*). A complex term with a good deal of cultural baggage, it refers to a wide-ranging social, emotional, psychological and political mixture, loosely gathered together under the heading 'poor taste'.

It encompasses (but is certainly not restricted to) the cruel, crude, vulgar, vain, loutish, gaudy, grubby, indecent, smutty, smug and sentimental. It is both a snob and a maudlin mess; uninformed, boorish and liable to complacency or mania. It is 'bourgeois' as Flaubert (rather than Marx) defined it: an attitude, not an ideology. Its reach extends from the triteness of trends and the predictability of fads and fashions – in goods, opinions or aphorisms – to political hype and the systematized crazes for deities, both celestial and worldly. Such are some of the salient features of *poshlost*, which Nabokov regards with his habitually mischievous contempt but also condemns more severely on both moral and aesthetic grounds – the dreary fiends of *poshlost* who lurk to consume compassionate civilization in a collective sludge of idiocy, coarseness and monotony.

In art and literature, *poshlost* is insincerely beautiful, fraudulently clever, and the list of literary giants Nabokov accordingly dismisses has become legendary: out go Camus, Sartre, Brecht; so, too, Faulkner, Galsworthy, Hemingway, D. H. Lawrence, Conrad, and many, many more. Perhaps most famously, Freud – 'the Viennese Witch Doctor' – is on the receiving end of a sustained volley of insults from the lofty Russian, and the father of psychoanalysis might be seen as the very embodiment of Nabokovian *poshlost*. In great literary works themselves, we can observe the vice and foible of *poshlost*: Claudius and Gertrude (*Hamlet*), Alexei Karenin (*Anna Karenina*), and Molly Bloom (*Ulysses*) – as well as Charlotte Haze (*Lolita*).

It should be clear that everything and everyone in *Invitation to a Beheading* that is not Cincinnatus C. is riddled with *poshlost*, making the multifaceted and inimitable protagonist a lonely, isolated figure. He is the genuine article in a world of forgery and phoniness. Cincinnatus materializes, amid the novel's bizarre, perplexing ether, as a Nabokovian exemplar of the true artist in conflict with the tyranny of aesthetic pretence. And yet this authenticity, this transcendence and legitimacy, is available to all of us, if we seek out –

discover – inspiration and integrity, discarding duplicity and conventionality.

The artist's role is to intensify the mystery of existence, not explain it, and this priceless, difficult book takes the obscurity of being to profound depths. It is an exploration of both prison life and prison flight, of human fusion and human seclusion, personality and banality, as the protagonist unsuccessfully attempts to break free from a jail constructed in his own mind. Cincinnatus recognizes that his looming execution may function as a vehicle for self-awareness or awakening, but that to achieve this he must overcome his immobilizing dread and anxiety, his panic of death and attachment to this world, ceasing to contribute credibility to the falsity that encloses him. Part of this process is Cincinnatus's dawning realization of his own nascent creative abilities and the need to cultivate his imaginative potentiality – which he does, from mangled first phrases to flourishing eloquence and a humble, prescient understanding of his craft and its role in his life:

> Envious of poets. How wonderful it must be to speed along a page and, right from the page, where only a shadow continues to run, to take off into the blue.

Cincinnatus realizes that he can refuse the invitation to his own beheading: he can turn down his affection for and bond to the physical world, and in so doing remove the dread of ultimate expiry. In his last written statement, he maintains that he is almost fearless of 'death', before crossing out the word, the double negative generating a positive, a restoration and a marvel.

The ending of *Invitation to a Beheading* – the execution itself – petitions us to forsake the literal for the emblematic, the banal for the special. Cincinnatus rebuffs the rules of his persecutors, their callous games, and professes himself as the unique being he is. The book itself begins to dream, allowing a dual Cincinnatus to exist. The makeshift stage set of his scaffold crumples, and he seems to join kindred spirits. The conclusion, like the novel, is indefinite, thought-provoking, disobedient: the very things Cincinnatus's tormentors reject and which great art always is.

9

The Gift
PUSHKIN AVENUE TO GOGOL STREET

Nabokov's last and longest Russian novel, *The Gift* (*Dar*, 1938) is the portrait of a young man becoming an artist, as well as a detailed picture of a time and place now forever vanished. *The Gift* is set in the émigré Weimar Berlin of 1926–29 and follows the emerging, diverse literary talent of Fyodor Godunov-Cherdyntsev, a Russian exile, as he progresses from authoring a slim collection of evocative verse, to an abortive memoir of his explorer father, to an extravagant and ruthlessly opinionated biography of a celebrated literary-historical figure (the novel's entire fourth chapter), before finally arriving at the conception of *The Gift* itself.

A stylish and gracious poet, if reasonably immature and frustrated at first as his reach and grasp fail to meet, Fyodor shares some of Nabokov's upbringing, penchants and peculiarities (though they are decisively far from identical). We witness – through a mixture of grim reality and sparkling creativity – his attempts to come to terms with life's slings and arrows that harass his mind and trouble his memory: the loss of kin and country;

the dingy, lifeless existence in a foreign land, with all its attendant irritations and inconveniences. We witness his destitution, his long, lonely city walks, his cramped and grimy accommodations, his tedious teaching. But, despite the hardships, Fyodor never surrenders to despair. We track not only his developing creative abilities but also his discovery of, and burgeoning love for, Zina, his muse and future wife.

If Zina's love and Fyodor's vocation are two possibilities for the 'gift' of the novel's title, there is a crucial third, that of literature itself. Nabokov's tale contains many incorporated texts: fragmentary and complete poems; biographies both merely drafted and actually published; critical reviews and journals; parodies or pastiches of literary traditions and their legacies. *The Gift* is a rampantly allusive festival of spirited references to and discussions with Proust and Joyce, the high priests of the modern novel, confronting the former's narrative of memory and lost or squandered time in *À la recherche du temps perdu* (1913–27), as well as the Homeric quest by a son for a father in the latter's *Ulysses* (1922). Yet, for all the pleasure of such multilingual, cross-cultural encounters, *The Gift* most meaningfully negotiates with the Russian inheritance of Pushkin, Gogol and Nikolai Chernyshevsky.

For Nabokov, the contemporary continuity of the classical Russian tradition necessitated conflict, debate and multiple rereadings of the canon (as well as frequent expansion or contraction). Modern Russian writers had to engage with, dispute and challenge accepted truths about authors and texts hitherto all too frequently received as official, uncontested masters and masterpieces. Nabokov vigilantly formed his own particular literary genetics, circumspectly picking his lineages and developing resistance to any invasive species. That said, Nabokov was a variegated, multicoloured specimen – no other writer of his generation devoted himself so much to the fertility and diversity of his literary culture, creating his work in response to his lush family tree, pruning and grafting as he went.

Alexander Pushkin (1799–1837), the *de facto* founder of Russian literature, reverberates throughout Nabokov's Russian work. His first novel, *Mary* (1926), begins with an epigraph from *Eugene Onegin* (1833); *King, Queen, Knave* (1928) re-enacts a scene from Pushkin's *The Stone Guest* (1830), itself based on the Spanish Don Juan legend; the hero of *Glory* (1932) recites verse and apes the adventures of Pushkin's epic fairy tale *Ruslan and Ludmila* (1820); haughty Hermann Hermann of *Despair* (1934), named for the gambling lunatic in Pushkin's short story 'The Queen of Spades' (1834), blasphemously likens himself to its author, but misquotes the poet's lines and fails to notice his own parodic existence.

In *The Gift* (1938) Pushkin matters urgently to the young writer Fyodor Godunov-Cherdyntsev, as a source of nourishment, stimulation and connectivity:

> Continuing his training programme during the whole of spring, he fed on Pushkin, inhaled Pushkin (the reader of Pushkin has the capacity of his lungs enlarged). He studied the accuracy of the words and absolute purity of their conjunction; he carried the transparency of prose to the limits of blank verse and then mastered it. ... To strengthen the muscles of his muse he took on his rambles

whole pages of *Pugachyov* learned by heart as a man using an iron bar instead of a walking stick. ... He was in that state of feeling and mind 'when reality, giving way to fancies, blends with them in the nebulous visions of first sleep'.

Pushkin entered his blood. With Pushkin's voice merged the voice of his father. He kissed Pushkin's hot little hand, taking it for another, large hand smelling of the breakfast *kalach* (a blond roll).

For all the filial adoration and Proustian revivifications (which here seem slyly parodic of the great Frenchmen's '*petites madeleines*'), Fyodor and Nabokov do not exclude criticism or competition from their honest engagement with Pushkin's intimidating silhouette over Russian writers of the nineteenth century and his continuing challenge to those of the twentieth. Fyodor's censorious examination of, and thrilled adulation for, Pushkin anticipates in microcosm Nabokov's own immense four-volume venture decades later, when he not only translated *Eugene Onegin* (1964) but supplemented his version with a vast, insightful (and often somewhat crotchety) scholarly commentary, praising the venerated poet's inventiveness while condemning the clichés, banalities and occasional borrowings.

Shortly before *The Gift*'s appearance, Nabokov gave a public lecture ('Pushkin, or the Real and the Plausible') in Paris for the Pushkin centenary in 1937. Nabokov not only lamented the poor acquaintance of the average Russian with their national poet but also warned of the dangers inherent to 'fictionalized biographies'. These inevitably turn the divine poet into a semi-authentic macabre doll fabricated from a series of plausible vignettes – a nightshirt, a hairy chest, scribbling verse by candlelight, sitting with a bullet in his belly. Reconciling the 'real' and the 'plausible' Pushkin is as impossible as reconciling his verse in translation: 'at the approach of the translator's pen, the soul of the poetry immediately flies off, and we are left holding but a little gilded cage.'

This literary evening at the Salle Chopin in Paris had a Nabokovian strangeness to it. A Hungarian writer – Jolán Földes – who had recently written a French bestseller, *La Rue du chat qui pêche*, fell ill and pulled out. Nabokov took her place with the Pushkin essay already written for the *Nouvelle Revue française*. As Nabokov mounted the stage, many of the audience, realizing their beloved Földes would not be speaking, got up to leave. Anticipating this, a number of Nabokov's friends had tried to round up as many people as they could to be in attendance. 'A source of unforgettable consolation,' Nabokov would later recollect, 'was the sight of James Joyce sitting, arms folded and glasses glinting, in the midst of the Hungarian football team.'

It is mind-boggling, not to say cranium-wobbling, to imagine what these two twentieth-century giants, who did the most in their art to blur and enrich the boundaries between fiction and biography, might have discussed over the post-lecture drinks. Joyce had made a point of attending, so as to save his young colleague the embarrassment of an empty hall, and Nabokov never forgot it.

In *The Gift*, Fyodor's development as a writer roughly corresponds to the track Russian literature took from the Golden Age of 1820s poetry and 1830s prose, through to Gogol in the 1840s, the utilitarian 1860s of Nikolai

Chernyshevsky (author of *What Is to Be Done?*), then the period of Tolstoy and Dostoevsky, before the Silver Age and interwar modernity. Thus Nabokov's novel is structured and dramatized as a history of Russian literature, with *The Gift*'s five long divisions charting Fyodor's literary apprenticeship against that of his antecedents: his own reminiscent and adolescent verse in chapter one, Pushkin and Gogol in chapters two and three, Chernyshevsky (via Fyodor's mock biography) in chapter four, before, in the fifth, Fyodor determines his own gift and generates the very book that we have been reading.

Fyodor's poems in chapter one are expressed in iambic tetrameter, the poetic metre Pushkin eternalized. Moreover, whole passages of the novel are written in verse form, either explicitly or obscured within prose, genetically and generically connecting *The Gift* to Pushkin's own experimental 'verse novel', *Eugene Onegin*. By the second chapter, Fyodor has begun his transition to prose via an imaginary journey in Asia, biographically retracing the steps of his adventurer-naturalist father, who disappeared in the region several years earlier. The prose is patterned like Pushkin's, alliteratively ringing and singing – itself by now a recognizable trademark of Nabokov's art – and throughout his imaginary expedition, Fyodor bends the image of his vanished father through Pushkin's verbal optics. Fyodor the writer accordingly has two fathers, a parental and a literary one (just as in *Ulysses*, Stephen Dedalus has a comically distant father, Simon, and a literary-paternal companion in Leopold Bloom).

The imaginary excursion Fyodor makes is a metaphysical voyage to the beyond so familiar in Nabokov's Russian fiction, and it is one that allows him to complete his father's journey as well as achieve considerable artistic maturity. Fyodor can progress on from Pushkin, and he literally moves house: 'The distance from the old residence to the new was about the same as, somewhere in Russia, that from Pushkin Avenue to Gogol Street.'

Chapter three of *The Gift* explores the banality and crudity of Berlin (the capital city of Nabokov's *poshlost*, that mysterious Russian word combining poor taste, vulgarity, smugness and sentimentality) through the grotesque prism of Gogol, master of the monstrous and absurd. This distorting of the margins between the real and the imagined, biography and fiction, is continued into chapter four, Fyodor's bogus biography of Chernyshevsky: a merciless, hilarious dissection (with a Gogolian scalpel) of the clunking utopian socialist later praised by Marx and Lenin. For Nabokov, the utilitarian dullness of Chernyshevsky destroyed much of the life and spirit of nineteenth-century Russian literature – and was straightforwardly liable for the dismal social realism of the 1930s, an iron fist crushing the glittering surprises of the Russian Silver Age.

Fyodor successfully finds a publisher for his *Life of Chernyshevsky*. Nabokov was not so fortunate: *The Gift* appeared in Russian, but without its fourth chapter – the left was not going to allow their liberal sweetheart to be so brutally and uproariously torn apart in public. *The Gift*'s fifth and final chapter predicts such squeamishness by opening with a series of negative reviews of Fyodor's book, fusty critics nitpicking his grammar (not noticing they are actually censuring a Pushkin quotation) and revealing their own cultural-ideological prejudices.

Having expelled the materialistic aesthetic ghoul from Russian literature, Fyodor, in chapter five, is ready to embark on a new challenge: to write a 'classical novel, with "types", love, fate, conversations' – and *The Gift*'s final chapter is replete with sardonic, spoofing resonances with Turgenev and Dostoevsky, writers about whom Nabokov had perpetually unstable and complex feelings (though we have tended to remember only the entertainingly disapproving elements of his lectures on the great Russians). These parodies and ironies push Fyodor forward into creating the very book we are holding. *The Gift* is born by its own end, its potentiality finally *becoming*, as it has always strenuously promised to do. We are reminded of this when Fyodor discusses with his mother his demanding literary project to memorialize his father:

> At times I feel that somewhere it has already been written by me, that it is here, hiding in this inky jungle, that I have only to free it part by part from the darkness and the parts will fall together of themselves ... But what is the use of that to me when this labour of liberation now seems to me so difficult and complicated and when I am so much afraid I might dirty it with a flashy phrase, or wear it out in the course of the transfer to paper, that I already doubt whether the book will be written at all.

Like *Eugene Onegin*, *The Gift* is aware of its own gestation and parturition, anticipating its completeness during and through its incomplete form. Both books, too, have their poets and heroes dance around one another in expectation and collaboration, shifting reader or character perspectives, making us exhilarated (if occasionally dizzy).

In *The Gift* we see all the characteristics of a writer's life and work, including samples of the exertions themselves. (Novels with poet-protagonists usually assume our confidence that they are as great as their enfolding narratives wish us to believe.) We see both the vast, imposing heritage and the singular, impertinent endowment which seeks to expand or subvert it; we see the child who triggers the adult artist and the evolution of connectivity between the two; we witness the arduous nature of creativity and the energetic, unstoppable brain at work in the quotidian world. We see an idea dawn in the mind, then glow and burn brightly, escalating and relishing its own advancement towards delivery. We see the postnatal progeny subject to attack and hostility before another work is born and the process can begin anew.

As Nabokov makes clear in the foreword to the 1962 English translation, *The Gift*'s heroine is Russian literature, the whole work a valedictory love letter to the language and books of its creator's homeland. Yet, as an instance of romantic fiction, *The Gift* also has a more orthodox hero and heroine, and the novel is additionally Fyodor's letter of tender gratitude to Zina for helping him to create *The Gift*.

As chapter three opens, Fyodor has moved lodging houses, from 'Pushkin Avenue to Gogol Street', and the hero lies in bed, acclimatizing to his new surroundings. A morning hullabaloo vibrates through the slender walls of his bedroom as he falls in and out of sleep: the landlord's daughter clearing her throat; stubborn gas flaring and hissing to life; a brief row; the clatter of a mop handle; a vacuum cleaner. Amid all this bustle and boredom comes concealed one of the most audacious entrances in literature, even for a novel written in the mid twentieth century, as Nabokov introduces his heroine by the sound of her flushing the toilet. This is realistic romance indeed. Crucially, the first mention of her is hidden (just the noise of a bathroom convenience), buried within the bustle of morning commotion so that the heroine of both Fyodor's life and *The Gift* continues to be tantalizingly absent from the narrative, as she has been for the book's first two (long) chapters.

As Russian literature needed to get beyond Pushkin, so Fyodor needed to move, at the end of chapter two, from 'Pushkin Avenue to Gogol Street'. Doing so allows him to progress from his drifting, directionless existence in the first half of the novel, and from the unrealized biography of his lost father, to his resolutely complete Chernyshevsky book and the chance to discover the love-muse of his life, Zina. Both Fyodor and Nabokov make us wait for her, reinforcing the tension of disillusioned literary-emotional ambition so that the narrative-passionate release, when it comes, is all the more satisfying. Moving house has not only been part of Fyodor's literary growth but his emotional development, too, this shift conveying Zina Mertz into his life. Her eventual naming is positioned at the very centre of the novel. As if to prophesy the significance of Fyodor's mid-novel relocation, *The Gift*'s very first sentence describes a removals van on a Berlin street.

Zina is connected to the ghost of Fyodor's adventuring, butterfly-chasing father through a succession of significant phantasmagoria: rainbows and other illuminatory effects shimmer through the narrative, especially in the long period before, and moment when, Fyodor meets his beloved. The second chapter, wherein Fyodor tries to capture his vibrant, quixotic father within the bounds of a book, opens with a rainbow 'in languorous self-wonder, pinkish-green with a purplish suffusion along its inner edge' hanging suspended over a field. His father inadvertently enters 'the base of [the] rainbow – the rarest occurrence!' and finds himself 'in coloured air, in a play of light as if in paradise'. When Fyodor finally meets Zina, he notes a rainbow on the wall of their building, and feels 'the strangeness of life, the strangeness of its magic', just as he had earlier wondered if, when he was alone, his father had ever contemplated 'the strangeness of human life'.

Zina and Fyodor's father are linked by rainbows and colours, but also by absence. Fyodor tries to rediscover his missing father by composing a prose biography, initially attempting to maintain the chronicler's peripheral objectivity but soon finding himself drawn further into his father's existence, sliding into scenes and eventually taking his father's own perspective. This, Fyodor realizes, won't do, and he abandons the enterprise before moving house, finding Zina, and embarking upon the fruitful Chernyshevsky project. The father remains elusive, lost; the muse and receptive soul, however, can be found.

The dinginess of Fyodor's Berlin existence, the dreary monotony of his daily life, is transformed by light, imagination, memory; by love, literature, loss. Towards the end of the novel, Fyodor goes sunbathing in the Grunewald forest west of the city. Naked, he experiences the sun licking him all over 'with its big smooth tongue', feeling he has become 'moltenly transparent ... permeated with flame'. He becomes transfigured, the sun's contact connecting him with his aesthetic purpose in life. He wanders back through the woods, distracted by invasive thoughts of death. Determined not to let these feelings, or the experiences which caused them, impair or constrain his life, he resolves to transmute them into art – the art of *The Gift*.

Art can recapture the colour of the past, the ephemeral moments, thoughts and feelings of existence lost to us as every instant of our lives slips away, devoured by hungry time. All Nabokov's Russian novels have been, to some extent, a challenge to catch and contain the past's tint and shade, like one of his butterflies pinned to a card. Or, to change the metaphor, they are all jewels in the crown that is his Russian work. Accordingly, *The Gift* is the monumental sapphire at the centre, gleaming with energy and radiating history, luxurious and life-affirming, magnificent and mysterious.

10

The Enchanter
PREGNANT WITH DEATH

Shakespeare's sources have been frequently and famously derided as worthless base metals next to the shimmering gold the great playwright transformed them into. Certainly, with a few exceptions, Shakespeare did not invent the plots of his plays, making the most of stories old and comparatively new, known or unfamiliar, to weave his own particular strands of magical literary tapestry. For *Othello* (*c.*1603) Shakespeare looked to Italian writer Cinthio's 'A Moorish Captain' (1565), where we have the same basic plot that the English dramatist would cultivate. We also – apart from 'Disdemona' – have a series of unnamed characters ('Moor', 'Ensign' and so on). Cinthio's is a compelling tale in the style of Boccaccio's *Decameron* (*c.*1353), but its chief interest today is in the light it sheds on Shakespeare's motivations and purposes in penning *Othello*. A notoriously elusive writer, Shakespeare makes departures and developments with his sources which can tell us a huge amount about the particular kind of tale he was trying to tell, though we want to avoid the pitfalls and limitations of attributing authorial intention.

Vladimir Nabokov's *The Enchanter* (*Volshebnik*, 1939) occupies the same position in relation to *Lolita* (1955) as 'A Moorish Captain' does to *Othello*, and is either Nabokov's longest story or a short novella, along with being his last Russian work of fiction. Writing shortly after the outbreak of World War II, Nabokov became discontented with *The Enchanter*, and the work was not published until nine years after his death, in an English translation by his son Dmitri Nabokov in 1986, which his father had suggested many decades earlier. Most published versions of the text now include two author's notes by Vladimir, in addition to Dmitri's essay 'On a Book Entitled *The Enchanter*' (echoing 'On a Book Entitled *Lolita*' - Nabokov's 1956 postscript to his scandalous novel).

The plot of *The Enchanter* is straightforwardly told. A middle-aged man is frustrated by his unfulfilled desire for pubescent children in early adolescence. He marries a terminally ill woman to secure access to her twelve-year-old daughter. After the mother's swift death, he elopes with the girl. On the first night, as she sleeps, he caresses her. She wakes and screams in terror, sending him hurrying out into the street, where he is hit by a truck.

Although Nabokov later called *The Enchanter* his 'pre-*Lolita*', he also - quite understandably - saw it as a separate work. Its own antecedent is wonderfully intertextual: in Nabokov's extraordinary culmination of his Russian novelistic career, *The Gift* (1938), the protagonist-writer's girlfriend's stepfather proposes a novel about an 'old goat' wedding a woman to obtain her child. *The Enchanter* also explores other concerns surveyed throughout Nabokov's work, specifically deception and games, as well as a dangerously ambiguous merging of sensual and aesthetic delight. In *The Enchanter*, the nameless villain's plan is to dupe his nameless girl into an affiliation of attraction and enchantment via a series of calculating subterfuges 'like a chess player'.

The anonymous nature of the characters in *The Enchanter* (as with Cinthio's 'A Moorish Captain') seems significant, not least when we think how the names Humbert Humbert and Lolita will reverberate throughout not only their book but English literature itself – and beyond. *Lolita* – from its opening words – fetishizes, formulates, dominates and deconstructs its subject-victim's name: a possession of power and deception by the narrator-hunter over both his prey and his reader. By choosing not to give his characters named identities, the Nabokov of *The Enchanter* removes them slightly from our affections, even as this also allows him to amplify them, not only as (sadly all too commonplace) examples of the corruptions and miseries of human existence, but as unreliably sterile subjects constantly threatening to mutate in the laboratory-text.

As with nomenclature, so with modes of storytelling. *The Enchanter*'s approach to narration, which may initially appear second-rate to that of *Lolita*, yields, upon closer inspection, significant harvest. If, in *The Enchanter*, we are far away from Humbert's tense, fizzing first-person narration of his own sordid story, this earlier work's omniscient third-person narration, and its intimate alliance with its protagonist's perspective, is still a considerably stimulating technique. In many ways it is actually a first-person narration in disguise, feigning objectivity in order to confuse or amuse us, scrutinizing lunacy through the lunatic's unstable mind and even more unpredictable text – as *Despair* (1934) had done and *Pale Fire* (1962) will do.

The Enchanter lacks many of the things that would enrich, magnify and mystify *Lolita*: no Annabel Leigh, no Clare Quilty, no resplendently hapless Charlotte Haze (nor her brilliantly structured demise). The scenery is static, unspecified (though Nabokov would later clarify it to be the French Riviera). There is no panorama for the imagination that Humbert creates from the vastness of the American landscape; no peephole for our prying, curious eye to stealthily observe *Lolita*'s impeccably captured small-town USA.

The more complex setting, psychology, tone and ambience of *Lolita* would come later. But *The Enchanter* need not be read only by those wishing to enhance their appreciation of the subsequent *magnum opus*. Its style and structure are fascinating – as enchanting as its title needs it to be. Let us remember: *The Enchanter* is not an immature work, some obscure juvenilia of interest only to scholars or unhinged obsessives, but the final Russian work of a writer who had already produced several significant masterpieces, dwarfing much of the literary output of his generation.

Lolita is pregnant with death, an electric text of constant bereavement. Lolita herself is pregnant with death – literally so, since she will die in childbirth. To some extent, *The Enchanter*, too, is pregnant with death, since by birthing *Lolita* it will destroy its own ability to live. But this should not be the case: the parent has not been killed by the offspring. Indeed, Nabokov himself was surprised when, in 1959, he rediscovered the manuscript he had thought lost, rereading it 'with considerably more pleasure than I experienced when recalling it as a dead scrap during my work on *Lolita*.'

Its autonomous interest, not merely its length, justifies this novella's independent presence outside the main collections of Nabokovian stories (though *The Enchanter* would serenely fit among their many riches) and at the end of the sequence of Russian novels. Meticulous, eloquent, beguiling: it is pure Nabokov.

PART TWO

THE ENGLISH NOVELS

11

The Real Life of Sebastian Knight
DEAD MEN & DEAD ENDS

What's in a title? Novels as diverse as *In Search of Lost Time, One Hundred Years of Solitude, The Woman in White, As I Lay Dying, Things Fall Apart* or *The Man without Qualities* intrigue and tease with their designations, inviting us into their mysterious machinations. Earlier, Shakespeare mixed the authority, certainty and ambiguity of the histories and tragedies (*Richard II, Henry V, Coriolanus*) with the playfully evasive maxims of the comedies (*As You Like It, All's Well That Ends Well*). *Measure for Measure*'s biblical dictum encourages discussion before the curtain has even gone up; *A Midsummer Night's Dream* and *The Winter's Tale* enthral and attract with their seasonal sprinklings. Elsewhere, *The Stranger, The Rainbow* and *The Trial* seem clear enough, but their assurances immediately evaporate as soon as we look away from their labels and step inside their pages.

Nabokov's first novel in English, *The Real Life of Sebastian Knight* (1941), was written in Paris in 1938–39, and its title looks like a game or, worse still, a literary trap ready to catch us out. Why does it feel the need to assert its authenticity or sincerity? What does the title's affirmation hide by its very claim to reality? The 'truth'? Or something more elusive?

The Real Life of Sebastian Knight claims to be the biography of the lately departed writer Sebastian Knight (1899–1936), researched and prepared via interviews, reminiscences, and instinctive guesswork, as well as Sebastian's own books, by his half-brother, 'V.' (1906–), an émigré who has been living among the Russian community in Paris since 1919.

Sebastian, we learn, detached himself from his linguistic and ancestral past, taking his English mother's name and language, signing his early poems with the elusive image of a chess knight, and studying at Cambridge. After university, in London, he meets the receptively ideal mistress-muse Clare Bishop, his fellow chess-namesake, and promptly flourishes as a novelist of rare insight and distinction. V. sees Sebastian twice, and only fleetingly, in 1924 and 1929, before receiving a letter (unexpectedly composed in Russian) from his sibling in January 1936, and soon afterwards an urgent telegram from Sebastian's doctor. V. rushes to be with his dying half-brother and performs a vigil by his side. (Or does he? The tale has a few Nabokovian twists up its sleeve.)

V. seeks to understand Sebastian's life, and above all his ostensibly unhappy later years, retracing his past (via the facts and fictions of Sebastian's life, interweaving historical 'reality' with the 'truths' of the writer's oeuvre). He visits Sebastian's London flat, quizzes college acquaintances, and attempts to locate an unidentified Russian love the half-Russian Knight met at the end of the 1920s. This forms the deep, sad heart of *The Real Life of Sebastian Knight*:

the obscurity and pain of the past, as well as the sanctity of the individual's life and art, both being familiar features of Nabokov's Russian-language narratives in the first half of his bilingual career.

Estrangement, glances, endings: loss and the desperate need to recapture the past dominates the narrative. Distant and aloof in life, Sebastian's death brings the two half-brothers together as V. tries to write his book in March 1936 – shortly after Sebastian's former secretary, a Mr Goodman, has brought out his own rushed, 'slapdash and very misleading' biography: *The Tragedy of Sebastian Knight*.

This biographer seems aware of neither V.'s existence nor the boys' shared father's remarriage, and although we might initially take V.'s side in slighting the opportune hack Mr Goodman, soon we begin to doubt whether V. is really related to Sebastian at all, and thus why he thirsts so much for his fraternal affection. A deranged admirer? A lunatic bookworm obsessed with his favourite author's enticing, peculiar books to such an extent that he has confused aspects of his own existence with that of the writer's? Perhaps V.'s dull work as a businessman, his demanding boss and unending administrative crises, have made him envy Sebastian's apparently free, glamorous life as a writer.

As a narrator V. is not, on the face of it, untrustworthy: he seems modest, thoughtful, consistent, if occasionally a little peevish and given to consternation. When referring to his and Sebastian's common paternal origin, V. usually writes the curious 'my father', and this man's death in 1913 from an injury generated by a duel over an earlier *affaire d'honneur* slyly suggests some uncertainty over their mutual paternity. The possibility that V. is or is not Sebastian's half-brother cannot be substantiated or refuted, and the text is too meagre in its factual particulars to help: V. tells us very little about their childhood, their families, their rare adult meetings. Characters we encounter in V.'s narration are unlikely either to be able to corroborate much of what he tells us, or to find evidence to prove him otherwise.

The truth of their relationship glows – now faint, now vivid – throughout the novel, flickering between meaning and possibility in our minds. This operates to make both Sebastian and V. – whoever they are – more mystifying, more inscrutable – and their predicament profoundly poignant because both extremes (that they really are alienated half-brothers or that V. is simply insane) are acutely upsetting.

The Real Life of Sebastian Knight is a comic torment of disappointments, vexations and fake footsteps, as one figure tries to retrieve the enigmas of another's life – with its mysteries and surprises that all lives will contain, daring us to investigate, defying our efforts. For all his modesty (which now seems unreliably false) about his 'complete lack of literary experience', V. is perceptive and erudite enough to counsel us about the nature of biographic art:

> Remember that what you are told is really threefold: shaped by the teller, reshaped by the listener, concealed from both by the dead man of the tale.

The Real Life of Sebastian Knight is a hyper-literary text, and V. makes constructive, insightful use of reference, citation and synopses from Sebastian's five books, with their elaborate, slightly affected prose and sometimes fastidiously self-conscious titles: *The Prismatic Bezel, Success,*

Lost Property, *The Funny Mountain*, *The Doubtful Asphodel*. Two sets of texts V. destroys at Sebastian's request (graciously but catastrophically, surely, as an aspirant biographer) are two bundles of love letters, between Sebastian and Clare Bishop and between Sebastian and the unknown Russian woman (his last and clandestine love, who seems – in her absence – to diffidently lure us into reading her as emblematic for all Russia, its language, culture and people).

This documentary evidence calamitously extinguished (via gorgeous, pirouetting prose) in the grate of Sebastian's London flat, V. heads to the continent. He picks up bogus clues and muddy trails, travelling down blind alleys, his narrative now in the guise of a spoof thriller or detective story, much as Sebastian's own first novel, *The Prismatic Bezel*, had been. V. often (and unsuspectingly) meets or hears about people who bear a resemblance, physical or otherwise, to characters Sebastian has included in his fictional worlds (which, naturally, we know about only from V.'s own narrative).

V.'s generally thwarted quest does produce a detective, Mr Silbermann, who locates a list of fellow guests from the hotel Sebastian stayed at when he met his mysterious love. This vital inventory is rendered peculiar by the bizarreness of Silbermann's behaviour, as well as his resemblance to 'Mr Siller', 'the most alive of Sebastian's creatures' from his short story 'The Back of the Moon', collected in *The Funny Mountain*. Silbermann destroys the limits and restrictions of a realistic novel, compelling us to see V. as either blindly deluded or as intentionally (and disingenuously) populating his own narrative with Sebastian's creatures to give his biographic tale credibility and connectivity between his subject's life and art.

Habitually confused, often apparently made gullible by his own narrative, V. is a parodic inspector in a windup whodunnit. But if *The Real Life of Sebastian Knight* is an exploration of the genres of biography and detective thriller, it is also, with its fluctuating nexus of irregular explanations, a delicate and disconcerting ghost story. Indeed, Sebastian's own final novel, *The Doubtful Asphodel*, seems to be a spectral, sardonic anticipation of *The Real Life of Sebastian Knight* itself. (Moreover, it is largely a hint from *The Doubtful Asphodel*'s plot, where a secret is to be disclosed by a dying man, that convinces V. that Sebastian would reveal all to his half-brother on his deathbed.)

Is *The Doubtful Asphodel* actually Sebastian's penultimate novel and *The Real Life of Sebastian Knight* his last? It is hard to be sure, and one of the pleasures of Nabokov's book is that we don't – and can't – know the answers to such conjectures. Parodies, Möbius strip narratives, and numerous strata of meaning, combined with exploratory reaches for otherworldly domains, link *The Real Life of Sebastian Knight* with all Nabokov's Russian novels and the English ones to come. Perhaps the most satisfying reading of *The Real Life of Sebastian Knight*, especially given its position at the central and biggest shift in his literary career, is to see the ambiguous synthesis between Sebastian and V. as a parable of artistic plasticity, of aesthetic and linguistic manoeuvrability – an agility which necessitates losses as much as it anticipates gains.

To some, *The Real Life of Sebastian Knight* exists as a cautionary manual for would-be commentators or biographers – particularly biographers of writers, and especially biographers of Nabokov. Yet Nabokov's novel is (unsurprisingly) far more than this. It *is* an admonitory tale for biographers, but one for readers, too, especially those too keen to connect the life with the art of a writer (through overconfidence, lack of confidence or mere literary idleness).

Nabokov, in his own life, constructed a fortress to fortify himself against the invasive forces of both biographical inquiry and the future's view of his past, especially the past of his creativity and its imaginative processes. Over time, this citadel is inevitably stormed, not least when its lord is no longer around to defend it. Yet novels like *The Real Life of Sebastian Knight* are Nabokov's booby traps and sprung snares, upholding his post-mortem and perpetual ability to defend his art from incursion or attempted conquest.

Ever courteous, *The Real Life of Sebastian Knight* extends this tenuous but very possible protection not just to writers but to us all, showing how our lives defy the external gossipy intrusions of 'reality'. Few of us will suffer biographers prising open our inner lives; at worst, some vacuous relatives might pry or blather. All of us, however, face daily skirmishes between truth and falsity, reality and fantasy, that which is typical or abnormal, blatant or disguised, intelligible or incomprehensible. The borders between these are blurred and unstable, as perspective or opinion or fashions shift, alter or revise.

In *The Real Life of Sebastian Knight*, the spuriousness of the non-noumenal world is laid bare and the vitality of the non-material, spaceless, timeless sphere is asserted – benefiting, as it does, from an existence beyond the reach of causality or misrepresentation. And art always allows us access to, or at least a glimpse of, these miraculous, transcendent truths.

Within *The Real Life of Sebastian Knight*, 'reality' and the 'real' will not settle or sit still. They are restless, anxious and annoyed, exasperated by the burdens placed upon them, irritated with their own inability to fix or resolve significance. Yet they are also mischievous, even malicious, luring us in before spitting us out. They invite vast constituencies of meaning – plus layers, ploys, digressions, collisions and *culs-de-sac*, each jostling for recognition and their say, whether to amuse, frustrate or falsify our reading.

To return to where we began, what are we to make of the book's title? Closely considered, every word it contains – *The Real Life of Sebastian Knight* – is open to misgivings and speculation, with the most industrious literary detective work ultimately finding only various shades of red herring. Even the usually straightforward article 'the', endeavouring to definitely define its subject, quivers and trembles, its certainty, fixity and exclusivity continually destabilized.

Other book titles might, or might not, offer us more help. Early on in the novel, when V. visits Sebastian's London apartment, with its dead notebooks, cold fireplace and 'foreign coins in a chocolate box', he also discovers his brother's bookshelves, one of which is noticeably tidier than the rest. The volumes it shoulders might serve here as a final symbol for the myths and mysteries of *The Real Life of Sebastian Knight*. They are a confounding assortment of the unquestionably real and the coyly unreal, their titles forming a 'vague musical phrase, oddly familiar'. They tempt us to read something into their particular inclusion – by Sebastian, by V., or by Nabokov.

Hamlet, La morte d'Arthur, The Bridge of San Luis Rey, Doctor Jekyll and Mr Hyde, South Wind, The Lady with the Dog, Madame Bovary, The Invisible

> *Man, Le Temps Retrouvé, Anglo-Persian Dictionary, The Author of Trixie, Alice in Wonderland, Ulysses, About Buying a Horse, King Lear ...*

Do these titles have meaning, or are they another false trail laid by one of the many potential authors of *The Real Life of Sebastian Knight*? Is one of the titles a hint that Sebastian himself is playing a game with us? Is he a ghost, an invisible man, communicating from beyond the grave, perhaps via the vivid network of flowers that perturb and adorn the narrative?

12

Bend Sinister

THE EMBASSY OF SILENCE

AMBASSADOR: The sight is dismal
And our affairs from England come too late.
The ears are senseless that should give us hearing
To tell him his commandment is fulfilled
That Rosencrantz and Guildenstern are dead.

(Hamlet, V.ii.351–355)

In June 1940, 59 rue Boileau – an apartment block on the south-east corner of the Bois de Boulogne in Paris's sixteenth arrondissement – was razed by the invading German army. A few weeks earlier a family of three – two adults and a child – had hurriedly left the building and hastened to a train station. From there, they took a first-class sleeper they could hardly afford in order to give their boy, aged six and with a temperature of 104, some additional rest as they plied him with medicinal concoctions every few hours. Because of the swift German advance, the family's destination was a moving target, shifting from Le Havre in Normandy, further west along the coast to Cherbourg, then finally settling on Saint-

Nazaire, a port town nestled under the protruding snout of Brittany and staring out across the Atlantic.

This anonymous trio emerged from the station and proceeded quickly along to the harbour, their son now fit and well and holding a parent in each paw. Despite their impecuniousness, they had managed to obtain, via a charitable organization for Jewish refugees, a first-class cabin on the *Champlain*, a migrant vessel bound for New York. The crossing was rough and tense: two German spies were discovered on board, and a surfacing whale was on one occasion mistaken for a warship.

Behind them, the little troika left colleagues, friends and family, many of whom would be swallowed up by either the Nazi military machine or the black hole of the extermination camps. One of the departing threesome left behind a trunk of books and papers as well as a collection of European Lepidoptera, meticulously accumulated over the years. The books and papers were to be reunited with their owner after a decade; the hoard of butterflies would be destroyed, its treasures revoked to dust.

On 28 May 1940 Vladimir, Véra and Dmitri Nabokov slid past the Statue of Liberty and docked at Manhattan. Months and years of impoverishment; the struggles to obtain exit visas from France and enough money for the boat fare; elusive, poorly paid teaching work: all were at an end. Nabokov had arrived in America, a country where he would make his family safe, his resources secure – and his name immortal.

This entrance into relative paradise allowed Nabokov's imagination to roam in the abyss he had left behind. In the decade prior to his arrival in America, Nabokov had written some seven novels and dozens of short stories. His next novel, *Bend Sinister* (1947), his second in English, would take him six years to write, his time now occupied by teaching, translating and obsessive entomological work, as well as the demands of imaginative composition. Although *The Real Life of Sebastian Knight* (1941) was his first English novel, it was written in Paris in 1938–39 and inhabits a slight no man's land between the Russian and the English Nabokov, with its rearward fixations on loss and the impossible retrieval of the past. *Bend Sinister* continues many of these themes of estrangement and adds those of confinement and liminality, hysteria and anguish.

Written during a period of great happiness as Nabokov settled into a country he very quickly loved and felt at home in, *Bend Sinister* – for all its luminosity – is a brutal book that betrays the conditions of its conception in 1940: the advancing force of a martial superpower bent on conquest, callousness and liquidation; the instinctive need for a parent to protect their child. With a Jewish wife and Jewish son, Nabokov was only too aware of what Nazis might do to them, and this bestowed the stimulus for *Bend Sinister*, as Nabokov and his immediate family fled a continent once again determined not only to tear itself apart but to sink into the most appalling depravity.

In *Bend Sinister*, Paduk is the recently inaugurated dictator of an unidentified Central European country, where German and Russian (as well as a blend of the two) are spoken, its citizens subjected to their leader's Lenin-like rants and Hitlerian agitations, together with a blend of Nazi-Soviet constitutional nonsenses. This unexceptional little country can claim a minor global celebrity in its ranks: a philosopher in his mid-forties, Adam Krug, former classmate of the despot and the novel's protagonist.

We meet Krug at a crisis point in his life: his beloved wife, Olga, has just died following an operation, and he is moreover being pressured to support the new regime, his international standing granting the administration much-needed respectability. Krug declines, certain his status will shield him from harm but also blinded by grief to the risks encircling him. Attempts to compel Krug to comply by persecuting his friends fail – so Paduk has some brutes abduct the philosopher's eight-year-old boy, David. Krug at once agrees to back the government the instant his child is freed, but disaster strikes and the child is murdered by blundering guards. Driven senseless, Krug attacks Paduk and is shot by the tyrant's adjuncts.

Bend Sinister complicates, and ultimately annihilates, its superficially political ('Orwellian' or 'Kafkaesque') narrative by making the powers that taunt Krug shambolic, frivolous – and dangerously nonsensical. The book bristles with farcical devices (talking scenery; self-aware stage directions; italicized clichés) that draw attention to its fictive nature. It wilfully and digressively discusses rarefied theories of tragedy, geology, cosmology, parapsychology. Nabokov even closes the novel by – at its ominous climax – melting away mid-sentence to reveal its author at his desk, finishing his most recent creation.

What seems to be a socio-political novel, to stand on the shelf next to *The Castle* (1926), *Brave New World* (1932) or *Nineteen Eighty-Four* (1949), is in fact a metaphysical tale arguing for the absence or elimination of politics from people's lives, the better to improve them. Nabokov's politics, such as they are, are of a far vaster schema than any urgent or immediate local anxieties concerning the Red Army, Wehrmacht, or Japanese imperial belligerence. Like *Invitation to a Beheading* (1936) but – as Nabokov put it – in a 'bass voice', *Bend Sinister* explores forms of subjugation subtler than the malice of martinets and affirms Nabokov's appeal for personal freedom in a diversity of ways.

Such an approach is not a cold-hearted disregard for the plight of the politically beleaguered or a lofty retreat into philosophical abstraction. Nabokov, as we have seen, was only too familiar with of the sufferings of his age. Shortly before the novel's publication, he would write to his sister:

> Much as one might want to hide in one's little ivory tower, there are things that torment too deeply, e.g. the German vileness, the burning of children in ovens – children as funny and as strongly loved as our children.

Yet his solution is not further antagonism by means of a choleric novel of degraded politics and human wickedness, but rather a vigilance towards the wonder of human sentience and creativity (which does, of course, carry political corollaries).

For Nabokov, true democracy should unburden the individual from the weight or force of politics: the analytical and inquisitive mind drifting freely, scurrying about, probing, doubting, dislocating. Imagination is rebellion, in its most chaste form, an intellectual insurgence from the persistent, habitual failures of our species towards a constancy of consciousness. (That being said, as we will see, Nabokov's novel is also keen to exhibit abuse and ill treatment for what it is; and the means by which he does it – utilizing a vibrant, animated language – is crucial to the aversion and disgust he feels.)

For Paduk, the norm is the ideal: he is, after all, leader of the preposterously named Party of the Average Man. His ambitions are for standardization, a desire to see individuals turned to cosy couples boxed within an expedient and conventional society of 'normality', brains pruned like bourgeois hedges to duplicate the minds of others. Everything is to be a neat replication and as such is false, a routine multiplication of tidy humanity based on the lie of contented proficiency. Paduk, and everything he stands for, is an untruth, an incongruity and an emptiness. When apprehending Krug's friend, the brilliant poet and translator Ember, Paduk believes 'an atmosphere of high life, flowers, the perfume of feminine beauty, might sweeten the ordeal' – so decrees that the pair of arresting officers be a chic lady sporting a designer outfit and a dapper gent with a silky crimson tulip in his buttonhole.

Such devotion to detail is common to bullies and skilful oppressors, but it also heightens the ridiculous caricature Nabokov wants Paduk and his subordinates to be. Take them seriously and we're in dire straits. Calling such figures 'monsters' or 'evil' simply gives them the attention and mania they crave. They are absurd, outwardly powerful, impressive only with props and propaganda – and should be mocked as Charlie Chaplin's *Great Dictator* (1940) did with Hitler. Without his armies, orchestrated rallies or breathtaking stubbornness, Hitler would have been nothing but a failed, annoying and rather unlovable artist, author of a wearisome brochure of lies and stupidity. But tenacity, a smart uniform and a message of hate can go a long way, not least in a culture where individuality and curious nonconformity have been stigmatized or eroded.

The conflict in *Bend Sinister* between distinctive consciousness and a harsh, acquiescent world clearly links it to *Hamlet* (*c.*1600), and Nabokov's novel performs a complex dialogue (both explicitly and more stealthily) with Shakespeare's loquacious tragedy of vengeance and surveillance, meditation and mediation. In our time, Prince Hamlet is still, despite fluctuating cultural and academic fashions, the prototype of the outsider-thinker, a dazzling erudite mind and lexical juggler subject to the ominous manoeuvrings of a corrupt state, just like scholars and writers are in Paduk's modern kingdom of cruelty and coercion.

In the realm of *Bend Sinister*, the dictator (and his devotees) view ideas as things to be submissively acknowledged, blandly balanced, equalized into inert orthodoxy and agreement. In opposition to the blank paucity of Paduk's ideology stand two individuals: first, Krug, a leading intellectual, with a multicoloured, fertile mind that refuses to obey or stand idle; second, Ember, delightful poet-decoder of *Hamlet*, ambassador of words across the verbal frontiers, set on diplomatically translating every vivid shade and mysterious pleasure of Shakespeare's great drama.

Paduk himself stages for his people an inept version of the play, based on a Professor Hamm's 'extraordinary work' entitled 'The Real Plot of *Hamlet*'. Here, the 'fine Nordic youth' Fortinbras is repositioned at the play's conceptual core, the noxious wordsmith Hamlet further ostracized. For Paduk and Hamm, clever use of language is something unhealthy, unreliable, a disease of 'decadent democracies' – 'everybody in the Denmark of the play suffers from a plethora of words.' Accordingly, the only way to save the state is for 'popular commonsense' to 'spit out the caviar of moonshine and poetry'.

Hamlet, of course, has been reinterpreted (and misinterpreted) more than practically any other work in literature, inviting a swarm of perverse and pedantic readings down the centuries, including Nabokov's *bête noir* Freud's infamously Oedipal assessment of the drama. In *Bend Sinister*, the intricacies of such debates and the details of Nabokov's literary heritage, especially the *Hamlet* deliberations undertaken in Goethe's *Wilhelm Meister* (1796) and Joyce's *Ulysses* (1922), are parodied and negotiated, debated and knocked about. Nabokov takes the scholarly considerations of his predecessors and vastly multiplies them, while simultaneously placing the whole comic discussion within the context of absolutely grave personal and political strife (comparable to the relationship between *Hamlet*'s 'rotten' Denmark and its defective first family).

Bend Sinister understands translation and interpretation as avenues of inevitable loss, but as spectacles for opportunity, too: new linguistic and thematic acrobatics; a spirited circus of art and imagination. Ember, and to a lesser extent Krug, is perceived by Nabokov as a Hamlet- or Shakespeare-like figure, seeing the world in general, and language in particular, as a paradise of playthings, teeming with possibility. Against these imaginative, honest dynamisms, Paduk is a malign, appropriating form.

His name has Shakespearean origins, though of a less appealing kind: in *Macbeth* (1606), the name of the second witch's familiar, 'Paddock', means 'toad'; in *Hamlet*, murderer-usurper Claudius is obliquely referred to by his avenging nephew as a 'paddock'. Darkly amphibian, then, Paduk is a gloomy figure familiar from worldwide folklore: swarthy of skin and bland of colour, at home in a range of environments, emerging noiselessly from murky cavities or sliding quietly into concealing water, neither attractive nor to be trusted.

Hamlet's belief in the 'divinity which shapes our ends' (V.ii.10) connects him to Krug's faith in the emancipating potential of fate – though for Nabokov's protagonist, it is the transcendent narrator/author, not Hamlet's unfathomable, predestining Protestant deity, that shapes fortune. Theology has metamorphosed into aesthetics. *Hamlet* is tragedy, generically and tonally, even as it tries to twist and destabilize the form. *Bend Sinister* is not so straightforward. It is structured on tragic lines – heinous misconduct shatters essentially blameless lives with multiple resultant deaths – but its ending, as Nabokov reveals his authorial hand, is more ambiguous.

The novel is ruthless, killing Krug's wife and child before wrecking his marvellous intellect and twisting his creative consciousness into a muddled and homicidal homogeny (since all mad minds are uniformly nonsensical), an appalling real psychosis which eclipses Hamlet's feigned one. In many respects, Krug's insanity is a relief to him, and we as readers are 'comforted' at the end that his life and woes are only a fiction (like a parent soothing their frightened child: 'there, there, little one, it's only a story'). The flagrant and self-conscious manner of this reassurance, however, serves only to darken the hope. It paradoxically reminds us of the very real recent sufferings of countless individuals under Nazism and Stalinism, and of innumerable other transient manifestations of ignorance and hatred across the course of human history.

Bend Sinister contains many horrific episodes, not least those involving the torture of children. At one point, unsure if his stolen boy is dead or alive, Krug learns of the sadistic goings-on at the 'Institute for Abnormal Children', where David might be being held. We see abuse and experimentation masquerading as sociology, maiming and murder exhibited as therapy or fun:

> Sometimes the 'squeezing game' started at once after the 'spitting game' but in other cases the development from harmless pinching and poking or mild sexual investigations to limb tearing, bone breaking, deoculation, etc. took a considerable time. Deaths of course unavoidable, but quite often the 'little person' was afterwards patched up and gamely made to return to the fray. Next Sunday, dear, you will play with the big boys again. A patched up 'little person' provided an especially satisfactory 'release'.

Horrors hide behind obscure words: 'deoculation' is the removal of the eyes (and we imagine the immobile, vacant horror of readers when they've gone to google it). Perversion and unimaginable distress are presented in nonchalant, easy-going language, smug and complacent, spiteful and sneering. It is not just malevolent; it is *nasty*. After presenting us with this litany of savagery, the narrator casually continues:

> Now we take all this, press it into a small ball, and fit it into the centre of Krug's brain where it gently expands.

Krug is obliged to envisage an infinite amount of undetermined pain, much like that of the mother who suffers over her son's mental agony in Nabokov's 1948 'Signs and Symbols' – one of his greatest short stories, written around the same time as *Bend Sinister*.

> She thought of the endless waves of pain that for some reason or other she and her husband had to endure; of the invisible giants hurting her boy in some unimaginable fashion; of the incalculable amount of tenderness contained in the world; of the fate of this tenderness, which is either crushed, or wasted, or transformed into madness …

Hearts physical or figurative thump and thud throughout *Bend Sinister*, the plot of the novel throbbing as sections communicating Krug's feelings equivocate with those documenting his thoughts or distractions and with those segments supplying interruptions or backgrounds to the protagonist's inner world. Such narrative-linguistic rhythms pump the blood of our imaginations, and the pulses in these cadences form gaps through which we peer into a chasm of dreadful terrestrial or everlasting unknown: parents fraught and frantic as they lose sight of their children in the street (or see them disappear into cattle trucks, gas chambers, incinerators).

Multilingual word games, punning idioms, jesting colloquialisms, intertextual amusements – all these and more cram and crowd the text, playing with our emotions as verbal ghosts come and go, insinuating connections, meetings and meanings. Memories of his wife and child flicker through Krug's guilt- and grief-stricken mind, recording his pain but representing it only momentarily, partially, inadequately.

Bend Sinister is an opaque, caliginous novel, replete with abundant images and instances of agonizing callousness that shock and disgust. It is also full of incongruously coexistent linguistic shenanigans and exuberant textual mischief: acts of unutterable brutality are in fact shaped and conveyed by way of a macabre verbal display. This is not to claim ironically that tyrants and persecutors are dim-witted, lacking style or sophistication (though of course they often are). More crucially, it is the notion that acts of iniquity, especially those of the types undertaken in *Bend Sinister* or the Holocaust, are actually indescribable, inexpressible, outside and far beyond language's ability to communicate meaning. Placing such tangible horrors in the synthetic framework of words to some extent sanctions or endorses them, even if it is the only tool at our disposal, since such events should never have occurred, never have the need for discussion. *Bend Sinister*'s buoyant, mischievous prose, and its glaringly self-aware conclusion, draws attention – with devastating power – to the moral baseness it describes.

Language and literature are processes of communication, envoys of meaning at the consulate of human engagement. The diplomatic mission of words is, for Nabokov, benevolent and beneficial, overcoming boundaries and transmitting rapture. The dense intertextual provocations of *Bend Sinister*, as well as its garrulous semantic antics and philological diversions, point to the interconnectedness, the essential integrity of language and its literary offspring. But language – even Nabokov's language – can do only so much to bear or reveal the nature and meaning of certain terrors perpetrated, crimes committed. Eventually we must become mute, as verbal ambassadors reach the embassy of silence.

13

Lolita

COMEDY, CATHARSIS
& COSMIC CRIME

Lolita (1955) is an exceptionally problematic book to design a cover for. Too gaudy or explicit and you distort the book's shrewder meanings and musings. If your layout is too conceptual, too intangible, do you improperly ignore the book's darker traits and challenging issues? Nabokov himself was, of course, all too conscious of the difficulty, writing to his publishers at Putnam for the forthcoming (1958) American edition:

> After thinking it over, I would rather not involve butterflies. Do you think it could be possible to find today in New York an artist who would not be influenced in his work by the general cartoonesque and primitivist style jacket illustration? Who would be capable of creating a romantic, delicately drawn, non-Freudian and non-juvenile, picture for LOLITA (a dissolving remoteness, a soft American landscape, a nostalgic highway – that sort of thing)? There is one subject which I am emphatically opposed to: any kind of representation of a little girl.

After receiving a small selection of sketches, he wrote back, declining all of them:

> I want pure colours, melting clouds, accurately drawn details, a sunburst above a receding road with the light reflected in furrows and ruts, after rain. And no girls. If we cannot find that kind of artistic and virile painting, let us settle for an immaculate white jacket (rough texture paper instead of the usual glossy kind), with LOLITA in bold black lettering.

Eventually, author and publisher settled on the white cover with a firm black typeface, as well as a Jackson Pollock-esque yellow frenzy behind the title, signifying, perhaps, the chaos and commotion within. The original Paris edition of 1955 had favoured a simple olive-green jacket and a distinctively academic design not unlike the Loeb Classical Library's. Deceptively restrained, discerningly understated, it solved the problem largely by avoiding it.

In truth, most covers for *Lolita* have probably failed to meet the enormous challenge laid down by the book's contents, and in the decades since its first publication we have had everything from the elusive, subtle and abstract to the obvious, vulgar and kitsch. The latter have been occasionally not just lurid but openly pornographic, frequently starring mature women (with gigantic chests and long-drawn-out legs), in a puzzling and lamentable disparity with both *Lolita*'s heroine and its protagonist's fantasies. Publishers, it seems, are willing to sacrifice all sense of propriety or obligation to accuracy in order to cash in on the immense success of Nabokov's novel, exploiting his text just as Humbert takes advantage of his stepchild, offering poor *Lolita* up either as voluptuous erotica or valueless smut.

Unfortunately, not least because of these misrepresentations, the refracted image of *Lolita* that has prevailed in popular culture (and few books have become so swiftly and comprehensively a component of the general nexus) is one of an aggressively sexual seductress, precociously flirtatious and almost entirely lacking any sense of victimization. Publishers might argue that Nabokov invited such eye-popping aggrandizements with his vivid imagery and sensational subject matter – which is, of course, to woefully misunderstand not only the book's subtleties but also Nabokov's intentions in writing the novel. *Lolita* ambushes us with Humbert's alluring mind and brilliant, extravagant prose, while simultaneously inviting – begging – us to escape, to envisage and comprehend Lolita's suffering.

Some exquisitely considered covers have grasped the wide-ranging connotations and shadowy poetics of *Lolita*, as well as its ability to trick, mislead and confuse. One appears to show the corner of a room, but close your eyes slightly and a girl's limbs and groin suggest themselves. Another bears the text of a legal statute covering sexual misdemeanours, with the letters L-O-L-I-T-A cut out like a child's school scrapbook, the *O* stylized as a heart. One edition evokes a stained-glass window, its bold colours mirroring Humbert's verbal vivacity, and gradually resolves into a trapped butterfly. Lolita's predicament is captured by one Polish version's simple drawing of a young girl standing in too-big high heels, while a Japanese release features a bored adolescent lounging on a giant sofa. Some publishers have attempted to conjure Nabokov's 'nostalgic highway' via blurry automobiles, lonely roadside diners, messy motel beds, or skeletal sequences of menacing telegraph poles. Elsewhere, designers have opted for the surreal: faceless figures or amalgamated abstractions which parallel the fantastical nature of *Lolita*'s narrative, encapsulating its preoccupied, obsessive strangeness and wistful disorientations.

Lolita is so familiar that a synopsis might seem superfluous, but a brief one, retaining only an outline of its main events, may be instructive, not least because of the dizzying density of Nabokov's novel and the way the book has been distorted in various media over the decades. Humbert Humbert is a middle-aged European scholar, now based in America, editing an academic textbook on French literature. In the summer of 1947 he lodges with widow Charlotte Haze in a small New England town and becomes obsessed with her twelve-year-old daughter, Dolores, known to the protagonist as Lolita. Eventually, Humbert marries Charlotte. One day she discovers his fixation but is killed before she can reveal it. Humbert and Lolita begin a series of journeys across and around America, in due course residing in 'Beardsley, New England' for work and school. After a time, they resume their cross-country travels and are tailed by an enigmatic car. In Colorado, Dolores is taken ill and is abducted one night from her hospital, thus vanishing completely from Humbert's life. Two years later, she unexpectedly writes to him, pleading for money: she is now seventeen, married and pregnant. He visits her, giving her funds but begging her to return to him. She rejects his proposal and reveals who it was that kidnapped her. Enraged, Humbert seeks out the culprit: Clare Quilty, playwright and love rival. He murders him, is incarcerated for his crime, and, imprisoned, writes the book we have been reading.

What this summary has left out – that Humbert rapes Lolita nearly every day for two years – is what, understandably, has made the book so controversial. Largely because of its contentious subject, the novel became a huge *succès de scandale*, earning Nabokov enough money to be able to retire from his Cornell professorship and devote his time solely to writing and butterflies. For its author, *Lolita* was a 'special favourite', but it remained the most difficult of his books to write, its theme being 'so distant, so remote' from his own settled, conventional emotional life.

Salacious (and careless) readers are always likely to be drawn to (and disappointed in) *Lolita*, their expectations reducing the text to an erotic memoir or drearily one-dimensional inspection of lust. In fact, of course, it is properly understood as an examination of cruelty and pain, as well as a feast of literary allusion and wordplay. Crucially, these two are intimately connected, the comedy and virtuosity of Humbert's narrative trapping us in pleasure and amusement but beseeching us to break free and grasp Lolita's misery. Although it is no longer necessary to defend *Lolita* against charges of juicy sensationalism, the function of the aesthetic and literary qualities of the novel in relation to its subject matter do need scrutiny.

The cathartic effect one experiences with this text, especially when reading *Lolita* for the first time, occurs because it forces us to re-evaluate attitudes that are threatened by the novel's ravishing raconteur. Readers' carnal inclinations are stimulated, provoked, and then (hopefully) expunged, allowing us to perceive the full extent of Humbert's cosmic crimes. It is Nabokov's delicate, treacherous balance between purgation/liberation and 'aesthetic bliss' that forms both the enjoyment and the continual eminence of *Lolita*, allowing it to endure as a triumphant, euphoric work of art and profoundly poignant study of sorrow.

This dangerous game begins before we have even reached Humbert's narrative, in the fake foreword, which - alas - many readers seem to skip, perhaps supposing it surplus to the novel, or possibly overeager to reach those famous opening words, 'Lolita, light of my life, fire of my loins'. That the prologue is penned by one 'John Ray, Jr, Ph.D.' should alert seasoned readers to his status as a confidence trickster. His drolly doubling name, his brandished doctorate, his absurdly (though significantly) titled article 'Do the Senses Make Sense?' (awarded the 'Poling Prize'), as well as his portentous manner - all alert us to his position essentially as a comic villain, his amusingly well-intentioned preface seeking to confuse and disorient us from the outset. He fills his foreword with clichés and banalities which we, *sophisticated readers*, feel we can do without:

> As a case history, 'Lolita' will become, no doubt, a classic in psychiatric circles. As a work of art, it transcends its expiatory aspects; and still more important to us than scientific significance and literary worth, is the ethical impact the book should have on the serious reader; for in this poignant personal study there lurks a general lesson; the wayward child, the egotistic mother, the panting maniac - these are not the only vivid characters in a vivid story: they warn us of dangerous trends; they point out potent evils. 'Lolita' should make all of us - parents, social workers, educators - apply

ourselves with still greater vigilance and vision to the task of bringing up a better generation in a safer world.

Ridiculously grandiloquent, its simplistic ethics might spring from any of a thousand ecclesiastical homilies or schoolmasterly speeches. We acknowledge his point, but his moralizing and patronizing tone instinctively make us want to contradict him, or at least problematize the straightforwardness he asserts. Thus Nabokov primes the trap before we've even reached Humbert's imperial dominion over us.

The first three-and-a-bit pages of *Lolita*, John Ray Jr's foreword, are some of Nabokov's finest parodic writing, precariously close to collapsing into affected farce but never doing so. Instead, we are given a simultaneous review and preview of the book to come, a spoof that anticipates and challenges the assumption of many readers that they are immune to either Humbert's sexual proclivities or his semantic charms. The foreword also allows Nabokov to furnish the reader with some of the loose ends left at the conclusion of Humbert's tale, on account of it being a first-person narrative. (One wonders how many of those first-time readers who *do* read John Ray Jr's preachy little preamble recognize exactly who 'Mrs Richard F. Schiller' is and why her expiration is so heartbreaking.)

The forewarnings of the foreword performed, we are free to launch into Humbert's delectable declaration, his euphoric misery memoir. Nabokov blends a variety of figures in Humbert Humbert – author, scholar, spouse, father, lover, charlatan and villain – enlarging and complicating our engagement with his character across the novel. It is always as a writer, however, that we meet Humbert, and we are permanently in his textual thrall as he saturates, and burdens, *Lolita* with a perilous momentum and outrageous persuasiveness.

There is a relaxed fluency to Humbert's prose, an accomplished confidence and buoyancy that only occasionally lapses into doubt or depression. There is, too, a disconcerting self-awareness, a revelatory vigilance, to his perception of his own shortcomings, now possible at the desk of his prison cell. (And which, to a degree, countenances this eloquent ogre to become a more honourable man: after all, *Lolita*'s subtitle, the '*Confession of a White Widowed Male*', is a clear admission of guilt in committing his crimes, in ethical terms a key stage in moral rehabilitation.)

Humbert as storyteller intersperses his reminiscences with hyperbolic remonstrations of regret and self-revulsion in his typically self-absorbed manner (until, potentially, realizing a more honest form of contrition by the novel's close). So ardent and verbally luxurious are Humbert's professions that we are liable to forget (or overlook?) the facts of what he is recounting – that is to say, exploitation and repeated sexual abuse.

> I recall certain moments, let us call them icebergs in paradise, when having had my fill of her – after fabulous, insane exertions that left me limp and azure barred – I would gather her in my arms with, at last, a mute moan of human tenderness ... – and the tenderness would deepen to shame and despair, and I would lull and rock my lone light Lolita in my marble arms, and moan in her warm hair, and caress her at random and mutely ask her blessing, and at the peak of this agonized selfless

> tenderness (with my soul actually hanging around her naked body and ready to repent), all at once, ironically, horribly, lust would swell again …

That 'ironically' is doing a lot of work. Out of context, Humbert's powers are somewhat diminished: when they are seen isolated and pinned to the page as our own 'Exhibit A', we are less liable to fall for Humbert's protestations and self-indulgent wailings. In the unbroken environment of reading the novel, however, we are enticed, ravished, overwhelmed – 'captivated' in both the modern sense of bewitched and the more archaic meaning of seized or captured. Moreover, for all its vice and criminality, it *is* a love story, and we feel it as such, enthralled to its hopes, dreams, joys, delusions and disappointments.

As Nabokov himself famously emphasized, *Lolita* is as much a record of his love affair with the English language as it is virtuoso attempt by Humbert to 'fix once for all the perilous magic of nymphets'. Both Humbert and Nabokov revel in the impediments and possibilities of their second or third tongue, and Humbert's prison-bound lament, 'Oh, my Lolita, I have only words to play with!', implicates Nabokov in Humbert's pertinacious desire for the English language, in which Lolita, *filia*, is target, fulfilment and allegory.

Verbal play is therapeutic but risky, liberating and confining at the same time, since the moral and textual tightrope Nabokov treads threatens to undermine or trivialize the molestation of a child. *Lolita*'s linguistic bacchanalia, in Humbert's dirty, erudite paws, is able to realize an Apollonian grace and perfection through its exquisite, inquisitive style and myriad allusions, which operate as twin cathartic vehicles.

Especially on repeated visits, *Lolita*'s style and intensely referential quality allow the reader to surrender to a calmer aesthetic and broader intellectual satisfaction, in addition to a more dynamic involvement in the fictional world Humbert and Nabokov have assembled. When rereading *Lolita*, the shock and pain remain – indeed, are intensified – but other perspectives or engagements more readily emerge and develop, too, both cerebral and moral. As Nabokov himself said: 'Curiously enough, one cannot read a book: one can only reread it. A good reader, a major reader, an active and creative reader is a rereader.'

An enormous range of authors and intertextual treasures lie buried in *Lolita*, from time to time protruding more obviously through the sly and secretive sands of the book, or appearing with devoted rereadings. But we might take just three examples to illustrate its literary debts and referential sport: Fyodor Dostoevsky, James Joyce and William Shakespeare.

Thanks to some provocatively snarky university lectures on Dostoevsky, Nabokov has been regarded as deeply critical of his Russian forefather. The truth is a little more complex, and in reality many of Nabokov's novels are a veiled tribute – as well as mock response – to Dostoevsky's legacy, especially in terms of engrained self-awareness, sarcasm, farce, hysteria, and a fruitful mixture of tragedy and comedy, the one continuously revising and reworking the other.

Nabokov has Humbert hijack Dostoevsky's method in *Notes from the Underground* (1864) by devising for his hero to consciously address an imagined audience while he tries to foil their jeering accusations via the artifices of his own egotism. Nabokov also echoes and goads Dostoevsky's paedophilic villain Stavrogin (*Demons*,

1873), in part via Humbert's perverse perception of the 'sweetness of shame', plus his glee in his own malice, as well as his lurch towards repentant sentimentality near the end of *Lolita*, weepily imagining the absence of Lolita's voice in a chorus of children. This Dostoevskian pathos, which Nabokov tended to decry, helps alert us to the textual, emotional and ethical games Humbert is playing, manipulating us into sympathizing with him and absolving him (as he'd done at the beginning of the novel by placing his sensual affinities within the context of losing his childhood love, Annabel Leigh, to typhus).

John Ray Jr's foreword mentions the 'monumental decision rendered December 6, 1933, by Hon. John M. Woolsey in regard to another, considerably more outspoken, book' – more outspoken, that is, than the one we have in our hands. Experienced bibliophiles will understand these details as indicating that the unnamed book is James Joyce's trailblazing *Ulysses* (1922), a novel sharing the legal hullabaloo *Lolita* anticipates for herself – and the critical and popular reception of both books has been disproportionately dominated by their controversial contents. Certainly, *Ulysses* shares *Lolita*'s allusive qualities and extended wordplay; yet *Ulysses* is a marvellously multi-voiced work, a congested swarm of compound particulars.

In terms of Joycean debt, *Lolita* probably owes more to the monomaniacal accent of *A Portrait of the Artist as a Young Man* (1916) and the dark sexual confusions of *Finnegans Wake* (1939), despite Nabokov's assertions that the former was 'feeble and garrulous' and the latter 'a formless and dull mass of phony folklore, a cold pudding'. As with Dostoevsky, influence, homage and sardonic reply go hand in hand, and *Lolita* acknowledges the *Wake* not only in its general fleshly murkiness but by having

Lolita and Humbert attend 'one fair mid-June evening' a 'trivial' alfresco entertainment by Clare Quilty and Vivian Darkbloom that has been, according to Humbert, 'lifted from a passage in James Joyce'. The timetable not only references *Ulysses*'s single-day narrative of 16 June 1904, especially its dramatic night-time hallucinations in the 'Circe' episode, but 'Vivian Darkbloom' also ominously echoes *Ulysses*'s hero, Leopold Bloom (and is, of course, an anagram of 'Vladimir Nabokov').

Yet the 'passage in James Joyce' is actually from *Finnegans Wake*, where a little boy, 'Shem', plays a game with his sisters wherein he must guess the colour of their underwear; he flunks the test and is teased, but this only arouses him. As in *Lolita*, failure and shame are eroticized, the sweat of lust and guilt merging. *Lolita* (and, to some extent, the *Wake*) dismantles love, exposing its primal origins free from society so that it can be restored, by the reader, to its authentic sense of value and care.

Undelivered letters also feature in both the *Wake* and *Lolita*: they structure their plots but also colour their themes of miscommunication and misfortune. In *Lolita* an inadvertently unsent letter spins the action from calamitous disaster to fortuitous opportunity at the turning point of the novel, when its incriminating sender is exterminated right in front of the mailbox, allowing the raptor-felon, Humbert, to swoop, 'clawing [the letters] to fragments in [his] trouser pocket' with his 'talons'.

Shakespearean connections are threaded throughout the luxuriant cloth of *Lolita*, from sly biographical hints – Quilty's cars' number plates are 'WS 1564' and 'SH 1616', Shakespeare's birth and death dates – to deeper textual associations and connotations. More obliquely, in *Pale Fire* (1962), the poet John Shade will refer to 1958:

> It was a year of Tempests: Hurricane
> Lolita swept from Florida to Maine.

From our cosy vantage point of decades hence, we can smugly imagine the shock and awe as Nabokov's turbulent novel barrels its way up the highbrow East Coast. Beyond the controversy greeting *Lolita*'s American publication, however, the verse also, of course, points to *The Tempest* (1611). Shakespeare's late tragicomic romance of magic, exile and self-referential authorship has clear thematic links in *Lolita*, and Nabokov peppers his novel with a number of allusions to the play. Lolita herself can be associated with the spirit Ariel's nymph-like qualities, ability to enchant, and quest for freedom. Humbert shares some of Caliban's more monstrous characteristics – but also his ambiguities, especially since Shakespeare's creature has been justly rehabilitated as a more complex individual than earlier stagings and scholarship supposed.

Equally compelling are the connections between the magicians Humbert and Prospero: both are puppet masters, exercising control over their worlds. Both have a complex relationship with their charges – with Humbert, explicitly sexual; with Prospero, there are suggestive incestuous undercurrents to his relationship with Miranda. Moreover, so long as we do not fall into the error Nabokov tempts us with – of confusing Humbert with his creator – there is also a clear rapport between Prospero, the playwright of his own drama, and Nabokov the novelist, an affinity itself paralleling and playing with the Romantic notion conflating Prospero with Shakespeare. Nabokov certainly stage-manages *Lolita* to a considerable extent, with deliberately artificial fabrications and coincidences which Humbert, as their co-creator, revels in.

Whatever the abundance of its allusions, Humbert's language is a fertile and festering kingdom of idiomatic ornaments, colloquial prevarications and rococo linguistic fripperies. It is an aberrant, embellished verbal empire with its own rules, its own codes, always open to flamboyant conflagration or rapturous dissolution. Humbert's imagination melts meaning into his liquid art, transforming or modifying words and phrases to his own meticulous vernacular in order to mock, amuse, mislead. His constant alliteration is catchy, charismatic, suave, rollicking and entirely memorable.

Although disdainful of cliché – in life or in lexes – Humbert does not discard it; rather, he plays with it, toys with it, taking it apart and putting it back together again, delighting not only in the components themselves but his ability to reconstruct them. Humbert exploits cliché to display his scorn and supremacy, but also his unceasing joy at discovery, as he unearths new sounds, rhythms and undertones to words.

Together with his delight comes derision, and frequently his attitude is one of bullying disrespect (even if his style still transfigures the object of his hauteur). During his coast-to-coast wanderings with Lolita, mid-century American eateries come in for much of Humbert's satiric bite:

> We passed and re-passed through the whole gamut of American roadside restaurants, from the lowly Eat with its deer head (dark trace of a long tear at the inner canthus), 'humorous' picture postcards of the posterior 'Kurot' type, impaled guest checks, life savers, sunglasses, adman visions of celestial sundaes, one half of a chocolate cake under glass, and several horribly experienced flies zigzagging over the sticky sugar-pour on the ignoble counter.

Bourgeois postures, fixtures and fittings are a constant target for Humbert's sneers. Charlotte's home comes in for particular contempt upon his initial arrival:

> a white-frame horror [appeared] looking dingy and old, more gray than white – the kind of place you know will have a rubber tube affixable to the tub faucet in lieu of shower. ... The front hall was graced with door chimes, a white-eyed thingamabob of commercial Mexican origin, and that banal darling of the arty middle class, van Gogh's 'Arlésienne.' ... The only bathroom, a tiny oblong between the landing and 'Lo's' room, with limp wet things overhanging the dubious tub (the question mark of a hair inside); and there were the expected coils of the rubber snake, and its complement – a pinkish cozy, coyly covering the toilet lid.

For Humbert, everything is irritatingly recognizable and too straightforwardly distinguished by what he perceives as its vulgarity, triviality and obviosity – its *poshlost*, to use the untranslatable Russian word so familiar from Nabokov's earlier books. And yet this peevish, irascible Humbert is typically usurped by the regal one who miraculously fashions a fantastical world out of the commonplace.

> It happened for instance that from my balcony I would notice a lighted window across the street and what looked like a nymphet in the act of undressing before a co-operative mirror. Thus isolated, thus removed, the vision acquired an especially keen charm that made me race with all

speed toward my lone gratification. But abruptly, fiendishly, the tender pattern of nudity I had adored would be transformed into the disgusting lamp-lit bare arm of a man in his underclothes reading his paper by the open window in the hot, damp, hopeless summer night.

Humbert's gifts are such that even when the fantasy has been uncovered, the dream soured to grubby reality, his verbal powers persist, preserving the magical metamorphosis of the world even as the illusion has collapsed, while also leaving a troubling sense of our own complicity in his corruption.

America is ripe for Humbert's wry, beguiling discernments, and he encounters pleasure in every facet of the United States he surveys, his habitual snobbery notwithstanding. Indeed, his perfectly observed surveillance of his New World surroundings is a fundamental characteristic of the textual fabric of *Lolita*: its people and places, its idioms and idiots, its pop culture and commercial desire, its innocence and animation, brashness and impropriety.

The world of '50s America is glaringly, affectionately, revealed to us, especially when Dolly and Hum are on the road, with their cheap accommodation and need for diversions, treats and bribes; comics, sweets and sodas. It would be all too easy for Humbert to be an acerbic European pedant, stuffily condescending towards American society and values. Although he can be so at times, more vitally, Humbert incorporates contemporary culture smoothly, joyously, into his chronicle. Effortlessly and engagingly, the cadences, shapes and textures of booming post-war America are paraded before us: the materialism, the conservatism, yes; but also the energy, spirit and fun which characterize this golden period. We are a world away from the grim modernist disapproval of fashions, trends and low art which features in many of the Russian novels of Nabokov's austere Berlin years, despite the verbal dexterity and luminosity with which he charged his Russian fiction.

Class lists and motel registers; road signs and shop signs; billboards, posters, leaflets with nifty slogans and corporate catchphrases crowd and cluster the text of *Lolita*, along with the letters, diaries, poems and reference books so typical of Nabokov's other novels. Lolita embodies this vivid, energetic Americanness: her vocabulary is coarse, rude, brazen – but also facetious, flippant, witty and entertaining. Her slang and jargon move Humbert immensely, partly due to their childish aspects – their freedom, naughtiness and simplicity – but also because of their vigour, so evocative of the country he has embraced.

Lolita is (tragically) just like any other American girl, and the way Nabokov prepares us to encounter this perfectly ordinary pre-teen is masterly. As Humbert scornfully tours the Haze house before meeting Lolita, we see her things scattered about: an old tennis ball, a white sock, magazines, a plum stone (still glistening from its recent emancipation by tantalizing teeth). These traces of Lolita, as Humbert nears his prey, alert us to her prepubescent presence, her routine normality, the ordinariness which makes her stolen future so sorrowful and cruel.

Later we are treated to extended glimpses of her talents, at fourteen, as a tennis player and actress – the former now one of the principal popular images of Lolita and affording a fascinating insight into Humbert's view of his stepchild; the latter important structurally and thematically in this world of invention, make-believe and deceit.

Nevertheless, Lolita's verbal dexterity and sassy jocularity permit her much more control over Humbert and her situation that might otherwise be the case. She is, for all her undeniable status as a victim, a formidable creative and erotic agent. Lo is no fool, and manages to dupe her stepfather on several occasions: he is, in fact, an unreliable reader of his own infatuation/requisition. Moreover, her generally sunny disposition is never completely clouded: for all that Humbert does to her, all the wickedness and abuse he inflicts, Lolita's spirit is never quite crumpled. Her goodness of character and refusal to be broken is one of the most touching things about the novel.

Humbert comes to realize how he has wronged Lolita, though the depth of his sincerity is doubtful. Certainly he sees their road trips as largely a waste of time, a ruination of not only Lolita's childhood but America and her landscapes:

> We had been everywhere. We had really seen nothing. And I catch myself thinking today that our long journey had only defiled with a sinuous trail of slime the lovely, trustful, dreamy, enormous country that by then, in retrospect, was no more to us than a collection of dog-eared maps, ruined tour books, old tires, and her sobs in the night.

In *Lolita*, America is recurrently evoked in terms of charts, atlases, paintings, models or toys, comparisons which always prove ineffective, inaccessible. Humbert cannot connect with an unaffected, natural, flowing, three-dimensional world, but only with the fabricated or artificial. America, like Lolita, always remains remote to him.

The novel has, of course, had several lives beyond the page. Nabokov was an intensely cinematic and pictorial writer: images and the visual dominate not just *Lolita* but all his works, and many of them have been adapted for film, though with very limited success, either commercially or artistically. Nonetheless, both mainstream motion picture versions of *Lolita* have something to say and do a fairly good job of transferring such a densely literary novel to the screen, even if both, for different reasons, underplay the abusive nature of Humbert and Lolita's relationship.

Stanley Kubrick (1962) opted to focus on the book's humorous and satirical elements, portraying Humbert as a vain pedant and expanding Quilty's role – essentially, though not entirely, rejecting a vast screenplay Nabokov himself offered. In his disturbing, problematically beautiful film, Adrian Lyne (1997) concentrated on the dark ambience and desperate agony of the protagonist, including a maudlin, manipulative score (which is not necessarily a criticism) from Ennio Morricone, though the film did allow some space for comedy as well. A one-man stage monologue by Richard Nelson (2009) was perhaps more successful than both Kubrick and Lyne in its capacity to comprehend Lolita herself as a lost possession, an unforgettable memory, forever locked in Humbert's mind.

Nelson's monologue excelled in capturing *Lolita*'s remarkable fixation on its two leading characters – an egotistic, fanatical storyteller will ensure this – but one of the special pleasures of the novel is the profusion of secondary eccentrics who, beyond their structural roles, on occasion mirror Humbertian peculiarities or function as relief from the claustrophobia of the villain-victim axis. We have not had space to discuss the great circus and sorrow of Charlotte; the weird riot of Quilty; the cuckolding taxi driver Maximovich (and his humiliating death, with Humbert's first wife); the unpredictable orthodoxy of the Farlows; the forlorn oddity of Rita, Humbert's post-Lo relationship; or the splendid carnival of Miss Pratt. Each of them enriches *Lolita*'s comic textures and waggish self-assurance, often surprising us in sadness or simply making us shake our head at Humbert's rudeness (while nodding, too, at his insights).

For all the wonder of its comedy, in its ironies of time and fate *Lolita* possesses a philosophical gravity to match Nabokov's other works. Coincidence, chance and providence play a decisive role in not only the novel's structure but its themes as well. Luck deals Humbert several fortuitous and fortunate hands, enabling him to evade punishment and augment debauchery – allowing, that is, the novel to exist. Such elements are part of the darkness of *Lolita*, as well as its fun. Nabokov and Humbert play with our sense of literary expectation, causation, suspense and probability, as well as how things are supposed to turn out. In *Lolita*, victims can rewrite their own tragedies, even under the gaze of their tormentors, but neither villain nor victim can dictate the tessellations of time or correct the configurations of destiny.

Towards the end of the novel, Humbert imagines that Lolita's unborn baby is 'dreaming already in her of becoming a big shot and retiring around 2020 A.D.' But the fictive structures and black themes of *Lolita* determine that neither Humbert nor Lolita nor her gestating child live to see 1953, never mind 2020. None even survives the novel's foreword, where John Ray Jr matter-of-factly informs us of their individual demises, along with those of a number of others. Everyone in *Lolita* is, so to speak, discreetly dead on arrival.

The bleakness of *Lolita* is matched only by its rhapsody, the two altering and amending each other, often in the same sentence, sometimes the same phrase. Together with its complex tonal fusions, *Lolita* utilizes a structural principle Nabokov used earlier in *Despair* (1934) and 'The Vane Sisters' (1951): a first-person narrator employs a battery of rhetoric to foist themselves on the reader; yet the events they depict, in due course, command an entirely different interpretation to their teller's experience. *Lolita*'s disconcerting first person contains delicate textual shifts that quietly warn us of Humbert's unreliability and fallibility. Inner and outer worlds coalesce and intersect – eclipsing, elucidating.

Like his echoing ancestor Hermann Hermann in *Despair*, Humbert Humbert writes his own story and has absolute jurisdiction over the charismatic text he creates. But within Humbert's own words Nabokov is able to assert his own verdict on the self-absorbed brute, casting him as a pathetic assassin, full of envy and spite, able to regret only after the event, not before. Chronology convicts Humbert and sanctions Lolita to live eternally. (Nevertheless, of course, Nabokov acknowledged that the later Humbert became, to a degree, a 'moral man', achieving some form of apotheosis which permits him an annual parole in paradise – something that will never occur with Hermann.)

Word after word, line after line, page after page, *Lolita* shocks us, enraptures us, embroils us, enmeshing us in Humbert's narcissistic snare, summoning us to abscond, to feel Lolita's agony as well as the misery of a million anonymous Lolitas and their infinities of pain. Nabokov's art shows that the fate of one little American girl, and the more familiar mass crimes on larger scales of time and space, are the same, each horrific and each deserving of our pity, compassion and understanding. Ethics, aesthetics and metaphysics combine to condemn all human wickedness.

In this essay we have lingered a little longer with *Lolita* than with Nabokov's other novels. His best-known work, *Lolita*'s attractions and distinctive, exceptional qualities justify the dawdling. Humbert possesses Lolita from his memoir's first word, taking her name and contorting it for his own devices. Yet he also captures *us*, detaining his readers for hundreds of pages of his electric recollections, zipping across the page to thrill, amuse and appal. 'You can always count on a murderer for a fancy prose style', Humbert promises us at the very beginning. He does not let us down. *Lolita*'s greatness is assured, its desolation, power and beauty guaranteed.

14

Pnin

THE FACULTY OF PAIN

Sports, games and play in general feature across Nabokov's work. In the opening scene of his first novel, *Mary* (1926), the protagonist Ganin – stuck in a lift – refuses to play a guessing game with his fellow inmate. The titles of the next two, *King, Queen, Knave* (1928) and *The Luzhin Defense* (1929), refer to cards and chess, with the board game a prominent element of the latter, while *Glory* (1932) includes varsity football and tennis. *Laughter in the Dark* (1932) has three people watch an 'ice hockey match at the sport palace'; the subject of *The Real Life of Sebastian Knight* (1941) is named for a chess piece; and the ferocity of *Bend Sinister* (1947) is prefigured by violent childhood football contests. *Lolita* (1955) has a now notorious tennis match at its centre; poet John Shade in *Pale Fire* (1962) pictures the gods playing a 'game of worlds'; incestuous lovers Ada and Van (*Ada*, 1969) relish games of Scrabble, while fretful insomniac Hugh Person in *Transparent Things* (1972) can find sleep only by pondering tennis techniques.

Nabokov's fourth English novel, *Pnin* (1957), sees its maligned, eponymous hero find quiet dignity and status in the game of croquet he plays with fellow Russian émigrés at a New England garden party. That much-mocked and ostracized figure – the 'funny foreigner' – Pnin suffers humiliation and desolation in both his professional and personal life, but put a croquet mallet in his hands and he comes to life:

> From his habitual, slow, ponderous, rather rigid self, he changed into a terrifically mobile, scampering, mute, sly-visaged hunchback. It seemed to be always his turn to play ...

Pnin can be regarded as the second part of Nabokov's American Trilogy or the central panel of an Academic Triptych. Framed on either side by the deviant lunatic narcissist-scholars Humbert Humbert (*Lolita*) and Charles Kinbote (*Pale Fire*), Professor Timofey Pnin is pedantic and peculiar, it is true, but compassionate and sane as well. Where exiled villains Humbert and Kinbote are masters of the English language, geographically and linguistically displaced Pnin is verbally clumsy, uproariously stumbling and floundering through his new life in the New World.

Pnin, too, is imbued with a warmth and comic brio, a world away from the obsessive claustrophobia and fanaticism of *Lolita* or the psychosis and whimsical fancies of *Pale Fire*. Yet this kind-heartedness and nimbleness of touch serve only to make *Pnin*'s depths deeper, its solemn hues a particularly ominous shade of black. Moreover, its straightforward episodic structure belies an intricate architecture and demanding narrative voice which bewilders and disorientates as we follow our hero's precarious, hilarious adventures.

For Nabokov, *Pnin*, initially serialized in the *New Yorker*, was constructed as a 'series of inner organic transitions'. It was to be a fused sequence of stories – certainly not a 'collection of sketches', which would be to misunderstand not only the novel's overall accord but the importance of several internal thematic links. Each of the first six chapters, before a crucial shift in the seventh, forms a self-sufficient short story, while also together assembling a novel with their arrangement of associations that support and maintain the wider organization. To use a metaphor close to *Pnin*'s world, the chapters are faculty buildings that together create the university/novel.

Nabokov is seldom interested in his characters' development: they rarely change in their books the way Dickens or Dostoevsky have their creations mature or transform, lapse or regress. In *Pnin* in particular this helps maintain not only the autonomy of each story but also the integrity and unity of the set, as well as more easily promoting the rearrangements and upheavals in genre, tone, location, time, story and narrator that the book will undergo. Just as Timofey Pnin is a relocated Russian professor in America, *Pnin* the novel experiences several displacements, underlining its sense of awkwardness and discomfort, but also its agility and protean fluidity – like Pnin at his croquet, darting over a country house lawn. Pnin remains the same but everything around him changes. He is a solar centre orbited by the planets of plot and narrative impulse.

As a bonding motif across each chapter, Nabokov employs that canny, erratic and fearless creature, the squirrel, a resilient rodent who will recur in various and surprising guises throughout the novel, as will a fickle narrative attitude to time management. Inventive reminiscences, chronological sliding and gliding, as well as a mixture of preliminary bagginess and then increasing density concerning supervisions of time: all inform *Pnin*'s aesthetic, ethical and metaphysical discussions. Here the common dependence of the stories, unseen on the episodic surface, begins to reveal itself, revealing the complex structural preparations that will eventually convict the capricious narrator – and us, the conspiratorial reader – and set Pnin free.

We first encounter our hero on 'that inexorably moving railway coach' as he blithely heads, on the wrong train, to give a guest lecture at Cremona Women's Club. Here we meet 'none other than' Professor Timofey Pnin – a wording redolent more of a dinner party anecdote than the opening of a novel. This Pnin is 'ideally bald', a sonically pleasing phrase combining peculiarity, purity and suitability, suggesting he is the target of mockery but the owner of integrity, too. This superlative, exemplary hairlessness grants Pnin – fond in his advancing years of sunbathing – a 'great brown dome' which remarkably surmounts him. Yet it is a grandeur which swiftly dwindles as we move down to his 'tortoiseshell glasses', 'thick neck', 'strong-man torso' and 'spindly legs' before arriving finally at his 'frail-looking, almost feminine feet'.

In the novel's opening paragraph, a sardonic, teasing description of Pnin and his obliviously hapless situation has not only displayed the narrator's literary gifts and established a character immediately and effortlessly before our eyes, but it has also made us a clandestine, colluding partner in laughter at Pnin's expense, a collaboration that Nabokov, author, will come to make us feel ashamed of.

Pnin obviously wants us to snigger and snicker at Pnin, joining in with the narrator's chuckles – why else relate the tale in such a way? We soon come to learn that Pnin is not only on the incorrect train but amusingly (for us) unaware of this fact, before being compelled to disembark and find alternative means of transportation. It is then that the novel has the first of its many tonal shifts, as Pnin crumples onto a park bench, sustains a small convulsion, and is mentally conveyed back to his Saint Petersburg childhood illness. The occurrence is intense, graphic, full of particulars: we see Pnin's elaborate inner life in a way comic farce and slapstick never allow. Pnin's pain abruptly carries some weight, its reality matters to us, even if we are speedily returned to the ill-fated sitcom of his Cremona Women's Club escapade.

The chapters of the novel progress through a series of essentially comical stories covering, in their main timeline, around four years of Pnin's perilous stretch as professor of Russian literature – in fact he is the entire department – at Waindell, a droll fictional merger between the Ivy League Cornell and women's liberal arts school Wellesley College. Pnin's present existence is exhibited to us, his wretched and ill-starred past filled in as we go. Campus life and the dire domestic politics of academic America are wryly painted: their familiarities, repetitions, disillusionments; their jaded and enthusiastic participants; their colours, rhythms and intrigues. Faculty luncheons, over-friendly Russophiles, co-worker conspiracies, the mysterious jumble of scholastic seclusion and breezy geniality – all are tenderly and acerbically stuffed, mounted and put on permanent display in the literary foyer.

Together with his professional activity, such as it is, we closely observe Pnin's home and personal life. Regarding the former, he is a nomadic, peripatetic soul, even in his asylum America; of the latter, we witness the sorrows and ignominies of his past – especially his émigré ex-wife, the psychotherapist and poet Liza Wind – which continue to shape, and inflict misery on, his present.

Pnin's sanctuary Waindell proves inconstant in its embrace, and he moves house nearly every semester, renting a succession of rooms in other people's homes, uprooted by life's caprice when trouble and misfortune strike his or his hosts' lives. By the penultimate chapter, he looks set to not only lease his first complete residence (hosting a 'house-heating' party) but perhaps purchase it too – though we, conniving readers, already know his job is about to become extinct.

In his domestic life, gadgets, devices and appliances plague and fascinate, besiege and elate the incredulous, pitiful Pnin. Refrigerators, washing machines, dentures, radiators, alarm clocks: all are part of the confusing, comfortable paraphernalia of the mid-'50s America that alien Pnin inhabits. And yet another modern convenience propels the novel's narrative and themes still further, manoeuvring us to its comic spots and down its darker routes: the motor car.

Pnin's fifth chapter sees our determined and indomitable hero learn to drive, that emblematic American occupation which doubly released Humbert Humbert from a marital penitentiary and allowed him to roam free with his stolen stepdaughter (an automobile inadvertently but fortuitously eliminated Lolita's mother, while another transported the toxic twosome around the States). However, unlike in *Lolita* – where the car actually becomes another prison, whatever liberties its mobility initially seems to offer – for Pnin a car advances a twofold escape: first, to more or less revisit his Russian homeland; second, to finally shake off his hostile narrator and the vindictive novel *Pnin*.

The drive to the biennial garden party of an émigré friend is, unsurprisingly, a comic delight, as Pnin gets lost and bungles his vehicle through the woods, his driving skills still unpredictable or non-existent, before in due course he finds a surfaced road and rusty sign just about setting him in the right direction. At the get-together, a commune of exiled Russian intelligentsia, Pnin is once again at home: socially, culturally, linguistically. This character, whose every utterance has hitherto been a source of mirth, is suddenly elegant, witty, distinguished, his pedantry no longer hair-splitting fixation but erudition, precision (he methodically corrects a wilfully casual reader of *Anna Karenina*). And, as we have seen, it is also here that he shines at the subtly vicious game of croquet, the sport of his youth rediscovered as Pnin outclasses all his contemporaries.

Amid this restoration of self-worth comes the poignant core of the novel, which has been quietly anticipated all the way through by means of a string of curious reappearances of squirrels. In chapter one, Pnin's reverie during his seizure removes him to his childhood bedroom, where a screen of decorated wood depicts a squirrel holding an enigmatic reddish object. This trance-memory resolves into present-day Pnin on his park bench, slowly recovering from his fit and staring at a real squirrel appraising a discarded peach stone. From here, Pnin's luckless journey to the Cremona Women's Club begins to improve. Could this be the fateful intrusion of the past through an interdimensional rodent?

In chapter two, following ongoing nasty conduct from his still-pined-for ex-wife, Pnin notices a squirrel climb up a drinking fountain and glower at him, seeming to demand he produce a beverage. Pnin obliges, fumbling the device. The squirrel watches him with disdain, then fast departs, as greedy and ungrateful as Liza Wind. This too, however, is a providential sign for Pnin to move on emotionally and materially from his avaricious ex-wife.

Each chapter has its own auspicious squirrel appearance, and by chapter five we are actively expecting its arrival. As Pnin drives hopelessly to his friend's house in the country, zigzagging through the wood, we observe him from a high tower with graffiti names ('Miranda', 'Mary', 'Almira' and so on) etched into its carpentry. We observe an ant on a timber banister, as hassled, perplexed and lost as the 'preposterous toy car progressing below'. Suddenly, a gunshot rings out, and the quick arboreal movements of a forest creature – clearly, our awaited squirrel – are described: evidently the animal has not been harmed. Immediately, the insect locates an upright beam and can march on, while Pnin finds both the road and the sign to his destination: 'The Pines'.

It is at this hard-won convivial haven in the woods, amid his peers and past, that Pnin suffers another mild seizure and the onslaught of unforgettable memories, this time brought on by meeting a mutual acquaintance of his ex-girlfriend, Mira Belochkin. Mira – her name prefigured by the girls' scratched appellations in the tower – had died in Buchenwald, and we are given a profoundly harrowing insight into the Holocaust's unrelenting agony. It is the painful, still-beating heart of *Pnin*/Pnin:

> In order to exist rationally, Pnin had taught himself, during the last ten years, never to remember Mira Belochkin – not because, in itself, the evocation of a youthful love affair, banal and brief, threatened his peace of mind (alas, recollections of his marriage

to Liza were imperious enough to crowd out any former romance), but because, if one were quite sincere with oneself, no conscience, and hence no consciousness, could be expected to subsist in a world where such things as Mira's death were possible. One had to forget – because one could not live with the thought that this graceful, fragile, tender young woman with those eyes, that smile, those gardens and snows in the background, had been brought in a cattle car to an extermination camp and killed by an injection of phenol into the heart, into the gentle heart one had heard beating under one's lips in the dusk of the past.

The detail that the love affair was 'banal and brief' is characteristic of Nabokov's ability to texture his novels with minutiae that reverberate in perpetuity. Not the obvious grandeur of a great lifelong passion; just one little romantic relationship ended by time. Then that lover annihilated by murder and cruelty before being even further eradicated as those who knew her cannot bear to think of her. 'Those eyes, that smile' – no corroborating adjectives are required. We know the beauty and wonder of those eyes, that smile, now extinguished forever.

For Pnin, the internal conflict between forgetting the past and his being unable to not recollect it is a physical affliction and immense emotional load. The Jewish element of Nabokov's work, and the terrible burden of the Holocaust, is still only a relatively embryonic part of Nabokov studies, but here we see the full force of its power. Accused of 'ignoring' such major historical events and/or political issues, Nabokov – like Shakespeare before him regarding the Reformation – in fact treats such vast, seemingly impenetrable, topics with an aesthetic subtlety that wields enormous clout. Far from overlooking the subject, Nabokov's perfectly formed comic novel compels the reader's attention via the art of deflection, the significance refracting and ricocheting off the ostensibly lighter touch to exert a considerably greater emotional punch.

Writing *Pnin* in the 1950s, Nabokov was pioneering in addressing the enduring trauma of the Holocaust, especially its bearing on memory and the act of remembrance. We live now in an age of self-conscious commemoration (as well as wilful forgetfulness), but the period immediately after the Second World War was particularly caught – like Pnin – between trying to escape the recent past and the need to remember it. Once again, Nabokov's ingenious sleight of hand, the conjuror's trick of diversion, proves to be a powerful weapon, whose impact prevails longer and stronger than many more direct approaches. In the decade of *Pnin*, émigré intellectuals like Theodor Adorno (*The Authoritarian Personality*, 1950) and Hannah Arendt (*The Origins of Totalitarianism*, 1951) were writing crucial socio-political studies examining the roots of Nazism and Stalinism, but Nabokov takes us into the savage, lonely heart of human pain and survivor's guilt, as bumbling Pnin remembers his beloved Mira.

Mira's surname 'Belochkin' is, needless to say, a derivative from the Russian *belochka*, a diminutive of *belka*, a squirrel. Accordingly, *Pnin*'s squirrels are revealed as designers of destiny, patterning pain through Pnin's life. But perhaps these squirrels are Mira's presence beyond the grave, transcendently beckoning and orientating him through his unlucky and jumbled life, disclosing her as something far more than 'banal and brief', but as an enduring tenderness, virtuously eclipsing the appalling

Liza. For all the immense sadness of Mira's place in the novel, she offers something positive and hopeful.

This optimistic function is taken further by Victor, Liza's son from her new marriage – a lanky teenager with a prodigious, exceptional artistic talent (reading *Pnin*, we really do lament that he is only a fictitious construction). Sweet-natured, kindly Pnin is keen to meet the boy, perhaps the son he never had, and invites Victor to visit. Pnin buys him a couple of presents (which turn out to be wildly unsuitable) and they have a nervous, friendly time together, occasionally awkward, but Victor's artistic instinct perceives the dignity that lies behind his mother's ex-husband's external gracelessness.

More successful than Pnin in the tricky business of gift giving, Victor sends Timofey a stunning aquamarine glass vessel as a thank you, which is then given pride of place as a glorious punchbowl during Pnin's 'househeating' party. When his guests have left, the host does the washing up, the great bowl softly soaking in the soapsuds. Clumsy Pnin drops a nutcracker into the basin, where 'an excruciating crack of broken glass follow[s] upon the plunge.' The novel pauses as we, and Pnin, ponder in furious despair. Gingerly retrieving the jagged glass from the bubbles, Pnin extricates a broken goblet: the resplendent bowl is undamaged. Victor's enchanting present becomes a victory for Pnin, something slyly foreshadowed by Pnin's earlier, finicky correction to a party guest that Cinderella's shoes were not originally made of 'greenish blue' glass, but 'Russian squirrel fur'. Victor's grand bowl becomes a sort of quasi-squirrel and thus a symbol of hope and triumph.

The deliverance of the bowl ends the sixth chapter of *Pnin*. The seventh (and final) chapter suddenly then makes known its ostensibly omniscient third-person narrator, until this time a well-nigh anonymous figure. We know this narrator has dabbled in lepidoptery, is now a novelist and has recently been appointed a Waindell professor. It is, of course, Vladimir Nabokov himself, thereby splitting *Pnin*'s creator into VN the Author and VN the Narrator, and it is this latter manifestation, as merely another (and not very nice) character, which causes *Pnin*'s preceding narrative to sway – destabilizing its metaphysics but stimulating its ethics.

How has this narrator come to know details concerning, say, the initial jinxed excursion to Cremona Women's Club or Pnin's dealings with his ex-wife? Perhaps specifics have slipped out through the usual gossip channels of workplace or small-town chatter. More momentously, how has this narrator, this actual character in the Waindell world, been party to Pnin's thoughts and innermost feelings? Intellect, suffering, pain – all are discreet, hidden, unknowable to anyone outside their proprietors. Has Narrator Nabokov merely concocted these thoughts and emotional states? If he has, we wonder why and feel a tad cheated. More decisively, and significantly, we must see that Narrator Nabokov is the invention of Author Nabokov. Pnin's pain exists only – in an extraordinary paradox – if we believe in and acknowledge the fictive nature of his story. We have to have faith in fiction to tell the truth.

Nabokov's mind-bogglingly complex metafiction and metaphysics here reach their apotheosis in what is superficially his most straightforward novel since *Mary* or *King, Queen, Knave*. But what of *Pnin*'s ethics and Pnin's escape? Our immoral literary collusion with this narrator has been in operation since the very beginning, as we have laughed along with his side-splitting chronicles of the doomed, dome-headed Professor Timofey Pnin. In the final chapter, Author Nabokov has upset the novel's episodic structure and torn open the cosy comfort of conventional storytelling, making us as readers acutely aware of our own enjoyment at Pnin's expense. The secure objectivity of narrative detachment has gone; in its place is a disconcertingly judgemental voice. A human. Like us. Arrogant, unfair. Yet this narrator-reader complicity cuts both ways: we have laughed at Pnin but we have also felt pity at his pain, particularly his memories of illness or his sweetheart Mira's horrendous death.

Chapter seven of *Pnin* largely consists of Narrator Nabokov arriving in town around the day Pnin is due to leave (his 'department' having being closed down) and becoming inebriated with his new boss, rude Pnin-mimic extraordinaire Jack Cockerell, Waindell's head of English. They drunkenly call Pnin in order to tease and ridicule him, but there is no answer. Cockerell suggests driving over to horse around outside Pnin's house, but Mrs Cockerell fortunately intercedes. Retiring to bed, the narrator somewhat regrets his actions, appearing to ask that we, too, repent our sordid participation in this tale, chortling at Pnin as we have been. The next morning Cockerell reignites the antics, ending the novel with his story of how Pnin rose to 'address the Cremona Women's Club and discover[ed] he had brought the wrong lecture.'

The book has come full circle – but Pnin has already obtained safe passage out of its narrative vortexes. Just before Cockerell's novel-closing breakfast anecdote, Narrator Nabokov has, after a restless night in the Cockerells' parody of a spare room, nipped out to find some freshly squeezed orange juice with which to '[confront] the rigours of the day'. Walking empty-handed back to his hosts, Narrator Nabokov notices a 'humble sedan' jam-packed with 'bundles and suitcases' heading out of town: it is Pnin. The narrator tries to catch up with the car to say hello, but Pnin is off, surging forward from the traffic lights, adroitly overtaking a pair of menacing beer trucks, and away into the distance, 'where there was simply no saying what miracle might happen.'

That 'miracle' is divulged in Author Nabokov's next novel, *Pale Fire* (1962): Pnin is fleetingly mentioned several times in this opaque, idiosyncratically organized book. We learn that he is now head of the 'bloated Russian Department' at Wordsmith College, New Wye, Appalachia. Pnin has not only escaped *Pnin*; he is thriving. Like the magnificent glass punchbowl, he has survived intact.

And is probably still demolishing people on the croquet lawn, watched over by benevolent squirrels.

15

Pale Fire

THE POET & THE KING

> I am but too conscious of the fact that we are born in an age when only the dull are treated seriously, and I live in terror of not being misunderstood. Don't degrade me into the position of giving you useful information.
>
> – Oscar Wilde, 'The Critic as Artist'

Novels, as their name suggests, have always sought out innovation and originality in their forms and techniques, breaking convention to excite, surprise and challenge. This fidgety and voracious medium has, from its inception, taken on a variety of formats – letters, pamphlets, diaries, journals, memoirs and biographies – to structure and organize itself. *Tristram Shandy* (1759) contained experiments in narrative and visual form that defied eighteenth-century expectations with its rejection of plot continuity and inclusion of inventive graphic devices: hyperactive, almost self-aware, punctuation disrupts narrative arrangements; an entirely black page mourns a character's death, tragicomically transforming form into nothingness.

In the twentieth century, polymorphous, polyglot *Ulysses* (1922) assaulted the proprieties of form with one chapter composed of newspaper headlines, another presented as a play script, and a third flaunted as a mathematical catechism of 309 questions and answers. More recently, Michael Ondaatje's *The Collected Works of Billy the Kid* (1970) synthesized prose and verse, blurring historical accounts, period photographs, dime novels and imaginative autobiography in order to prise open and deconstruct the outlaw's legend, immersing us in Billy's inner being. Anne Carson's verse novel *Autobiography of Red* (1998) fused modern life with Greek myth and is both a scholarly study of classical literature and examination of present-day adolescent sexuality.

In France, resurrecting practices enjoyed as far back as ancient Rome, Greece and China, the 'Oulipo' ('Ouvroir de littérature potentielle', 'workshop of potential literature') sought to create new literature via constrained writing techniques which, ironically, allowed for adventures in form and meaning, via a maze of literary conundrums and splendidly irresponsible games. Literary bondage becomes literary fetish and fun. For example, in the Oulipo's 'N+7' system, texts are 'translated' via substituting for each noun the word found seven places below in a dictionary. Thus, 'To be, or not to be, that is the quiche' or 'Mrs Dalloway said she would buy the flugelhorn herself.'

And the Oulipo's disruptive mischief worked on even larger scales as well. Georges Perec's *La Disparition* (1969) is a three-hundred-page novel written without the letter *e*; Raymond Queneau's *Exercices de style* (1947)[6] retells the same story (an inane anecdote) ninety-nine times, each in a different style, while his *Cent mille milliards de poèmes*

---

6 Nabokov himself thought *Exercices de style* 'a thrilling masterpiece'.

(1961) has ten sonnets, all with the same rhyme scheme, with each of the fourteen lines printed on a separate strip, allowing them to be reconfigured into approximately 100,000,000,000,000 new poems.

Yet, for all the surface amusement of the Oulipo – founded, in part, to reconcile the split between C. P. Snow's 'two cultures' of science and the humanities – darker implications lurk beneath. We are invited to question sense and significance, integrity and interpretation, seeing words and the world in flux, often dangerously unstable – perhaps even unhinged or deranged?

Nabokov's *Pale Fire* (1962) is a novel which tricks us into believing it is a scholarly edition of a new poem, complete with a foreword, commentary and index. This critical apparatus conceals the layers of narrative embedding that the author has ingeniously constructed, and the book explores, tantalizes and manipulates the complex affiliation between the internal text and its external frame.

It is an elaborate, devious game not just requesting but requiring multiple rereadings. This is not in order to 'solve' the 'puzzle' of *Pale Fire*, for there is no definite solution, but rather to fully uncover its limitless playful and paradoxical possibilities, for the novel is fundamentally concerned with that key Nabokovian interest: discovery.

Pale Fire is a reading game, one where we should observe and embrace particulars more than ever in Nabokov, delighting in the intricate details within the text, skipping back and forth between different parts of the book. Indeed, in many ways, *Pale Fire* cannot be read cover to cover, starting on the first page and working through to the final one (although first-time readers must, trusting in both their and Nabokov's ability for the story to gradually reveal itself). It is designed to be repeatedly re-examined and rediscovered in a dynamic non-linear fashion as one moves between its different sections, looking around, solving local puzzles on the way but not eventually locating any definitive exit from the literary labyrinth.

If the riddle of *Pale Fire* could be cracked or deciphered, it would be consumed, sapped of its magical spirit, dead and finished. Yet *Pale Fire*, structurally and thematically, fights against death, against the inevitability of the final whistle or the departure of the circus for the next town. It invites us to continually replay its sport, revisit its literary fairground, climb aboard its textual carousel.

Merry-go-rounds can cause dizziness, of course, and *Pale Fire* might leave us with a queasy sense of textual circuitousness or purposelessness if we do not properly understand it as less an amusement ride than a game with rules and restrictions which do not constrain but heighten the enjoyment of participation. Games without rules tend towards hostility and resentment. Regulations and conventions allow talent, dexterity, a development of skills and understanding.

Nevertheless, like in any game, volatile, unpredictable elements loom to throw proceedings into chaos and confusion. *Pale Fire* has ominous, ever-present storm clouds that might call off play. Moreover, the playing field is uneven and experiences frequent earthquakes and the occasional flood and fire, as well as player strikes and management disputes. As participants, we cannot afford to be sullen on the sidelines, bemoaning bad luck, the referee's decision or a niggling injury. This is professional literature. It is hard work, determined and unsparing – but the rewards are immense.

For all the competitive, confrontational and demanding features of *Pale Fire*, Nabokov wants reader and writer to not only be in creative concord but eventually to merge, reader becoming a sister-writer and fellow-inventor, obscuring, then eliminating, distinctions between players, teams, officials, spectators and pundits. But before the post-match pint: the game.

Summer 1959. New Wye, Appalachia. American poet John Shade has been murdered. His last poem, the 999-line 'Pale Fire', has been issued – together with a peculiar foreword, extensive annotations and a quixotic index – by his neighbour and academic colleague Charles Kinbote. Kinbote's notes are self-important, intrusive and wildly digressive, mingling and conflating public, private and fantastical worlds. In the foreword, Kinbote's precise and knowledgeable introduction almost immediately begins to break down, rupturing into crabbiness, erratic paranoia and haughty self-promotion.

Who is this editor, and why is his behaviour so strange, so capricious, so linguistically licentious? Why does he have such a personal and particular interest in Shade's manuscript and final poem? How has he come to be so well informed regarding the genesis and execution of the text?

It is not long into the foreword before we encounter the first of countless and recurrent dilemmas in our perusal of *Pale Fire*. Kinbote directs us to his note on one of the poem's last lines and its reference to 'horseshoes'. Should we turn to the commentary or proceed with the foreword? If we choose the former, very tempting, path, we are nearly at the end of the book and come across a lengthy annotation – focused but oddly unsound – claiming to relate a walk between Shade and Kinbote, along with anomalous remarks about something called Zembla. Midway through this note, we are also bidden to an earlier and vast nine-page annotation concerning the architecture of the poet's house, which, in turn, cites the commentary to line 691. Turning here, we find an incongruous reference to a disguised king parachuting into America.

Lost on this awkward trail of references and cross references, the reader might be forgiven for forgetting the foreword ever existed. But we need to drag ourselves back there, trying to pick up where we left off, striving to read the novel straight through, though now with an unsettling awareness of not only our editor's abnormal relationship to his subject, but various unusual internal and external goings-on.[7]

Intrigued though they might be, at this point many readers may throw down the book, exasperated by the taunting show-off Nabokov, lording his intellectual pre-eminence over us. But this should not be the case. Nabokov believes in us, in our abilities as resourceful, conscientious readers, in our capacity for curiosity, discovery and confidence (in ourselves and our author). *Pale Fire* is not going to be tranquil or uncomplicated – truth never is – but with a spirit of inquisitive adventure, it will be invigorating, spine-tingling, breathtaking – and entertaining, for it is a very funny novel.

Meanings and literary networks are progressively disclosed to us. Sometimes only in a tantalizing half-light, then in the full glare of sudden exposure. Take the

---

7 To complicate matters further, at the end of the foreword Kinbote even gives us his own tips on how to proceed – advice which, the reader is by now probably aware, needs to be taken with a small mountain of salt.

huge annotation to line 130 (or rather, to a rejected draft Kinbote seizes upon), involving the childhood discovery of a secret tunnel. It is a master stroke of design, patience and anticipation, the ploys and pleasures shifting with not only each reader, but each reader's reread.

Two boys hear strange voices on the other side of a locked green door at the end of the tunnel: angry and violent, then suddenly disconcertingly soft. These voices mystify us, too, until their provenance is beautifully revealed to us later on. Revisiting the text affords the rereader the insider's gratification of knowing what the boys do not – or, perhaps, the alluring thrill of only half-remembering what is beyond the passageway's fastened door (it is, of course, a portal to several kinds of dramatic fantasy and imaginative flight).

Such are the manoeuvrings of the commentator's sprawling, excursive tales that we often lose sight of the poet and the poem supposedly under consideration. John Shade himself is a poet of the Robert Frost type: a sly, measured wit; colloquial, unpretentious and languidly romantic. He teaches at Wordsmith College, New Wye, specializing in the satirical and discursive poetry of Alexander Pope (a writer whose works are woven into the finer textures of *Pale Fire*). He still lives in the house he grew up in and has been married to Sybil, his childhood sweetheart, for forty years. Their daughter, Hazel, committed suicide two years ago. Recently, as we have seen, Shade has heard tales about a legendary land, Zembla, during sunset walks with his new neighbour, Charles Kinbote – who also claims to be this fabled, faraway country's recently deposed king, Charles II ('the Beloved').

'Pale Fire' itself is a 'poem in heroic couplets, of nine hundred ninety-nine lines, divided into four cantos'. It is intrepid, shrewd and sharp, but gentle too, its verses harmoniously rhyming, as it sensitively probes its subjects. It was composed during the last three weeks of Shade's existence and is a reflection on this homely poet's life, its wonder and contentment, tragedies and disappointments, as well as his daily routines and creative processes.

'Pale Fire' is pervaded by the exquisite, intricate and realistic appearances of birds and butterflies, all authentically indigenous to Shade's location, and which function, too, as emissaries of mortality and are complex representatives of transience, change and prospective regeneration. The poem's famous opening – 'I was the shadow of the waxwing slain / By the false azure in the windowpane' – references Shade's departed ornithologist parents, who died when the poet was an infant; the *Vanessa* butterfly is frequently associated with Shade's wife, Sybil, and their deceased daughter, Hazel, and this 'velvet-and-flame' insect will make a gorgeous, elusive appearance at the novel's climax. Nabokov does not assert these birds and butterflies are literal reincarnations of the dead – such things are too mysterious, too inherently unknowable – or that they are merely clumsy symbols; rather, he indicates that they suggest the intangible presence and persistent existence of the dead.

Shade has recently suffered a health scare and, at sixty-one, is contemplating death more than ever before. His poem ruminates on apparent glimpses of the supernatural, the afterlife, the 'faint hope' of higher powers playing a 'game of worlds', which might explain life's many coincidences. On 21 July 1959, he completes the poem, looking optimistically to the twin futures of the next day and the hereafter:

> I'm reasonably sure that we survive
> And that my darling somewhere is alive,
> As I am reasonably sure that I
> Shall wake at six tomorrow, on July
> The twenty-second, nineteen fifty-nine,
> And that the day will probably be fine ...

That same day, however, he is killed by an assassin, on Kinbote's doorstep, as the two prepare for a glass of surreptitious celebratory wine to toast the poem.

Kinbote has apprehended the manuscript of 'Pale Fire', believing it his duty to do so. Surveying the text, however, and expecting to find his fascinating Zemblan material (revealed on those evening strolls with Shade) transformed by a poet's skill, he sees nothing of his majestic story or the magical kingdom he presumed his neighbour to have been putting into verse:

> I started to read the poem. I read faster and faster. I sped through it, snarling, as a furious young heir through an old deceiver's testament. Where were the battlements of my sunset castle? Where was Zembla the Fair? Where her spine of mountains? ... The complex contribution I had been pressing upon him with a hypnotist's patience and a lover's urge was simply not there.

Fighting back the 'bitter hot mist of disappointment', Kinbote concludes that the distant realm of Zembla and its adored sovereign must lie buried in the text, which he has now arranged for publication, along with his notes. These annotations, he believes, are the only way to make sense of the poem's cavernous layers and concealed meanings.

We can - and should - follow the text in an essentially linear route, but Kinbote tempts us, irresistibly propelling us back and forth, hither and thither, across his annotated edition of 'Pale Fire', with meandering diversions in a circuitous riot of scholarly caprice and convoluted detours. Nonetheless, Kinbote's style is quite straightforward, with only occasional insertions of irksomely (and humorously) uncommon English words or bits of exotic, nostalgic Zemblan vocab. His language is often bizarre, protective and pontifical, but it is also entrancing, bright and inventive, with gorgeous images, poignant wordplay and brilliant gags.

The commentary mixes Kinbote's recollection of his Zemblan past with his recent New Wye present. We see the enchanted, beautiful Kingdom of Zembla: the youth of its promiscuous prince; its revolution; the imprisonment and escape of its much-loved monarch via a covert course and across the picturesque mountains. This is juxtaposed with Kinbote's spell living next door to Shade, their dusk walks and apparently flourishing friendship, along with remarks and annotations concerning their academic life and colleagues. We hear, too, of Kinbote's appeal to Shade to compose an epic poem recounting his magical, distressing tales of Zembla.

As the commentary and its Zemblan background/ hinterland progress, we begin to learn more of Shade's poem and its creation, along with Kinbote's frenetic spying upon its composition. These two blended stories - Zembla and New Wye - are quietly pervaded by a third: the cautious, gradual but unremitting advance into the texture of the text of one Jakob Gradus, an assassin dispatched by Zembla's new regime to locate and then eliminate the exiled King Charles. This is the man who has shot John Shade – apparently missing the king and killing the poet.

Gradus's pursuit, Kinbote and Shade's acquaintance, the ousting and exodus of King Charles: all three stories are permitted to progress through the commentary. As the novel reaches its climax, the composition of the poem 'Pale Fire' that fateful July and Gradus's simultaneous unyielding journey from Zembla to New Wye become more and more frequently placed side by jarring side, so that poet's line and hitman's quest grate and fuse in the text. Comedy and tragedy, error and terror, align themselves in magnificently mismatched union – as do parodies of detective fiction and erudite scholarly analysis. Nabokov's art is reaching its supreme apogee.

Each reader, on each reading and subsequent rereading, has to decide how adventurous or conventional they are prepared to be in flipping between poem, commentary and index, as well as occasional returns to the foreword. The story is relentless and exciting, but every now and then we have to be courageous, sometimes venturing where Kinbote sends us, juggling different parts of the text, filing away certain things to memory or returning, again and again, to particular spots.

Whatever fluctuating and divergent choices are made regarding the process and practice of reading *Pale Fire*, it is clear that poet and editor, poem and commentary, are wildly, preposterously, ill-matched. One is humble, composed, sane; the other conceited, agitated, ridiculous. One seems to exist in a Norman Rockwell painting, a close-knit community of humdrum, everyday life; the other inhabits a fantasy dominion of lurid extravagance, colourful occurrences and dreadful isolation.

As a literary critic, Kinbote is a comic concoction of disconcerting narcissism and benign megalomania, ruthlessly parodied. He claims to be the poem's origin, subject and muse; he steals, then misappropriates, the text, wheedling himself into it, obstructively placing himself between verse and reader; he points out improvements, mistakes or misconceptions; he constantly reminds us how indispensable he is to understanding and decoding the text. He is every writer's worst nightmare and every reader's worst enemy. He is envious, vindictive, resentful, distrustful – but also a rather tragic and pathetic creature, desperately redirecting us from Shade's life and work to his own. A lonely hijacker, terrorizing others to fulfil his fanatical caprice.

Yet there is something unusually, even uniquely, captivating about Charles Kinbote. In part this is the voyeurism of the car crash: it is exciting to watch someone founder quite so spectacularly, to so magnificently get it wrong and humiliate himself in public and in print (though whenever we snigger at Kinbote for missing a point or pun, we should remind ourselves that we, too, will have missed several ourselves, whether in 'Pale Fire' or *Pale Fire*). But Kinbote and his strange tale are bewitching, and he charms us with his unending extraneous details concerning Zemblan customs, history, landscape and language.

There is an eerie radiance to Kinbote's sad saga, his dramatic, audacious escape, and his extravagant elucidation of John Shade's last work. There is something peculiarly touching and troubling, too, in his dauntless, dogged belief in his friendship with the poet, which never seems to be quite reciprocated. Kinbote always seems to be popping up out of nowhere, a sudden and unwanted new best friend: boorish, bothersome, perverse.

Kinbote's story, such as it is, seems far-fetched, incredible and full of holes. For a start, if his reign was so beloved, how has a revolution managed to take hold? (His vain, indulgent commentary gives us a clue.) But, more crucially, Kinbote's constant bids for self-justification and validity tend to backfire and cultivate further misgivings about the accuracy, or indeed reality, of what he documents in his commentary.

The way the novel is constructed, and the way in which we have to read and reread it, means that our own sense of the veracity of Kinbote's annotations changes. For the most part, things become clearer the better acquainted we are with the text, but occasionally matters muddy as we acquire auxiliary details that complicate or refute earlier assumptions. We have to reassemble the widely dispersed splinters of evidence that Kinbote's commentary has littered across *Pale Fire*, carefully reading between his defensive, disingenuous lines.

As we do this, the discrepancies in Kinbote's story mount up, and John Shade emerges as a kind, patient man, more accepting than everyone else of Kinbote the tedious, unnerving oddball. Shade rather enjoys Kinbote's unbalanced, gaudy flights of imagination but is not blind to his self-absorption and thoughtlessness.

There is comedy and irony here, of course, as we (and Shade) see what Kinbote, in his egotism, cannot. Kinbote's inability to decode poetry or recognize literary references provides repeated occasions for humour, as well as pity: an early reference to the Sherlock Holmes story 'The Final Problem' (1893) and its long-awaited sequel, 'The Adventure of the Empty House' (1903), is woefully missed (along with their crafty connections to the themes of death and rebirth in 'Pale Fire'). Later, Kinbote seems completely unaware of the scandal involving a certain book entitled *Lolita* ...

On the other hand, we need to be careful not to pat ourselves on the back too fondly either, marvelling at our own ability to spot the in-jokes and allusions or sneering at Kinbote's misinterpretations of Shade's verses. For this is a monstrously playful text – turning wit inside out and upside down – which will trip us up and twist our heads off if we don't pay attention.

There is also a tender ethics at work here as we resolve the tangled contrast between Kinbote's appalling conduct and noxious imagination (his snooping on his neighbour; his convoluted commentary) and Shade's mellow tolerance, something he seems able to do even after death, gently rolling his eyes and shaking his head at the grotesque perversions inflicted upon his text. A touching line in 'Pale Fire' about the poet's daughter's suicide is commandeered by Kinbote's commentary into a hilarious (and lusciously lyrical) discourse on methods of self-murder. We melt and enjoy the observer's deviation, but Shade's line, and its depths, still haunt us, perhaps even more so because of what Kinbote has either missed or chosen to ignore.

Eventually, we discover that Shade's killer, Jakob Gradus, the assassin sent by the radical new Zemblan rulers, claims to the New Wye police to be plain 'Jack Grey'. He has recently absconded from a prison for the criminally insane and intended to kill a different man entirely: Judge Goldsworth, who put him away, whose house Kinbote rents, and who resembles John Shade in appearance. Grey was in the right place but has killed the wrong man. Gradus – and the whole intricate, elaborate history Kinbote has devised for him – evidently doesn't exist. Nothing Kinbote has claimed makes sense or holds together. His credibility is in tatters, his mind surely in shreds.

Where, then, does this leave our interpretation of *Pale Fire*, and indeed 'Pale Fire'? Several explanations have been put forward: that John Shade's daughter, Hazel, is the spectral inspiration behind Kinbote and Zembla; that Shade himself has staged his own death and deliberately invented Kinbote as a literary device for his new poem; that Kinbote is a figment of Shade's unhinged imagination, splitting his personality Dr Jekyll and Mr Hyde–like into the kind, sensitive poet and his alter ego, the unpleasant, inconsiderate critic.

The most prevalent rationalization, and one that Nabokov himself seemed to endorse, is that Kinbote and his whole Zemblan past are nothing but the manic delusions of one 'V. Botkin', an émigré Russian professor on the staff at Wordsmith College, who is mentioned very briefly in the commentary and index. His anguish at exile may have caused him to flamboyantly construct the complex network of Zembla as a psychological recompense for the terrible loss of his homeland.

The key to *Pale Fire*, however, seems to lie not in identifying which of these 'solutions' – or one of the many others that have been offered – resolve the riddle of the text, settling the puzzle like a completed crossword. Rather, each of these elucidations, with variant degrees of plausibility and possibility, offers a distinctive way to experience the text and its meanings, which vary with every revisit. We are not restricted to one explanation, but granted a limitless number of potential reinterpretations.

On whichever reading we choose, the disparity between poet and commentator has a quiet moral strength, asserting the silent victory of luminous, sensitive creativity sheltered in a balanced, loving mind. Shade's imaginative self-liberation contrasts with and triumphs over Kinbote's confining fancy, which incarcerates everything we read within the madman's obsessive, irrational prison of ego. But is such a separation between Kinbote's iniquity and Shade's innocence possible – even desirable? Is John Shade as blameless as we suppose?

Loss, trauma and hope are Nabokov's perennial themes, and each of the layers or interpretations of *Pale Fire* surveys the inescapable bereavements at the heart of life, seeking explication and transcendence. Shade's poem tries to explain his daughter's suicide (ostensibly perpetrated because of her unattractiveness) as the poet struggles to process this devastating event as well as to comprehend the apparent waste of all human life and potential in death.

Yet, just as Kinbote's commentary incestuously desires Shade's poem, incessantly attempting to promote its own status from offspring to spouse, does 'Pale Fire' itself also try to hide a dark Oedipal drama lying behind Hazel's death, even if an unconscious, unrealized one? This is not to suggest that Shade in any way abused his daughter, but rather that there existed certain cultural and sexual tensions which contributed to the daughter's own feelings of inadequacy and thence suicide. Here, *Pale Fire*'s Hazel Shade becomes a lost American sister with *Lolita*'s Dolores Haze, their sad, short lives as mirrored as their names: L. Haze and Haze-l.

The pity of Hazel's plight, and Shade's pain, lies at the heart of 'Pale Fire', if not *Pale Fire*, as Kinbote's own fantastical inventions strive to justify the sorrows of mortal existence: in effect, they act as a coping mechanism or pressure valve for *his* pain. It is obvious that the cultural-geographic losses of Kinbote's Zembla (and Botkin's

Russia), as well as Shade's mistaken, futile murder, evoke the two great losses of Nabokov's own life: his Russian homeland in the Revolution and his beloved father in 1922. (His statesman father was slain in Berlin as he intervened in the attempted murder of liberal politician Pavel Milyukov.)

Nabokov's father's birthday was 21 July, the day his son chose for John Shade's murder, and his successor as head of the émigré associations in Berlin was one S. D. Botkin. Forty years on from personal disarray and overwhelming loss, Nabokov would create a complex art of order and exultation, transfiguring an appalling moment into an aesthetic wonder that endlessly explores the brink between life and death, sense and folly, artifice and authenticity.

Pale Fire asks us to reconsider the fickle margins between original art and opportunistic criticism, as well as the unstable borders between characters, variant perspectives and multiple creative works. For all the evident and persistently invoked differences between them, Shade and Kinbote are mirrors, doubles, zombies and parodies of each other, each 'the shadow of the waxwing slain' in the first line of 'Pale Fire', each asserting and reasserting an afterlife for himself in the gruelling game of existence.

Kinbote creates his eccentric commentary solely to demonstrate that Shade's poem is about Zembla and he its usurped king: 'Pale Fire' is the only 'proof' of Kinbote's true being. It is here that the boundaries between illusion and reality, sanity and madness, poet and critic, rapidly begin to break down, for it is far too easy to merely dismiss Kinbote as a madman, however much he appears to be corroborated as such by his own text. He is after all, to some extent, a scrupulous, highly intelligent storyteller and narrative architect. Kinbote is clear on his vocation:

> I do not consider myself a true artist, save in one matter: I can do what only a true artist can do – pounce upon the forgotten butterfly of a revelation, wean myself abruptly from the habit of things, see the web of the world, and the warp and weft of that web.

At the very end of his commentary, Kinbote mischievously suggests he might write a play about 'a lunatic who intends to kill an imaginary king' and 'another lunatic who imagines himself to be that king'. Kinbote might not be playing with a full deck, but he is far from being a complete madman, and *Pale Fire* quietly urges that we recognize the fluidity between the poet and the critic-king.[8]

At a summer cocktail party, John Shade kindly recognizes as 'a fellow poet' a local madman who thinks himself God and, defending him against his detractors, asks that people do not see this unstable man's behaviour as madness. For Shade this is 'the wrong word' and should not be applied to someone 'who deliberately peels off a drab and unhappy past and replaces it with a brilliant invention'. That 'drab and unhappy past', the text – and surely John Shade – invites us to imagine,

---

8 Shade has a predilection for 'word golf' – a game moving from an initial word to a target one, via a series of 'shots' changing one letter at a time, and using only legitimate words. Usually the aim is to play between two words which are in some form of relationship – synonymous, antonymous, etc. For example, you can go from 'hate' to 'love' in three shots: hate > have > hove > love. Such games show the mischievous fluidity between words and their meanings and have important thematic significance for *Pale Fire*. (Lewis Carroll, a figure who looms behind the novel – and Nabokov in general – as a kind of benevolent, playful godfather, is said to have invented the game on Christmas Day in 1877.)

undoubtedly refers to Kinbote's, too, and the 'brilliant invention' to not only his amusing, delusional Zembla but Kinbote's literary annotations as a whole, pedantic and violently engorged, diligently distended to the point of insanity.

Nabokov recognized the commentator's thoroughness as being the same as the artist's love of detail, a component so vital to the texture of his own art. As he wrote the novel, Nabokov was also engaged on the massive project of translating Pushkin's *Eugene Onegin* and providing a vast multivolume commentary to go with it, and *Pale Fire* is a form of self-mocking response to this undertaking. Though clearly a satiric lesson on the labours and resentments of ill-conceived criticism, *Pale Fire* is also a parodic game in praise of punctiliousness. Nabokov celebrated the art of commentary in an essay on translation written around the same time, arguing for

> translations with copious footnotes, footnotes reaching up like skyscrapers to the top of this or that page so as to leave only the gleam of one textual line between commentary and eternity.

Nabokov's point refines and purifies the connection between poet and reader/commentator: each has an afterlife dependant on the other's word games.

Pale Fire is ceaselessly intertextual, riffing on the infinite potential for texts to spawn afterlives for themselves as well as on their inherent interconnectivity. *Pale Fire*'s own title stems from Shakespeare's relatively little-known play about generosity and alienation, *Timon of Athens* (c.1605), a derivation Kinbote comically fails to perceive due to the pitfalls of translation.[9] In the play, Timon – now destitute and ignored after a lifetime of largesse – cynically illustrates how everything in the world (and therefore by implication in literature) is indebted to something else:

> The sun's a thief, and with his great attraction
> Robs the vast sea; the moon's an arrant thief,
> And her pale fire she snatches from the sun;
> The sea's a thief, whose liquid surge resolves
> The moon into salt tears.
>   (IV.iii.431–435)

Clearly Kinbote is trying to steal some of Shade's poetic sunlight via his commentary, and he is a literal thief when he purloins the manuscript of 'Pale Fire' from Shade's bleeding body (later comically sewing it into his coat pockets to evade detection). As indicated by the novel's epigraph, Shade is Dr Johnson to Kinbote's James Boswell – the Scot Boswell also, of course, coming from a 'distant northern land'.

Nabokov, however, also transcends this misanthropic literary larceny by showing the positive, playful, collective relationship between texts in general. The same year Nabokov's father was slain, 1922, *Ulysses* and *The Waste Land* arrived as brilliant, chaotic, revolutionary works in pursuit of organization and coherence. Like them, *Pale Fire* is a mock epic, as are Pope's *The Rape of the Lock* (1714) and *Dunciad* (1728), texts at the heart of John Shade's academic field and which inform so many of the deeper strata of the novel.

---

9 There is also a reference in *Hamlet*, when the ghost remarks to the prince how, as the day starts to dawn, the night-time glow-worm '[be]gins to pale his uneffectual fire' (I.v.90).

Each of these works – *Ulysses*, *The Waste Land*, *The Rape of the Lock*, the *Dunciad* – seeks to playfully register the ordinary against the extraordinary, ironically teasing out complex correlations and disparities between alternative texts and histories in order to generate new values or contexts. Texts are never dead. Authors' works always have afterlives, and their shadows lie across literature.

Just as Joyce's novel and Eliot's poem summon a gigantic and cacophonous range of literatures and cultures with their constantly varying voices, *Pale Fire* appeals to and exemplifies the multilayered, interrelated and ever-changing nature of literary interpretation, reputation and prominence. As fickle as the moon, a work's appraisals will wax and wane as orbiting opinions shift over time. Moreover, a moon's fire might be pale, pinched and wavering, but it is still cherished as a striking indicator of space, time and meaning.

People, places, and texts continuously correspond, recall and engage with each other in *Pale Fire*, offering not quite reflections in partial, fluid or unstable mirrors. John Shade often shades into Charles Kinbote (and vice versa), just as his Appalachia evokes, though does not disappear into, his neighbour's Zembla (something taken even further in Nabokov's next novel, *Ada*, as global cartography is reconfigured, augmented, eliminated). At the same time, Kinbote's commentary is distinct but inseparable from Shade's 'Pale Fire', the biographer, editor and commentator locked in a dangerous relationship with his subject that is at once parasitic and affectionate, opportunistic and altruistic.

Similarly, Western literature, and especially literary rivalry and/or literary biography, infiltrates *Pale Fire*, a text which itself has since cast its own shadows and resentments onto postmodernism. There are the aforementioned Boswell/Johnson tensions, as well as – more comically – those between Sherlock Holmes (Shade) and his biographer, Dr Watson (Kinbote), *Pale Fire* being a latter-day detective thriller to match those from Arthur Conan Doyle's pen. There are innumerable connections between Swift (Kinbote) and Pope (Shade), in addition to Shakespeare's 'old' Timon (Shade) and Tennyson's homosexual, ill-informed, ill-mannered 'New Timon' (Kinbote) of 1846 – which itself was a stinging, satirical response to an opponent's spiteful denigration.

Pale Fire is alive to these squirming jealousies and intertextual suspicions, impudently parodying the ideals and idiocies of biography, criticism, and the whole petty business of literary clashes, something Nabokov's English-language novels in particular are fascinated by, from *The Real Life of Sebastian Knight* right through to the final *Look at the Harlequins!* (and even beyond, in the unfinished *Original of Laura*'s acts of self-bowdlerization).

Spiritual disagreements also track and trail the novel, partly as an ironic commentary on the 'blasphemy' of editing/expounding texts (a clear analogy is drawn between literary and theological discourse), but also in shrewder, more directly religious, ways. *Pale Fire* contains many subtle, subtextual theological discussions – in particular, engagements with Saint Augustine's *De Trinitate* (*c*.417) and Thomas Aquinas's *Summa Theologica* (1274) – that are only now beginning to be taken seriously by scholarship. Nabokov's self-fashioned apathy towards religion is, itself, another game: the concepts, sources, debates and disputes of faith are fascinating elements of *Pale Fire*'s ongoing interrogation of the relationship between writer, critic and reader.

This is important because readers cast shadows, too, as they construct their own ways of reading and rereading, especially when it comes to *Pale Fire*. No two readers or rereadings are alike, and they move variously between annotations and poem, identifying some, none or different allusions and connections on each visit. They become, as Nabokov expected, authors of their own reading, co-writers with the novelist, projecting their own hues of meaning onto a limitless series of personal rereadings.

Ludic and ludicrous, the regal poetics of *Pale Fire* invite frustration and satisfaction, pleasure and pain, as we navigate its tiers and trapdoors, marvelling at its gemlike beauty and encrusted perfection. Along with *The Gift* and *Lolita*, it is surely Nabokov's supreme achievement: in the countless mountains of his art, an Everest to their K2 and Kilimanjaro. It rises prominent, resilient, peculiar, showcasing all the facets of his brilliance – in language, plotting, precision, detail, character, texture, structure and theme – better than anywhere else. And its magnitude only grows, as its author envisioned, with every new visit, every fresh ascent of its treacherous slopes.

Yet, for all its might and reach, games and flames, *Pale Fire* remains a simple love story. Like all Nabokov's writing, it is captivated by the mystery of happiness and the enigma of death, the one as elusive as the other. 'Pale Fire', if not *Pale Fire*, seems to offer an answer to both, and from the same source. Charles Kinbote's desolate life is placed in stark contrast to John Shade's idyllic marriage to Sybil, the recipient and true muse of 'Pale Fire'. Their happy union seems to be a vision, a foretaste, of the otherworldly bliss we might attain in death.

Kinbote resents Sybil both emotionally, as Shade's wife, but also textually, since he believes she has censored

'Pale Fire', expurgating the Zemblan elements. In fact, of course, they were never there, and 'Pale Fire' is actually a paean to art and tenderness, hope and transcendence. Nothing could better encapsulate Kinbote's solitude and his woeful misreading of 'Pale Fire' than the terse, bitter entry he gives the poem's addressee in his otherwise voluminous index:

Shade, Sybil, S's wife, *passim.*

16

Ada or Ardor

LETTERS FROM AN AMBIDEXTROUS UNIVERSE

Rich, sumptuous, delicious? Or stodgy, unpalatable, indigestible? Perhaps even revolting, poisonous and evil? *Ada or Ardor: A Family Chronicle* (1969) is Nabokov's longest and most ambitious novel. Vast and plentiful, romantic and extravagant, it presents incestuous lovers who enjoy a lavish lifelong affair on an alternate Planet Earth, dying together in their nineties. It is a strange and sickly world: poetic and inspired, dazzling but disturbing, shot through with paradox, controversy and the dissonance of audacious proficiency.

Ada is preoccupied with time: the way we sense it, suffer it, are perplexed and consumed by it. Time dominates our lives yet remains a mystery to us. We determine it via clocks and calendars, but asked what it is, we can only shrug and mutter incomprehensibly about 'progress' or 'things happening'. Time is something we experience immediately and yet – at the same time – we cannot quite grasp, still less delineate. We know about causality, how events seem connected through time and how it also seems to be irreversible. But what is the true nature or meaning of time? Is it only an illusion? What is the reality behind its mystical appearance?

Human perceptions of subjective time change during our lives, as events and images become more familiar, less surprising, and *Ada* measures this. Indeed, subjectivity is built into the novel's very structure, through the radical differences in size of each section of the book as it progresses: part five is only one-sixteenth the dimensions of part one, which itself is half the novel. Across *Ada*'s pages we witness the vastness of youthful time, where anything is possible (and everything can wait). Then the hastening, hurrying bankruptcy of time as we grow up (and realize we won't live forever). The stockpiles of memory begin to overwhelm us, stacked high and deep, time speeding by as we age, lament and mourn.

Nabokov's novel divulges the lifelong love story of Van Veen (1870–1967) and his sister Ada (1872–1967). They first meet when she is eleven and he fourteen, initially believing themselves to be cousins but later discovering they are actually siblings. They begin a sexual affair, and *Ada* charts the numerous and protracted disruptions and fleeting resumptions of their relationship over the decades. They are wealthy, well educated, cultivated, highly intelligent. Van goes on to become a world-famous psychologist-philosopher; *Ada* takes the form of his memoirs, written in his nineties. The text is interspersed with his own and Ada's marginalia, and in parts with annotations by an unidentified editor, perhaps indicating the manuscript was incomplete or unfinished at their death.

Ada begins in the second half of the nineteenth century on an alternative Earth called Demonia or Antiterra. The planet's geography is the same as that of our own, as is much of its history, but with blips and disparities.

The English-speaking USA extends across the Americas (although there is a Russian-speaking province in what we know as western Canada and a French-speaking one in the east). Most of Asia is Russian; Europe and Africa are British (and ruled by a King Victor). Aristocracy remains extensive. Technology seems occasionally ahead of, though sometimes behind, our own timeline: there are cars and aeroplanes, but no television or telephones. Electricity has been banned since the ominously elusive 'L disaster', and hydro-kinetic systems now provide Antiterra's energy needs.

Throughout Antiterra lurks the abnormal belief in the existence of a twin world, 'Terra'. This planet seems to have a history much more like our own, something we discover due to the fact that adherents to this cult-like creed form an important part of Van's early psychological research. Van's subjects/patients dream, or hallucinate, about Terra, believing themselves in some way in communication with it.

This is the Antiterran world that Van and Ada are born into. In part one of the book we witness the two adolescents falling in love. The sweethearts tenderly pool resources to tell the story of their past, its patterns and contentment, its blissful sexual summers and harsh disappointments as they are compelled to spend considerable lengths of time apart (as cousins often do). Memory reconstructs past time, mislaid pleasures, evoking them in minute detail and linking them to the future happiness the couple will share in their later lives. Part one has been called the last nineteenth-century Russian novel: *Ada*'s sonorities, atmosphere, subject, visual landscape and narrative edifice all converse and negotiate with her mighty literary predecessors, while also conserving the artefacts of the previous century's novels in a vigorous, ironic museum.

But between the older couple and the ardent young lovers falls a severe and expansive chasm that *Ada* also navigates. Parts two and three have ragged, jagged edges, irregular vacillations and frayed textures. This is time in flux and anguish, jealous and aggrieved. Van and Ada hardly see each other across the long decades and when they do are aghast, repelled, awkward, irritated. Part four is Van's lecture on time, dictated as he drives across Europe to see Ada. Near its end, we feel that Van and Ada's love (and their lives) has been squandered. Only the slim, intolerably slight, final section awaits. But it will triumph over time (and space).

Part five begins on Van's ninety-seventh birthday. We learn that the couple, after decades apart, have spent the last forty years together in beatific, luminous love. After the immeasurable years of separation and recrimination, it hardly seems possible that they can still have time for so long together, but they do (and the maths, when we do it, adds up and summons tears). It is this final victory, and the almost appallingly slight amount of space we have to experience and enjoy it – 16 meagre pages out of a hefty 461 – which is the meaning and achievement of *Ada*.

It is not just that Van and Ada finally reunite, as they might in any number of pensioner-led romcoms where combatant former lovers get back together. *Ada* is not just a love story with a happy ending, a winter with flowers. *Ada* is about time and the way it manipulates us, and we manipulate it. There is mistreatment on both sides, and Nabokov explores and exploits this mutual manoeuvring. Like a rusty accordion, *Ada* pulls and squeezes time: dozens of pages are devoted to a few hours; a handful of slender sheets encompass decades. Expanded and condensed this way, our experience of, and involvement with, time changes.

Life, as human beings experience it, is not a one-way street or an arrow relentlessly moving through time, its point tapering and finally striking an inevitable target in death. It is much looser, with periods of torpor; then the shakes, shocks and changes of direction that make up the distinctive shape and particular texture of an individual's destiny from cradle to crematorium, womb to tomb. Viewed externally, life seems determined and obvious, undeviating. From within, however, it is restless, fluid, multidirectional, disorientating and disconcerting.

In *Ada*, Nabokov fuses shifting scientific approaches to time, quite properly portraying our perception of time as a synthesis of several models. Time was long regarded as unbending and universal, calculated by Newton's clock in the sky, which all could see. Yet by the twentieth century, Einstein's relativity, and quantum mechanics, shattered our notions of set, absolute time and defined spatial dependence. Einstein's picture of reality as a network of relationships seemed to complement, if not corroborate, much of the peculiarity of time that we live through. Here fixity is repudiated for dynamic uncertainty, a more subjective, intrusive system closer to our own emotional-psychological experience.

At the same time (as it were), *Ada* recognizes that, for all the strangeness, time marches on: the sun still rises and sets with a Newtonian regularity, while the planets orbit our star like cars endlessly circling a roundabout. But there are also discrepancies, idiosyncrasies, that match the dilating, tightening, crawling or careering time we feel with flummoxing familiarity, as we humans are variously busy, bored, young, old, in love or in pain.

Ada's language is as ornately ironic and diversely fertile as its temporal deliberations (it begins by mangling the famous opening words of a famous nineteenth-century Russian novel). Like *Romeo and Juliet*'s (*c.*1595) semantic compressions and inversions, or the dangerous harmonics and lurid tonalities of Wagner's *Tristan und Isolde* (1865), *Ada*'s gaudy, heterogeneous language both conveys and conceals its meanings.

In *Ada*, time and sentences seem to proceed for just a little too long. They are nebulous, incestuous, ambiguous, often losing our attention, straying into hallucinations and deliriums, the text becoming excited, animated, overwrought. They can also be pithy and laconic, lethargically slouching, apathetic, blasé, blank. *Ada* muddles language and time just as it jumbles comedy and tragedy, dreams and realities, Terra and Antiterra. With laughter and tears, *Ada* tries (and perhaps succeeds) to cleanse guilt and history, flouting gravity, disregarding space and time.

Yet it can only rinse so much. Dark, complex or controversial figures from our world haunt and menace *Ada* via delectably bad puns or worse jokes: early on we encounter a stalking Sigmund Freud, 'Dr Sig Heiler'; near the end, the Führer slithers by as 'Athaulf Hindler'. Fantasy worlds, like childhood, can seem all sunlit summers and elations, but youth is often sickly and revolting as well, full of ghosts and shadows, and *Ada*'s frequently infantile language contrasts sharply to its typically sophisticated prose and fervid philosophizing. Like a succubus it enchants and terrifies, alternately demonic and angelic, vigorous and exhausted, original and clichéd, logical and absurd.

In part, this helps explain why *Ada* is so indecipherable, almost unreadable for many diligent bibliophiles and attentive Nabokovians. By blending beauty and horror, infancy and maturity, art and science, brother/sister and husband/wife, and our world and another, Nabokov mixes meanings to such an extent that partition and comprehension become elusive, remote. *Ada* asks us to transcend time-bound limitations and terrestrial parameters – beyond taste, convention, laws, memories, and into true freedom, the frank abandon and abundant inventiveness of the primordial experience.

During the short final section of *Ada*, revelations of Van and Ada's ultimate decades-long happiness are interspersed with observations on the havoc and consequences of time, especially on the fleshly self. Cancer advances excruciatingly within Van, the disease being one of the book's many 'engine[s] of agony', as he and Ada rearrange eighty years of splintered and reforged time into a dialogue on death.

Van ceases tweaking his largely finished (but not yet entirely perfected) work, and the text of *Ada* starts to become distorted, indistinct. The novel no longer refers to Van and Ada as separate beings, but begins to variously amalgamate them into 'Dava or Vada, Anda or Vanda' as they 'overlap, intergrade, interache' and inaugurate their own termination, dissolving into the finished book. They move into a state of maximum entropy, thermodynamic equilibrium, where everything ceases, including time, since there is now no way to measure it: nothing changes; everything stays the same. A timeless state, an eternal existence, unfathomable to our hominid imaginations.

This ultimate romantic union of Van and Ada, and their eventual metaphysical merger, is not brought about solely by the gambling fortunes of fate or by latent feelings finally surfacing. All Nabokov's works hint at otherworldly connections or intercessions, exhorting us to think beyond the prisons of human time. The distinctive, exceptional textures of his art encourage us to backtrack across the story, retracing our narrative steps to discover interdimensional clues that invite and provide meanings. These otherworldly mediations tend to work in conjunction with pain and loss, for at the heart of Nabokov's works lie secrets and sorrows: absent, usually dead, girls who nevertheless continue to structure and inform the texts in which they do not actually figure.

Mira, murdered by the Nazis, endures to protect her youthful lover Pnin, shepherding him via a succession of interventionist squirrels (*Pnin*, 1957); Hazel, lost to suicide, guides her father (poet John Shade) in his art and eschatological musings (*Pale Fire*, 1962); the eponymous siblings in 'The Vane Sisters' (1951) speak with startling power across the cosmic and dimensional divide. In *Ada*, this function is occupied by flame-haired-girl-in-green Lucette, Van and Ada's kindly kid sister. In this case, she is a present and vital character for much of the novel, until her structural and thematic exit, which paradoxically opens up her much larger organizing role and significance.

In the midst of their passion, Van and Ada tease their little sister and exclude her from their sexual and intellectual games, cruelly using or manipulating her for their own ends and amusements. She is by turns a convenient tool or a troublesome obstruction (as little sisters tend to be) to their love and desire:

> Lucette, the shadow, followed them from lawn to loft, from gatehouse to stable, from a modern

shower booth near the pool to the ancient bathroom upstairs. Lucette-in-the-box came out of the trunk. Lucette desired they take her for walks. Lucette insisted on their playing 'leaptoad' with her – and Ada and Van exchanged dark looks.

By the time she is eight, Lucette has fallen for Van, who she believes her cousin, spellbound by his charm, captured and enraptured in a dangerous and fatidic adult game that will ultimately kill her. A few years later, determined to seduce Van on a transatlantic liner, she is thwarted partly by fate's malice (actress Ada's unexpected appearance on the ship's cinema screen) and her own kindness in politely helping others (boorish family friends). Frustrated in her amorous mission and rejected by a now sexually sober Van, she consumes a vast quantity of sleeping pills and jumps overboard.

Lucette is one of Nabokov's most attractive creations: physically stunning, she is also witty, caring, courteous. While her death is horrendous, the episode is told in some of Nabokov's greatest prose. Van's final rebuff of Lucette is a virtuous thing in itself (betraying one sister with another will hardly improve a complicated situation), but it exposes his (and Ada's) overall treatment of their sister and the way in which their ardour disregards all feeling for others. It is an infatuation which devours us as well, morally blinding us with its glare, since we, too, frequently wish Lucette out of the way of the erotic shenanigans *Ada* will have us behold.

Although the incestuous lovers – dazzling, passionate, articulate – think they are uniquely extraordinary, inhabiting their own world of difference, we can see past their dreadful glamour. Amid all the charisma, colour and romance of Ada and Van – and we are certainly seduced – we can distinguish the conceit, the cruelty, the way they have manipulated Lucette into becoming a manic, fragile, sex-fixated young woman (who dies a virgin). They have essentially teased her to death, as they half-admit.

Yet it would be too easy for Nabokov to simply denounce Van and Ada for their callousness. They are punished for their behaviour, suffering lonely decades of remorse and regret as they live their own lives apart. But Lucette's kindness and humanity endure beyond her Atlantic suicide and watery grave, and she tears through the textures of time to help reunite the lovers. Lucette is a silent but persuasive narrative presence, a subtly forceful hue amid the infinite intensity of Van and Ada's electric chromatism and brash designs.

Two themes – letters and water – form a peculiar pattern throughout *Ada*, determining the destiny of not just Lucette but Van and Ada too. They underscore both the novel's scrutiny of ethical obligation and its probe of metaphysical possibilities outside human perception. Nabokov links up written messages across the novel's formidable span: texts within the text that we are asked first to observe, later remember and finally connect. A poem Lucette is made to go away and memorize (so that Van and Ada can have their fun) returns in a letter Lucette writes at the end of her life, still desperate to display her love and devotion. During the disturbing scenes aboard the ship, which flourish in farce and desolation, this letter – written before the tragic sea voyage but read only after it – forms an omnidirectional compass around which *Ada*'s codes orientate and evolve.

Letters and water are further invoked by the many intertextual games the novel plays with dozens of other works of English, French and Russian literature, as well as with itself. *Ada* quips and riffs, playing frequently and at length on the role of correspondence and water in *Hamlet*, most especially via Ophelia's exchanges with the prince and her aqueous demise. Letters alphabetical as well as epistolary figure in *Ada* – in the novel's many (often purposefully bad) puns or in the Russian Scrabble that Van, Ada and Lucette play.

The initial character of Lucette's name also connects to the wider metaphysics at play: the mysterious 'L disaster', which occurred at some point in the mid nineteenth century, not only discredited electricity but made talk of it taboo. Since then water has been the source of Antiterra's power; but one other strange corollary of the L disaster was the rise of the bizarre, quasi-religious belief in the existence of 'Terra', a world physically akin to Antiterra but apparently sharing our planet's narrative. Van is a world expert on this outlook and its believers' vague, uncanny convictions (his work being a sorrowful sanctuary during his absences from Ada). He even writes a novel on the subject, *Letters from Terra*, under the jesting pseudonym 'Voltemand' (the name of a letter-conveying courtier in *Hamlet*), and it is to this alias's address that Lucette deliberately sends her final missive to Van.

Ada abounds with images that anticipate or recall Lucette's death by drowning, and her aquatic departure is emblematically linked to Antiterra's narrative and the novel's metaphysics. It is no coincidence that the L disaster, which has caused Antiterra's history to diverge from our own, has led to both the rise of hydro-dynamic energy and the perturbing belief in another world beyond Antiterra. Water is literally powering the planet, but subliminally it is also driving the energies, via kind-hearted Lucette's transcendental intercessions into the fabric of space-time, that will reunite Van and Ada. Nabokov suggests that the dead Lucette exists on Terra, which is largely inaccessible to those on Antiterra, apart from an unsettled special few.

Van, flamboyant, impressive authority on Terra though he is, cannot initially grasp the connections that will allow his and Ada's lives to have true meaning in happiness together. He eventually does, however, at the hotel in Mont Roux where the lovers' reunion finally takes place. The novel's hidden messages converge in scenes where luck, writing, dejection, the direction of time and the renewal of hope each play their own role, as do punning allusions and sly subliminal references to a 'mermaid's message' (from Lucette, by now twenty-one years dead). Details from across the novel suddenly snap together, the rhythms of Ada and Van's fickle, disordered lives revealed and rejoiced in. Now fifty and fifty-two respectively, they can spend their remaining decades by each other's side, writing many books together – including the one we are holding.

The extent of Van and Ada's redemption is limited. Their book, *Ada*, is not a narcissistic attempt at self-justification like Humbert's memoir *Lolita* (1955), nor is it a dictionary of moral monstrosity like Hermann's *Despair* (1934). Van and Ada are not exclusively outstanding freaks or fiends, and their book ironically indicts them as, in fact, the quite ordinarily flawed human beings we all are and participants in a really quite ordinary love affair (which, like all love affairs, from the inside feels astonishing and unique).

Lucette haunts their remaining years but benignly, even benevolently. By skilfully transferring the centre of the novel away from Van and Ada to Lucette's quiet kindliness, Nabokov mutes the lovers' vibrant voices and permits them to properly listen to each other and themselves, working together and discovering true happiness. We can see what Van and Ada cannot: the delicate filaments that Nabokov has entwined into the texture-web of *Ada*, which suggest the drowned Lucette has influenced Van's and Ada's lives, sending signals from a province outside perishable space-time – particularly at the decisive point when their reunification at the hotel seems to have been unsuccessful.

Ada is opulent comedy and a complex essay in Nabokov's lifelong art of parody. Family sagas, fairy tales, epistolary literature, erotic fiction, the art of narrative exposition, even the role of attics in the nineteenth-century novel – all these and many more are lampooned and given new meanings in the rich riot of *Ada*'s fabulously designed universe, which engages with, as well as taunts and mimics, our own. In many ways, as a summation of Nabokov's art, *Ada* is also a parody of his own parodies, playing with the ironies of his own making, disintegrating into itself and reconstituting further meanings concerning the comic and the cosmic.

Despite all its clowning and wit, *Ada* will always be an immensely difficult book. Like its author-subjects, Van and Ada, it is infuriating, exasperating, incessantly smug in its opacities and esoteric insinuations. It revolves around its own force, self-circumnavigating in a frenzied, violent desire to be different and to assert that difference. Yet it needs to do this to allow its discreet moral strength to glimmer and to intuit (not preach) transcendent, timeless realms of being and connectivity. In his work in general, and *Ada* in particular, Nabokov unites ethics, aesthetics and metaphysics into a continuum of belief rather than distinct categories. They are inseparable aspects to his art, forming a triune literary divinity: three-in-one, intimately related and indivisible.

Many seasoned Nabokovians are quite reasonably never able to fully enjoy *Ada*'s piquant pleasures or prevail over its tantalizing challenges. Nevertheless, with a certain amount of patience and persistence, it yields its intentionally subtle delectations, its rich and riveting delights. Though not Nabokov's last novel, it is his final feast, served up by an ambidextrous, omni-talented chef.

17
Transparent Things
PROOFREADING THE PAST

Dmitri Nabokov (1934–2012), a fine mountaineer (as well as opera singer, semi-professional race car driver, part-time movie star and translator of his father's works) used to surprise his parents by inexplicably materializing in their living room at the Montreux Palace Hotel, having climbed diagonally outside from his own room on the floor below. At home in his own body as well as the spatial sphere around him, flourishing in his musical, intellectual and physical pursuits, Dmitri enjoyed a string of glamorous and protracted love affairs. He also maintained a close personal and working relationship with his father, living nearby when Vladimir returned to Europe from America following the success of *Lolita* at the end of the 1950s. An English version of *Invitation to a Beheading*, under its author's supervision, as well as a collaborative translation of Lermontov's *A Hero of Our Time* (1840) sealed the affectionate and mutually stimulating rapport father and son shared.

Dmitri's joyful self-assurance must have seemed almost an upturned spoof of some of his father's gauche and gawky early heroes. Dmitri was as confident, successful and compassionate as Ganin (*Mary*, 1926), Franz (*King, Queen, Knave*, 1928), Smurov (*The Eye*, 1930) and Martin (*Glory*, 1932) are diffident and disagreeable, alienated from not only themselves but their families and surroundings. As one might expect, as Nabokov grew older, and especially after Dmitri's birth in 1934, the writer largely left behind younger male protagonists, the notable exception being Fyodor in *The Gift* (1938), since here he wanted to chart the whole passage of a young artist's evolution. Instead, the middle-aged Nabokov focused on the more mature figures of philosopher Adam Krug (*Bend Sinister*, 1947), academics Humbert, Pnin and Kinbote (*Lolita*, 1955; *Pnin*, 1957; *Pale Fire*, 1962) and psychologist Van Veen (*Ada*, 1969). For his next novel, however, Nabokov would return to the theme of the maladroit, disaffected youth.

How do you write about sons after you have one of your own? If Nabokov had used his own life as inspiration for his awkward early heroes, now, at the other end of his career, he turned to and – as he had done with so many of his comic creations – outrageously inverted a type he knew well. This time, in *Transparent Things* (1972), he reversed his son's character to create a warped antithesis of his own offspring. Nabokov *père* transformed Nabokov *fils* to invent sullen, impatient, physically uncomfortable and amorously ineffective Hugh Person.

If not, perhaps, a true genius, Dmitri was an artist – on slopes, stage, page and bed – in his brilliance, attitude and salubrious imaginative energy. Hugh, by contrast, is a glum and lacklustre publisher's assistant and is as frustrated in his poetic articulation as in his romantic.

Transparent Things is the tragicomedy of a smart young man who squanders his life on routine, monotonous tasks, improving the work of others at the expense of enhancing his own existence. Hugh's mental momentum, not spent on any bold artistic undertaking that might relieve the itch of his being, ferociously explodes while his consciousness is unaware. A lifelong insomniac and somnambulist, he throttles his wife in his sleep, muddling nightmare and reality, before himself dying oddly in a fire, his death as clumsy, infuriating and curiously uncooperative as his life.

This novel, sombre and short but filled with sly wit and weirdness, serves as an unequivocal presentation of a number of Nabokov's fundamental literary, ethical and metaphysical concerns, his perpetual themes and techniques distilled into a slender, anxious masterpiece (as taut and slim as *Ada* was fat and digressive). Art and expiry, past and present, phantom and flesh, clarity and opacity, sparkle and tedium – *Transparent Things* surveys a variety of conflicts both on its surface and in the range of subtexts furiously buried within its psychic depths. It patterns fires and falls, rooms and romance, the torpid hostility of inert entities and the dysfunction of matter, in order to scrutinize our mystical relationship with the weary world we inhabit, its essential unknowability and elusiveness.

To explore these encounters, Nabokov engages not only an eccentric and unpredictable narrator but a host of puzzling and spectral storytellers, who have the otherworldly knack of being able to ramble and roam below the external present of objects and individuals. (The biography and constitution of a timeworn pencil is perused in nearly as much detail as the novel's protagonist.) These shadowy, ethereal narrators are a continuation, and development, of much of his earlier work, Nabokov again employing narrative ghosts from departed characters – in this short novel, some sixteen deaths are reported – to haunt the surviving ones, troubling and, from time to time, apparently directing their lives (think of Mira in *Pnin*, Hazel in *Pale Fire*, or Lucette in *Ada*).

In *Transparent Things*, these chronicler-spirits seem to maintain an active, flippant participation in their tale, and are facetious, eerie authorities throughout the text. This is especially so in the novel's opening and closing lines:

> Here's the person I want. Hullo, person! Doesn't hear me.
>
> Easy, you know, does it, son.

Between these two disconcerting and ungainly lines, *Transparent Things* charts the life of Hugh Person through four journeys he makes to Switzerland, a setting familiar to Nabokov from his sojourns in alpine resort hotels, where he ceaselessly butterfly hunted on the meadows and deep in the forests. He had been resettled in Europe for over a decade, finishing *Pale Fire* and *Ada* there, as well as his gargantuan edition of *Eugene Onegin* (1964). Nabokov continued to have frequent dealings with American publishers and chose to make his new hero a young, US-based editor/proofreader, Hugh Person.

On his first trip, as a twenty-two-year-old student, Hugh morosely escorts his recently widowed father, who dies absurdly while trying on a pair of trousers in a drab boutique. The now orphaned son commemorates the event by that night mislaying his virginity with a prostitute in a dingy guesthouse. Upon his return to America, Hugh obtains employment for a New York publisher and is assigned to work with Mr R., an unconventional German-born novelist who lives in Switzerland.

R., who pens English far better than he speaks it, is the focus of Hugh's second Swiss trip, where he nervously tries to perform his nascent occupation while the roaring, sardonic R. bellows misshapen idioms all over the place, murdering the very language he writes in. This second excursion is also where Hugh meets Armande, a superficial, bad-tempered and austerely promiscuous mademoiselle who, after an unlikely courtship, marries him, having misapprehended the young man's prospects. On their honeymoon, Armande is disturbed by a TV report of a hotel fire and coerces devoted Hugh into rehearsing with her a mock drill. The pair farcically descend the hotel's facade, and commotion and incompetence ensue, but acrobatic Armande has already accessed a third-floor room, where she fornicates with a stranger. Despite this wifely fickleness, Hugh's idolization of Armande continues, on their return to the East Coast, to shield him from her continuing licentious conduct and bizarre sexual proclivities.

A third Swiss trip follows, Armande to visit her terminally ill mother, Hugh his clients. An odd and occasionally inimical meeting with an ailing, irascible R. takes place in the library of the latter's 'big, old, and ugly' house, its walls lined with 'the author's copies of the author's books' in numerous editions and translations. Soon after returning home to America, Hugh strangles Armande one night, during a dream in which he saves her from a burning building. He is found guilty of her murder and spends several years shambling between jail and lunatic asylum.

Eventually released, Hugh makes a fourth and final pilgrimage to Switzerland, to recover what he (falsely, fondly) reminisces on as his happy first days with Armande. Hitches and glitches arise as he tries to pinpoint the exact location of their first kiss and secure the very hotel room they once stayed in. Events intervene, but in the end he is granted the sacred chamber. Retiring early, he visualizes his wife, and as he begins to fall asleep, his drifting imagination soars. Armande appears in a dream as a flight attendant before the jet explodes in mid-air. Hugh awakes in a fit of coughs to discover the hotel is on fire, set ablaze by a disgruntled former employee. Having mistaken the door for a window, he chokes to death.

In these excursions to Switzerland we witness, in excruciating detail and a harsh bright light, Hugh's irritation and misery as well as his indefatigability and the misplaced mawkishness which later lead him to try to revisit his past. Expectation turns to repetition, then termination (and potential emancipation into another state of being). Through these arrangements in time, the novel mocks the notion of prophecy and return as the spectral storytellers who narrate *Transparent Things* present a series of comically self-confident forewarnings about the particulars of their protagonist's demise.

But these prove to be erroneous: Hugh dies not by falling from the fire but by smoke inhalation (his suffocation matching Armande's death and forming another pattern). This comes about through an event that demonstrates the fundamental randomness of the human experience: a last-minute change of hotel rooms alters how Hugh will die, sidestepping the narratorial calculations. Nabokov, as the novel's creator, exerts authority over his narrators, and their naivety in believing they can predict the future, by changing the exact nature of Hugh's death in an authorial overruling.

This unpredictability extends across time's tenses. The future *and* the past are both unknown. To return to the past is impossible; it is a fabled cul-de-sac Nabokov's heroes have been failing to locate since *Mary*. The past is fluid, unstable, unrecoverable, and should be celebrated as such: an elegant, sinuous dimension of continued creativity and rediscovery, not a static prison of history.

By placing the story in the excitable hands of a rookie troupe of supernatural raconteurs, Nabokov ridicules the mythical prospect of knowing what the future holds while at the same time disrupting the corresponding dishonest illusion of being able to recapture the past. The bumbling, gossipy spirit-narrators tell tales, literally and figuratively. They utilize their knowledge to access all of Hugh's past and present life and, with this, try to find the coincidences and recurrences (conflagration, asphyxiation) that have patterned his personhood.

These narrative elves then pass on their findings to none other than elaborately idiosyncratic novelist Mr R., who seems, in death, to be head of this band of apprentice phantom narrators, utilizing his literary skill to spin the fragile, translucent web of *Transparent Things*. R. is both dead and alive, a truly spectral and liminal presence: he has died during the events of the book he narrates, in which he is a lively, living character, allowing him to apparently travel outside the fixed parameters of time and space. But there are limits, Nabokov tells us.

Undoubtedly, it is R.'s eerily distinctive hand behind the peculiar first and last lines of the novel cited above. Garrulous, sonorous R. begins the book with a warning: having taken on the role of a surrogate father, he tries to alert Hugh to the impending hotel fire. R. fails in his oblique counsel, so he and the other narrators idly wait for Hugh's apparent destiny to unfold, killing time by exploring his life, mischievously or mistakenly impersonating the messages of fate. However, the future does not yet exist: it is merely a void to be occupied subsequently, and appropriately, by the countless possibilities that every instant offers.

The ghostly group of trainee storytellers know their shortcomings. They identify suggestive shapes of quirk, fluke and echo – hotels, infernos – and aid R. in constructing his system of thematic motifs, but neither they nor R. can accurately ascertain that which is yet to come. Fires, love and futures are capricious, erratic things, some more predictable than others, but all essentially undetermined until they take place. Any accurate divination otherworldly beings might make, even regarding their own story, and with the assistance of gifted novelist R., is limited.

Ironically, the ghost-narrators see too much. Not limited by rigid bodily boundaries or the regimented flow of history (both of which hamper poor Hugh so much), they can see through everything: visibly into objects and across time into the past. The novice narrators must control and focus their sagacious powers to avoid irrelevancy or regression in their pattern making, entrusting the narrative principally to the experienced author R. (and to the even more practised Nabokov, who appears anagrammatically, as a 'sly scramble', via the incidental character 'Adam von Librikov' in one of R.'s books).

True omniscience and omnipotence lie solely with the creator-author, outside the restricted dimensions of the narrative, as he alone shapes his characters' future. It is this superior power that allows Nabokov to control the aesthetics (and therefore ethics) of first-person modes of storytelling by mad or malevolent narrators such as Kinbote and Humbert, thus granting their prisoner-subjects (John Shade, Dolores Haze) a freedom, integrity and moral victory over their outwardly almighty jailer-narrators. In *Transparent Things*, R. and his assistants narrate with a mysteriously apathetic tenderness refracted through a strange grey light, whereby Nabokov confuses and complicates our sympathies for dour, brooding Hugh.

On the whole, Hugh's life is mundane and unambitious, but he is of a melancholic, bookish bent and has his thoughts and dreams, flashes of dogged perception, mind-trapped verse and periodic insight. There is an inventive dynamism within, but it is locked away, caught inside him and unable to escape through the communication of art, which might otherwise act as a safety valve for his worries and diminish his persistent and violent dreams. Whatever his internal energy, Hugh is not a true artist and as such has a bogus, disloyal relationship with time as he tries to recreate a non-existent blissful past he never had.

Hugh navigates his life badly, choosing an unsatisfying, niggling career and attaching himself to a phony, unfaithful wife. This frustrating and habitually humdrum life ends with protracted drama, in a sort of perverse parody of *Romeo and Juliet*, something portended by the name of the Italian courtesan Hugh procures on the night of his father's death – Giulia Romeo – and the grim absurdist theatre of Hugh and Armande's lovemaking. A wretched distortion of the world's most famous romantic couple, lukewarm Hugh and wanton Armande pointedly contrast with ardent Romeo and chaste Juliet. In both tragedies the participants die apart, one at a time, but whereas in Shakespeare's play only a few minutes separate the sweethearts' deaths, in *Transparent Things* this partition is prolonged into an agonizing whirlpool of insanity, incarceration and self-delusional homecoming.

Ominous, enigmatic, and gorgeously gloomy, *Transparent Things* peers ruthlessly at a cumbersome, ham-fisted life, watching its graceless hero burp up a breakfast Coke or peel at raw skin after wearing too-tight boots. He is mortified in life, humiliated in death. Passing over the threshold into a new state of being, he will, if he's lucky, likely be compelled to check other people's lives as a spectral proofreader of mortal content, much like the other ghostly inspectors that narrate the novel. (His first name, 'Hugh', suggests the interrogative 'who?' or, with a Swiss French accent, the perspective 'you', confirming the novel's relentless, unsparing examinations of identity and narrative voice. His surname, 'Person', further taunts his ordinariness, his brutal normality.)

We zoom in and out of Hugh's ghastly lifespan with a hyper-cinematic lens, travelling effortlessly across time and space, darting to and fro, plummeting into objects and veering into the past. The novel's shapes and decorations are explicit, even aggressively insisted upon, paradoxically organized to disturb or propagandize a formless future. Its language emanates a rococo radiance mixed with a stark colloquialism, relaxed virtuosity jumbled with a jarring, uneasy and troubled hesitancy. The narrators shuffle between indifference and inquisitiveness, distance and proximity, formality and familiarity, whisking us back through Hugh's life before he is shoved, indecorously, across the timid frontier between life and death.

Nabokov's penultimate completed novel is delicate, elusive, concise, with a size, texture and tone far from the woozy opulence of *Ada*, the euphoric refinement of *Lolita*, or the sumptuous mappings of *The Gift*. A diaphanous text, the themes and meanings of *Transparent Things* transpire most clearly when held up against the light of his earlier work, whose complex narrative strategies, vibrant patterns and preoccupation with a vanished past here achieve a dazzling apotheosis.

A reliquary of sadness, *Transparent Things* is precious and exquisite, a tantalizing study of precarious humanity. It is also bleak, inconvenient, unfriendly. The conventional relationships between character, narrator, author and reader are sadistically shattered to reinvestigate time, memory and design, as well as the inscrutability of individuality and mortality. It is superficially unattractive but highly addictive, its tremors and networks matching the inestimable lost thoughts, feelings and sensations we all face during the grisly business of existence.

18

Look at the Harlequins!
INVENT REALITY!

Imaginative writers, whether of poetry or prose, must be prepared for naive readers and idle critics to maliciously or mundanely connect their artistic inspirations with their own lives. Although authors naturally draw on their own personal histories – 'write what you know!' – for stimulation, they also make things up. They create, compose, invent, contrive and devise, while also drawing on experience – using it, developing it, twisting it or throwing it aside.

Sometimes, understanding a writer's life can be the key to appreciating a work, not least when the text distorts or changes that life: the manner and degree of those changes can promote our comprehension of the aesthetic purposes behind the fictive handiwork. Too often, however, readers and commentators seek an easy biographical solution to textual problems or literary provenance, attributing them to a simple inspiration/correlation located in the life of the author.

Nabokov was no stranger to such facile connectivity. His own fiction drew heavily on, exploited and played with, his own biography, as well as his own fictional creations within that biography. Not only do Nabokov-like figures populate his books, but his own characters seek to indecently infiltrate their sister texts, so that a network of self-referential auto-allusions warp and blur our sense of narrative and biographic propriety.

The most famous (and damaging) linkage between life and work occurred, of course, with *Lolita* (1955), the work Nabokov always asserted was the most difficult to write because of the psychological-emotional distance between himself and his deviant brute, Humbert Humbert. It was all too easy for public and press to argue that, whatever his protestations to the contrary, the creator of *Lolita* must share some of its narrator's dark inclinations. Never mind that Shakespeare had never been a Danish prince or Scottish king, a Venetian moor or merry wife of Windsor; never mind that Dante had never been to hell, nor Milton to paradise. Nabokov *must* have some sexual perversions if he was to construct (so brilliantly and believably) the protagonist of the scandalous *Lolita*.

So go the usual misconceptions and self-defeating arguments. Typically, critical derision derives from a fear or insecurity on the reader's part. A simple way to deny the challenges (sexual or literary) of the creation in question is to claim its creator is a pervert/fascist/communist (etc.) and that one wants nothing to do with it. Works of art, if they are any good, confront, confound and complicate, and if we can unilaterally declare their creators evil, it saves us a lot of trouble – in time, morals, or brainpower.

Lazy and misleading erotic associations with *Lolita*, although occasionally vexing, tended to amuse Nabokov, secure as he was in his impassioned but stable and contented monogamy with Véra. Indeed, the misperceptions between art and life, imagination and reality, were always the lifeblood of his literary productivity, not least in his first English novel, *The Real Life of Sebastian Knight* (1941).

In the early 1970s, however, Nabokov was reading and correcting the draft of Andrew Field's *Nabokov: His Life in Part* and became increasingly displeased by Field's (albeit erudite) theoretical explorations of his subject's personal past, as well as the sheer quantity of factual mistakes.

Nabokov and his art understood the vitality of both biography and autobiography – he himself had written one of the masterpieces of the latter's genre in *Speak, Memory* (1951; 1966). The exiled Russian's memoir is shrewd and well crafted, sophisticated and astonishingly beautiful, but nonetheless unforthcoming when it comes to delving deeply into its subject's emotional life or work. Evasive with regard to emotions and elusive about aesthetics, it is itself a work of art. His frustrations with Field's book and the inherent complications between life and composition seem, we might tentatively suggest, to lead Nabokov to what would be his last completed novel, *Look at the Harlequins!* (1974), which probes and parodies the very notion of self-writing, as well as the way readers of novels seek to fallaciously affix life and art.

Look at the Harlequins! (hereafter *LATH*) plays the usual Nabokovian tricks: fickle perspectives, giddy reversals and untrustworthy guides. But it does so not simply to amuse or confuse, nor to mock naive or one-dimensional readers. Rather, it is to cunningly affirm Nabokov's overall (and inseparable) literary-ethical-metaphysical philosophy, as well as pay a final, understated tribute to his wife (and editor) of nearly fifty years, Véra.

Throughout his literary career, Nabokov had proclaimed not only the beauty, luck and vitality he felt in his own life, but also its inversion or negation, portraying and interrogating the testing of that energetic bliss as it faced internal or external dangers. His life in the twentieth century had witnessed an enormous amount of fluctuation, his repeated exiles most notably punctuating and puncturing his mutable existence. But whatever the assaults on the castle of his happiness, Nabokov never lost his love for literary invention, nor his passion for his wife, both of which he saw as (hopefully but uncertainly) prefiguring some eventual escape from the temporary prisons of time and the self into some potential otherworldly existence – a theme all his works survey.

LATH takes the form of the memoirs of Vadim Vadimovich (hereafter VV), an eminent Anglo-Russian author. He is born in 1899 in pre-Revolutionary Saint Petersburg, where, he claims, he is abandoned by his parents and raised by a great-aunt. Following the Revolution, VV shoots a Red Army guard and escapes to England, where he encounters his patron, Count Starov, who pays for VV to attend Cambridge. Here he meets fellow student Ivor Black and then, in France, Ivor's sister Iris, who becomes VV's first wife. They move to Paris, where VV's literary career begins.

After Iris's death (she is murdered by a half-mad Russian émigré) he marries his typist Annette. They have a daughter together, Isabel, and emigrate to the United States, where VV lectures at Quirn University. The marriage is not a success, in part due to VV's dalliances with an eleven-year-old, the devious Dolly von Borg. After Annette's death in a flood, VV and Isabel (now aged eleven herself and known as Bel) travel around the country, contentedly drifting from motel to motel.

To neutralize gossip about the exact nature of his relationship with his daughter, VV marries greedy and rapacious Louise, while Bel herself later elopes with an

American to Soviet Russia. VV consoles himself writing his most successful and scandalous novel, *A Kingdom by the Sea* (*Lolita*'s working title). After this third marriage collapses, VV marries once more, this time to a Bel lookalike (who was, indeed, born on the same day as his daughter), mentioned in the text only as 'you'. She is VV's true and last love, found as he has reached old age.

This is the basic plot of *LATH*, structured matrimonially by VV's four marriages. Along with the quartet of wives, VV also mentions an enigmatic heroine 'Dementia', who he claims is his mistress and muse. Two other closely related elements are also crucial to the narrative: VV's various psychological maladies and his disturbed sense of authorial dualism. Regarding the former, VV's autobiography has apparently been written following a traumatic brain event; formerly, VV had been beset throughout his life by a related and indefinite mental condition that circled close to insanity and was characterized by headaches, dizziness, visions and deliriums. Regarding authorial dualism, VV's memoirs all the way through seem haunted by one 'Vladimir Vladimirovich', a writer possessing even more mysterious biographical and bibliographical resemblances to Nabokov than VV.

In *LATH*, it is as though Nabokov has been twice through the laundry, the first wash (Vladimir Vladimirovich) rendering him bright and sparkling, the second (VV) fading the garment. Or it is as though Nabokov has been photocopied twice, the second occasion using not the original but the copy, making the second duplicate (VV) second-rate compared to both the first copy (Vladimir Vladimirovich) and its original (Nabokov). Thus, there are three figures to distinguish here: First, Nabokov, the actual writer of *LATH*. Second, Vladimir Vladimirovich, his near copy. Third, VV, the narrator.

VV's titles and chronology imitate or reference Nabokov's own output, and VV's oeuvre is included at the beginning of the novel as 'Other Books by the Narrator' in a play on publishers' preliminary and promotional spiel 'By the Same Author'. Here are VV's novels, as *LATH* presents them, with Nabokov's (which are, to some extent, also Vladimir Vladimirovich's) added in approximate parallel for comparison:

Vadim Vadimovich (VV)		**Nabokov's Corresponding Text**	
In Russian			
Tamara	1925	*Mary*	1926
Pawn Takes Queen	1927	*King, Queen, Knave*	1928
Plenilune	1929	*The Luzhin Defense*	1929
Camera Lucida (*Slaughter in the Sun*)	1931	*Camera Obscura* (*Laughter in the Dark*)	1932
The Red Top Hat	1934	*Invitation to a Beheading*	1936
The Dare	1950	*Glory*; *The Gift* (Russian: *Dar*)	1932/38
In English			
See under Real	1939	*The Real Life of Sebastian Knight*	1941
Esmeralda and Her Parandrus	1941	*Lolita*	1955
Dr Olga Repnin	1946	*Pnin*	1957
Exile from Mayda	1947	*Pale Fire* (+ short stories)	1962
A Kingdom by the Sea	1962	*Lolita*	1955
Ardis	1970	*Ada*	1969

Nevertheless, *LATH*'s sinister Nabokovian persona, Vladimir Vladimirovich, is just that: a character, and he should not be mistaken for the real Nabokov, however identical their lives and art often seem to be. The crucial point here is that both VV and Vladimir Vladimirovich are imagined creations that are part of the fictional created world of *LATH*. For example, the former's titles bring to mind Nabokov's, and the latter's are the same as Nabokov's, but neither character is the genuine Nabokov who wrote the book.

But, as if this wasn't enough, Nabokov has another dizzying layer to add to the novel. In *LATH*, fictional author Vladimir Vladimirovich suffers from hallucinations and schizophrenic episodes where he imagines himself to be narrator Vadim Vadimovich (VV). Everything we read in *LATH* about VV's life is in fact the distorted delusion of Vladimir Vladimirovich. VV's novels are fictional, inferior phantoms of the 'real' novels written by the (equally fictional) Vladimir Vladimirovich, himself a close copy of the actual Nabokov.

VV, our ostensible narrator, is really a low-grade version of Vladimir Vladimirovich, created by the insane half of the latter's personality. VV has involuntarily created his own autobiography via the unbalanced intellect of the fictional Vladimir Vladimirovich. Throughout *LATH*, VV is anxious and paranoid that he has a superior twin, but in fact it is the other way round: Vladimir Vladimirovich's disturbed mind has created an inferior double, VV.

Many of the inversions and connections involved in the relationship between these characters are to be recognized by the reader via the shadowy and incestuous network of VV's wives, who are themselves furtively linked to VV's original benefactor, Count Starov. This Count Starov, an insatiable global diplomat, seems to be the progenitor of several of *LATH*'s characters, including VV and some of his spouses, an affiliation discernible through an anagrammatic stellar motif. Unlike the first three, however, VV's fourth wife is not held in progeny-planetary orbit around the lustrous Count Starov. Referred to only as 'you', this fourth and final wife becomes increasingly identified with 'the real' and 'reality', terms absent from the earlier consorts. Moreover, with this partner VV is noticeably disinclined to reveal lurid conjugal details for fear of adulterating or contaminating 'reality'.

None of VV's wives, except 'you', really exist. Nor do his novels (nor his aunt, who urged her young charge to 'invent reality!'). Neither does the count, nor the heroine Dementia, whose copulating with the former has in fact spawned the narrative we encounter. Characters not part of the mentally engendered Starov clan are aware of the VV / Vladimir Vladimirovich split: family friends mention VV's frequent bouts of psychosis or, in the humorous case of the mischievous book dealer Oksman, deliberately get the titles of VV's books wrong. VV's narration is the schizophrenic contrivance of the fictional author Vladimir Vladimirovich, himself the imaginary creation of Nabokov. VV invents no reality, but rather is merely one level in a multistorey car park of fictive fabrications, either in the basement or on the roof, depending on the reader's point of view (which is unstable).

As VV returns to health (and to the true Vladimir Vladimirovich side of his personality) towards the end of *LATH*, his mental disturbance (as well as his invention) dies down. His psychologically concocted wives, novels and behaviour dissolve back into the reality of his true wife, 'you', and the actual novels which he has written: *Mary*,

Camera Obscura, *Lolita* and so on. Helping to orientate us amid this tangle of perspectives are the links back to Nabokov's own life: the true wife, 'you', can be linked to Nabokov's Véra by the author's use of 'you' throughout *Speak, Memory* to refer to her. Additionally, the novels are here authenticated by their true Nabokovian titles.

Intense interrogations of identity and reality crowd and shuffle across *LATH*. Uncertainty is the watchword, muddle and mix-up the slogan, these mottoes articulated via what may seem a particularly disconcerting game of drunk Chinese whispers. With its cumbersome, exclamation-marked title and its intricate, multilayered narrative structure, *Look at the Harlequins!* is – even by Nabokov's standards – a ferociously problematic novel to navigate and comprehend. It asks us to explore, accept or reject various versions of the creator of the very thing we are reading, sometimes simultaneously. Its fictive layers are not only intentionally false, but doubly so, tremendously frustrating our attempts to maintain our greasy grip on several slippery forms of reality.

Nabokov does this neither because he wanted to hide himself in narrator-character Russian dolls, nor because he wanted to ridicule those readers and critics unable to divorce his literary creations from the events, people and conduct of his own life (even if this mockery might be a jovial by-product). As a chess player and composer of chess problems, Nabokov is always several steps ahead of us, plotting, planning, playing. But, as in *Pale Fire* or *King, Queen, Knave* (or almost anywhere else in Nabokov), *LATH* is more than a textual game or literary labyrinth. As always, aesthetical and eschatological, moral and marital concerns are made one, merged in an intimate union.

Nabokov's last completed novel is not only a salute to the fertile, metamorphic and endlessly inventive possibilities of the creative imagination, but a celebration of his faithful, enduring love for Véra. For all its mind-bending narrative ruses and artifice, *LATH* is in truth a tender, profoundly moving love letter and thank-you note to its author's lifelong companion. Death would intervene to prevent the completion of another novel dedicated, as they all had been, 'to Véra', so *Look at the Harlequins!* stands as Nabokov's final testament to love and art. It is an impish, nimble and ardent comic gem: a harlequin, in fact.

19
The Original of Laura
SMIRK IN PROGRESS

The 2009 publication of *The Original of Laura (Dying Is Fun)*, Nabokov's last, unfinished novel, which he began writing in the mid-1970s, hit the literary planet like the proverbial meteorite. Everyone had an opinion: some raving and rejoicing; others despairing and disparaging. The book itself came with a shrewd, if understandably rather defensive, introduction by Nabokov's son and literary executor, Dmitri. He had been the man charged, after his mother's death in 1991, with resolving the dilemma of the book's liberation from a decades-long incarceration in a Swiss bank vault. For nearly twenty years, he agonized between his desire to uphold his beloved father's wishes – that the manuscript be burnt – and his inclination not to go down in history as a literary arsonist. In the end, filial infidelity won over textual pyromania.

In the edition finally published in 2009, what we get are Dmitri's loose arrangement of his father's drafts: 138 scans of the index cards on which Nabokov habitually pencilled his novels, with the printed text included on the page below. Fascinatingly, the scanned cards are perforated so that the reader may, should they wish, remove the cards and rearrange them into a different order: Dmitri acknowledged that his organization was, while logical, only one potential configuration.

(The detachable cards in the form we have them, though alien to Nabokov's intentions, call to mind B. S. Johnson's experimental work *The Unfortunates* (1969), the so-called 'book in a box' where readers are invited to rearrange the twenty-seven unbound sections of a novel in any order they please, save the first and last parts, giving trillions of possible ways the book can be read.)

The images of *The Original of Laura* themselves afford a tantalizing insight into Nabokov's work processes: his self-editing, marginal notes and, thrillingly, his oblique, looping handwriting. Crossings-out and corrections litter the text, as we see the writer thinking, pondering, improving his thoughts and his words. Nabokov once famously maintained to have rewritten – sometimes several times – every word he had ever published: his pencils outlasted his erasers, he said. Here, we can sometimes see the vestiges of these alterations in the form of ominous and mysterious blemishes behind the tidy redrafted text, rubbings-out which poignantly echo the elusiveness of the whole novel itself. Indeed, there is something intangible, playful and strikingly intelligent to this book's overall design which matches its author's other works.

For the first sixty or so cards we have some sort of coherent narrative – we have to accept that this is a draft – and it seems to be presented in a plausibly correct order. Then things begin to wobble and collapse, the story disintegrating into something much scrappier and more sporadic, often just notes and jottings. Yet this fragmentary form intriguingly endorses both the subject and structure of the developing novel itself, which explores the fragmentary nature of both identity and art. In it, we are told the story of an affair between an unnamed 'man of letters' and a girl called Flora, now a young woman of twenty-four. But what we get, the narrator tells us, is only the original – the raw material, so to speak – of a fictional novel (*My Laura*) which was later published with Flora's name changed to Laura and which was, naturally, a huge bestseller savaged by the critics.

The Original of Laura tempts us to ask: If Flora is the original of Laura, who is the original of Flora? And the original before that? We are pulled into reaching back and back for an ultimate 'original', an ur-Laura, in the author's life. Nabokov is, one last time, teasing our desire to locate authorial biography in fiction – which is why he revisits the risky subject matter of nubile young girls and professorial lovers. This, of course, was the theme of *Lolita* (1955), the controversial novel which invited so many to conflate Humbert and Nabokov. (The inclusion of a predatory 'Mr Hubert H. Hubert' in *The Original of Laura* may not be one of Nabokov's best jokes – but that is rather his self-parodying point.)

As in so much of Nabokov's art, we have several competing layers of truth and reality here, each clamouring for attention and authenticity. The incomplete nature of this book only multiplies its inherent disorientation and the possibilities of interpretation, even luring us into thinking the novel was *intended* to be partial. It was not, of course: Nabokov was clear the book was unfinished and would have developed further. Within *The Original of Laura*, perilously incomplete novels, lives and loves slink across the page, migrate through our minds, their creator smirking from the grave as we laugh, smile, shriek or frown in response.

In the book's language, so far as we can tell, Nabokov's familiarly baroque weirdness is intact, as is his gift for images that are simultaneously exact and suggestive: as Flora tetchily prepares to make love, she finds her morocco slippers 'foetally folded in their zippered pouch'. Shortly afterwards, Flora and her annoying 'man of letters' lover begin their act of carnal union. Nabokov, scientist, is on hand to describe it with an agonizing precision; Nabokov, author, slides in some sly hints at his novel's layers and games:

> That first surrender of hers was a little sudden, if not downright unnerving. A pause for some light caresses, concealed embarrassment, feigned amusement, prefactory contemplation. She was an extravagantly slender girl. Her ribs showed. The conspicuous knobs of her hipbones framed a hollowed abdomen, so flat as to belie the notion of 'belly'. Her exquisite bone structure immediately slipped into a novel – became in fact the secret structure of that novel, besides supporting a number of poems.

Laura's images are delectable and repellent, thoughtful and unsettling, immediate and calculated. Moreover, there is something splendidly, alarmingly, Nabokovian in the status of this work as fragmentary, as well as in its themes of artistic provenance, the unknown, and physical and mental breakdown. Flora's husband, portly neurologist Philip Wild, has an aberrant fantasy of self-deletion. We learn of him when the hitherto relatively complete narrative breaks off into the neurotic nerve doctor's tormented internal monologue. He is obsessed with his own self-obliteration, picturing himself as a stick figure on a blackboard rubbing himself out from the feet up.

It is not, of course, clear exactly how this section would have fitted into the final novel. However, its arcane compulsions about the representation and erasure of the self tally not only with Smurov's splintered identity in *The Eye* (1930) and the paranoid impulses of *Despair* (1934), but even more closely with the eerily brittle personality of the hero, Hugh, in *Transparent Things* and the devious, schizophrenic realities of *Look at the Harlequins!* – Nabokov's last two completed novels.

Although all Nabokov's fiction might be considered 'late' in the sense of its maturity and idiosyncrasy, there is a particular peculiarity to his final three novels. Indeed, just as many have come to see *Lolita* (1955), *Pnin* (1957) and *Pale Fire* (1962) as his 'American trilogy', *Transparent Things* (1972), *Look at the Harlequins!* (1974) and *The Original of Laura* (1970s), can be considered a second trilogy. (*Ada*, 1969, floats alone in Terra-time, an incomparable pinwheeling galaxy from Nabokov's cosmic imagination.) This second trio forms a three-part study of identity, with *Laura* the final, alluringly unfinished panel of the personality triptych, its very incompleteness accentuating the depictions of fissured and fractured identity these three works exhibit.

All three of these final novels portray a type of sardonic postmodern self-portraiture, complete with premeditated rips and scratches, knowing transpositions, sly abstractions, self-assured auto-references, Warhol-like proliferations and negative inversions, and an inside-out, label-on-display exuberance in presenting their own processes of identity construction and annihilation. By *Laura*, even and perhaps especially in its unfinished state, the artwork resembles an infinite series of broken mirrors into which we can gaze upon the authentically distorted, and now entirely irretrievable, portrait of the artist.

Even as it stands, save any further material evidence coming to light, *The Original of Laura* is more than a literary curio or final gift for faithful Nabokovians. It continues its author's journey into new ways of discussing and presenting fiction, mingling metaphysics and metafiction through absorbing techniques and innovative ideas. As it is, it cannot be considered a masterpiece. But it comes close, rebuking us, exciting us, asking us to ponder what might have been (suggesting, too, that we be thankful for what came before).

BEYOND THE NOVELS

MEMOIR, STORIES & OTHER WORKS

20

Speak, Memory

> Because all hangs together – shape and sound, heather and honey, vessel and content.
>
> – Nabokov, 'An Evening of Russian Poetry'

Novelists like Nabokov make excellent ventriloquists: they can create the illusion that their voice is coming from somewhere else. Nabokov appears to throw his voice, his life and his personality into the puppets of his characters, asking them to articulate for him – with parodic, comedic or cataclysmic results. These autobiographical dummies, these fictive selves, disorientate and amuse, seeming to speak to or from other worlds and dimensions of being, the unliving Nabokov conversing with the past and future Nabokov, at once philosophical and entertaining.

Nabokov's novels, stories, poems and plays contain a wealth of what might be loosely described as 'autobiographic' material, drawing on and projecting the author's own life to a considerable extent (though his creatures are seldom his spokesmen). If few writers have been as gifted as this one in conceiving, *ex nihilo*, characters, events or emotions, Nabokov's life, too, is at the centre of his art. His universes are ones generated from an intrepid and immensely resourceful imagination, juxtaposing, then distorting, fact and fiction. From Ganin in *Mary* (1926) to Vadim in *Look at the Harlequins!* (1974), Nabokov's characters often seem to be incarnations, inversions, avatars, caricatures of the writer himself.

By *Harlequins*, the personal parody has become a vertiginous inverted game of biographic deceit, operating as a form of Escher illusion in prose, exploring infinity, impossibility, symmetry, reflection, refraction and corrosion. As Nabokov's characters jerk and stutter through reversals and burlesques of their creator across their silky pages, they also seem to deny the very possibility of autobiography. The mirages and deceptions of fiction constantly undermine certainty as veracity or authenticity become increasingly elusive, indefinable, meaningless terms.

If fictive assertions of the self appeal to truth via falsification, what can we make of Nabokov's presentation of his own life and being in the autobiographical memoir *Speak, Memory* (1951), and what bearing does it have on understanding his other work? Drifting around the mellifluous lagoons of the past, Nabokov takes us on a sunlit journey into lost time with a suggestion of timelessness, his smooth and enchanting elegance on display like never before or after in his writing.

In many respects, *Speak, Memory* is unsullied style, pure prose; but if we suppose that this means it will contain none of the familiar grotesque characters, helix structures or complex narrative designs, we will be wrong. Nabokov patterns his autobiography as meticulously as his fiction, fusing his powers of verbalization and determination with those of inspiration and decoration, the dim, often sinister past turned into a fluorescent eternity. *Speak, Memory* seeks to transcend time, yet it acknowledges time as the medium through which we must all exist.

Nabokov's autobiography starts with its author's birth in Saint Petersburg in 1899 and travels four decades, until his departure for America in the spring of 1940 as another war ravaged Europe. Although he lived through one of the most tumultuous periods in history, we rarely see politics ('major ideas in minor minds') discussed and certainly view no glib Nabokovian newsreel of the times. On occasion, the figures and happenings of the age flicker and flash before us: at four, Vladimir runs toy trains over frozen puddles to emulate the simultaneous Russian army's traversing an iced-over Lake Baikal to fight the Japanese; in 1930s Berlin, his son sees the ever-present obsidian moustache of the Führer repeated in a bed of pansies.

Speak, Memory exists in various forms (parts were published separately in English, French and Russian), but the same basic themes exist throughout all editions. The version most familiar to English readers presents fifteen chapters in a complex interplay between chronological order and thematic concern, which we might provisionally label as follows:

1. Father
2. Mother
3. English Education
4. Ancestors
5. French Education
6. Butterflies
7. Love I
8. Russian Education

9. School
10. Adolescence
11. Poems
12. Love II
13. University
14. Exile
15. Parenthood

(In later editions, a sixteenth chapter, 'On *Conclusive Evidence*' – one of the book's alternative titles – takes the form of a pseudo-review.)

Within this chronological-thematic structure, Nabokov evokes the past with a seductive sweep and almost miraculous recall of delectable detail, the text bearing a familiar strangeness, its memories at once common and recognizable as well as alien and anomalous. *Speak, Memory* has a confrontational fastidiousness, a provocatively pedantic tone that ostentatiously asserts itself and its social world at the expense of all others. With Nabokov's powers of re-creation and customary sense of humour, however, this superficial conceit and surface self-satisfaction is never permitted to curdle into coarse arrogance. The haughtiness has a peculiar modesty about it. The arrangement of *Speak, Memory* into subject zones and symmetries produces an objective humility, which further countenances Nabokov to coalesce both his own growth within time and his unruffled rising above it.

Even the slightest acquaintance with Nabokov's fiction reveals a writer preoccupied, obsessed even, by the quirks and coincidences of life, its codes and forms, repetitions and encryptions. In *Speak, Memory*, Nabokov devises (without fabricating facts) a rich, varied texture of recurrence and reverberation, investigating with an observant metaphysics and ravenous sensibility the idiosyncratic shapes of the past. Themes emerge and transform over time. Chronology is subservient to epistemology, methodology and morphology.

In part, this helps Nabokov to distance himself from his own life even as he places it under the microscope of memory. Unlike his narcissistic, agitated narrators Hermann Hermann (*Despair*, 1934) and Humbert Humbert (*Lolita*, 1955), who pant and smear their lives and egos all over us, Nabokov discreetly presumes his life to be of no significance, still less worthy of our sympathy. What is of interest is not the person at the centre of the life, but the patterns of its retelling, its aesthetic modelling into an abstraction of eschatological speculation and ontological vigilance. *Speak, Memory* is as much a work of art as anything in Nabokov's fictional oeuvre.

This does not mean Nabokov's autobiography is an opaque curio or irritating mystery tour down impenetrable lanes of personal flashback. Indeed, its very artistry discloses the mind of its architect more revealingly than any candid record of recollection might. Nabokov's style – in *Speak, Memory* and everywhere else – is highly considered: hyper-conscious, über-aware, exuberantly deliberate. For some, this is mere stylistic attention-seeking, and as such is debarred from offering any real honesty or emotional sincerity. Yet there is truth telling in Nabokov's vigorous verbal expertise. Its sophisticated opacity allows it to connect and combine with infinitely more bonds than blunt banalities or risqué revelations, which are limited by their very directness and apparent candour, would.

Nabokov's technique in *Speak, Memory* permits the elusiveness of the past to function alongside the detailed brilliance of his reminiscences. His text is able to explore both the boundless facility of human consciousness and its farcical existential inadequacy: the war of finite being with infinite imagination, its many skirmishes leaving memory lesions and scars of happiness. Time, a ruthless, capricious and belligerent major general, thrusts us into a battle where Nabokov seeks victory (or at least survival) through ecstatic individual tranquillity and an intense conception of the beyond.

Nabokov declines to be time's obedient foot soldier, so although the chapters succeed sequentially they are slack and baggy by design, refusing alignment with time's severely linear arrow. We might meet a meditative boy Vladimir, daydreaming in the lavatory, before suddenly sliding forward to another brooding bathroom ten years hence, the two safe spaces linked and recollected across the years. We leap in an instant from place to place, time to time, following Vladimir as he chases a boyhood butterfly into a marsh near his family's Vyra estate and emerging decades later as the soon-to-be world-famous author performs the same pursuit in the Rocky Mountains (the man still really a boy, retaining the ardour of youth).

Nabokov's father is a persistent refrain, his energetic life and appalling (though heroic) death interrelated, revisited with an intoxicating vitality but spellbound grief. Its variegated theme buds, then unfurls to blossom across the text. Nabokov's mother, meanwhile, represents a different kind of passing, in which loss is attached to a tenacious fortitude and the understanding (which is an art) of what one can always retain: the intangible resources of memory, nurtured and preserved for future retrieval. After the Revolution, in Berlin and Prague, the exiled matriarch endures as the guardian of the family's memories, and a haunting simile, evoking Shakespeare, connects mother and son:

> A soapbox covered with green cloth supported the dim little photographs in crumbling frames she liked to have near her couch. She did not really need them, for nothing had been lost. As a company of travelling players carry with them everywhere, while they still remember their lines, a windy heath, a misty castle, an enchanted island, so she had with her all that her soul had stored.

Nabokov *mère* is strongly linked to her son's developing literary consciousness. Among Nabokov's first readers, his adored and adoring mother was always keen to hear her son's poetical endeavours. She would beam rapturously, with tears flowing down her face, as he recited his latest adolescent verse. 'How wonderful, how beautiful ...'

The strength of Nabokov's passion for life, love and language only deepened the degree to which he felt their inexorable absences due to exile, brutality, sleep or death. (A lover of light and thinking, Nabokov despised sleep almost as much as he despised death, regarding it as demeaning 'mental torture', a 'moronic fraternity' and 'nightly betrayal of reason, humanity, genius'.) In truth, bliss and misery are so intimately connected in Nabokov as to be inseparable, an inexorable partnership of pleasure and pain. Every moment, every colour, sight and sound, is impeccable, priceless, its immediate and inescapable loss a burden, a silent sorrow. This is no mere hysteric hyperbole or adolescent posturing to pester the swiftly produced past. It is the savage and horrific wonder tightly bound into all our existence. Nonetheless there *is* something hysterical about this, something distraught and frantic. *Speak, Memory* opens with a shocking double nothingness:

> The cradle rocks above an abyss, and common sense tells us that our existence is but a brief crack of light between two eternities of darkness. Although the two are identical twins, man, as a rule, views the prenatal abyss with more calm than the one he is heading for (at some forty-five hundred heartbeats an hour).

These shadow-oblivions threaten and consume everything: yawning, then swallowing every beauty and tragedy of our lives, every instant, and the immeasurable number of thoughts, feelings and sensations our beings have captured in life and memory. Art and imagination allow us to glimpse release from this confrontation between finitude and eternity. Consciousness and artistic creation can object to the discord and seek to elevate life above the tawdry conflict and towards its inherent splendour. Yet life's phenomenal and never-ending ingenuity is visible not only in a sonnet or sonata, book or black hole, but also in a smudge of ink, burnt match or the translucent broken wing of an obsolete insect.

Love and beauty signify so much for Nabokov that their loss is almost unbearable. This is his obstinate theme. His works locate absence at their centres: the eponymous Mary (1926), the old couple's son in 'Signs and Symbols' (1948), Humbert's sweetheart Annabel in *Lolita* (1955), and John and Sybil Shade's daughter, Hazel, in *Pale Fire* (1962) are all characters pivotally present through their absence. For all their pain, these works also celebrate love, whether in the honest simplicity of the old couple, the Shades' lifelong companionship, or even the bogus union of Humbert and Lo, the rupture of which still exerts an astonishing devastation on the reader when Lolita absconds with Quilty.

In *Speak, Memory* the loss of Nabokov's homeland, and eventually his language, never ceases to sting. His father's death, too, is a cut Nabokov constantly reopens, an experience he is unable to ignore, its agony at once exquisite and excruciating. Pain in literature is artificial and part of the pleasure (the greater Othello's anguishes, the more our theatrical enjoyment), but here Nabokov's grief touches close to grim reality while nevertheless remaining part of the brilliantly devised aesthetic architecture. Memory repeatedly resurrects his father, only to continually kill him, again and again, in an artistic pattern that enriches the text as well as our understanding of personal loss.

Nabokov's passion for patterns and themes extends to sports, hobbies and leisure pursuits, where they are no mere pastimes, but opportunities for discovery and for further permutations of those patterns. Games – sporting, recreational, literary – are crucial to Nabokov's constructions, in part for their playfulness but also for their malice and caprice. They are precedents in pathology, metaphors for the cruel competitive battle of life. In *Speak, Memory*, for instance, the father theme is frequently connected to the chess theme: in 1919, as their boat navigates out of a beleaguered Sevastopol harbour, with bullets raining down around them, Nabokov *père et fils* sit on deck playing a game. At Cambridge, football – in particular the isolation and lunacy of the goalkeeper – becomes related to the theme of exile. And, as we saw earlier, butterfly hunting as a child in Vyra develops into semi-professional lepidoptery as an adult in Colorado, enlarging the subject of exile before America itself becomes a new theme, which is triumphantly sounded at the end of the book.

In *Speak, Memory* themes evolve and metamorphose, changing their shape and significance across the text, much like Wagner's musical leitmotifs in *Der Ring des Nibelungen* (1848–74), which derive from a common source before taking on new and independent lives of their own while nevertheless remaining networked to their origins, a vast coral reef of meaning and interconnectivity. Like Wagner, Nabokov is a master of juxtaposition, fluid and subtle, jarring and alarming, able to relate events, emotions and people across cosmic spans but in the most intimate way, each of them resonant with individual distinction and fine detail.

These arts of transition and correlation are matched by Nabokov's ability to illuminate his world. This is achieved not least via colour, for *Speak, Memory* – like his fictive worlds – shines with a vivid spectrum in which its author's synaesthesia aids communication and exchange. Stained glass glints and gleams in poems and the past; rainbows are wrought in the sharpest hues of Nabokov's language and are the purest links to aspiration or remembrance; a mother's jewels are first luminous toys, then urgent émigré currency, the theme of colour here shifting to that of exile.

Childhood is the primary focus of *Speak, Memory*: its incandescence, its radiance, its paradisiacal function as a liberating playground and as the originating locus of consciousness. Humbert Humbert wrote 'Lolita, or the Confession of a White Widowed Male' in order to 'fix once for all the perilous magic of nymphets'. Nabokov wrote *Speak, Memory* to keep forever a memento of the idyllic pre-Revolutionary Russia of his childhood, to retain in perpetuity the keys to his own particular Eden. In *Speak, Memory* the transient personal paradise becomes universal, eternal. It is at once a specimen, preserved by the past, and a liquid narration, ever advancing and attaching to newfound time.

Despite the obvious fact of his own maturation, through his series of associations and correspondences Nabokov is able to end his autobiography with childhood. Little Dmitri, Vladimir and Véra's son, marshals his locomotive abilities, ascertaining how to walk as his parents prepare to flee a continent re-destroying itself in war. The themes of gardens, colours, puzzles, boats, steps and exile circle, spin and then merge before exploding into the release of America, where the ache of exile can be extinguished by the discovery of a new home, a new environment, a new language.

Irony, landscape, pedantry, bewitching phobias and beguiling kinfolk – all and more populate *Speak, Memory*'s conscientious, multicoloured cosmos. The book is a central component of Nabokov's immense literary legacy, a melancholic marvel that is never tragic or saccharine: its humour and sophistication thwart mawkishness. Nabokov's jests can sometimes strain the reader, at times feeling more like private jokes (which they are) for the book's addressee, the dedicatee of all his books, his wife, Véra.

Nabokov's manner and tone of voice can vex and peeve, but his assiduous style allows for subtlety to rely under no circumstances on obscurity. The fleeting, uncertain phantoms of exile and memory, which deceive and disfigure, are never allowed to be unintelligible in Nabokov. Whatever their inherent ambiguity, they must be conveyed to the reader with clarity and lucidity, luminosity and love.

Across his works, Nabokov contends that we can disobey time, space, history, mortality and the penitentiary of the person, thus partaking of multiple lives, if we allow art and imagination to exist. Moreover, by cherishing and re-encapsulating existence in all its minute particulars and limitless potential (from a broken window to a galaxy to a child's first word), we can look again at the universe: reassessing it, surveying it, appreciating it anew.

Nabokov's art, including and especially *Speak, Memory*, takes us beyond ourselves as well as beyond the dusk of death. In it we can travel in dimensions of time and space, inhabit other bodies, experience other minds, suffer other souls. The merely temporal and bodily prison is destroyed, its bars dissolved through aesthetic action and invention. It might only be a provisional escape from the burden of being, but our autonomy can be summoned at any time, re-examined and re-explored. If the past is a foreign country, visits are visa-less. For Nabokov, however, the past is not remote but always local, always family, always home, activated not via the involuntary – à la Proust's madeleines – but by the intentional: the courageous will of memory and imagination.

Exile, émigré and refugee, Nabokov was buffeted by the tides of the twentieth century, but personal anarchy can be converted into delicate harmony by conjuring creativity and crafting art. Nabokov uncovered, via *Speak, Memory*, an intricate design in his own life, and he urges us to discover the same in our own lives. By ransacking the warehouse of our pasts to furnish the present, we, too, can perceive a pattern in our lives, as complex and ordered as any fictional creation. We must let memory speak and imagination flourish.

21

Short Stories

Vladimir Nabokov's short fiction is a significant and mesmerizing component of his output, especially the earlier Russian work and two extraordinary tales in English. The stories shimmer like the iridescent wings of the author's beloved butterflies, the prose style bright and quivering. But they haunt our imagination, too, their stealthy plots prowling in the dark: elusive, enigmatic, inscrutable.

Nabokov engages readers in an inventive enterprise of literary hide-and-seek, the main narrative and its sub-layers intriguing, then confounding, our attempts to vacate the network of mystery and memory, lure and decoy. Yet these deliberate obstacles in the structures are part of the pleasure, the rewards all the more satisfying (and flattering) when the riddles are detected, deciphered.

The short story form in general urges us to crack its codes: everything is emphasized, irrelevance edited out, selections purposeful and disciplined. This automatically invites the reader to believe in the potential (and essential) meaning of the entirety of the text: every character, word or happening must have meaning, or why include it? Compared to longer literary forms, we can more straightforwardly read and reread short stories, agonizing over a small detail or vague phrase, our tormented interpretation magnified by the diminutive extent of the text.

Nabokov exploits this paradox between size and significance, inclusion and elusion. He variously called the short story a 'small Alpine form' or 'dwarf' of the novel. These are appropriate analogies for Nabokov in particular since, despite their size, his stories nevertheless maintain most of his techniques and abiding thematic concerns – not least patterns, loss, exile, the 'otherworld', and the metamorphosis of anguish into art. If Chekhov perfected the 'slice of life' short story, in which the unresolved narrative matches life's lack of neatness, Nabokov gave his stories a resolution, but a puzzling one. Consciously shadowy, their ludic nature provides something self-contained and potentially fathomable. Cryptic tales, by definition, have a solution buried within them, however enigmatic or ambiguous it might be, and in Nabokov meanings are there to be discovered beneath the surface text.

The Russian Stories

In the early Russian stories, fantasy, caprice and make-believe play an important role, especially by repeatedly exploring nostalgia and the myth of an idyllic Russian past: Nabokov had begun writing his stories in his early twenties, in the first years of his lifelong exile from his homeland. 'The Wood-Sprite' (1921) features a figure from Russia who is brutally forced into exile when his forest is destroyed; 'The Dragon' (1923) sees its eponymous beast leave its cave only to perish in the modern world. In 'A Nursery Tale' (1926), a young man in Berlin desires women he glimpses from the tram, only to be promised them by the devil in the guise of an old woman, quirkiness and the erotic charging the tale with a peculiar energy.

The threats and hazards of expatriation are also explored in more realist stories involving refugee Russians. In the humorous 'Russian Spoken Here' (1923), an émigré family capture and detain a Soviet agent, keeping him for years in their bathroom. 'The Seaport' (1924) visits exiles trapped in southern France, the bright sunlight both beguiling and generous, confusing and comforting to their grey lives. In 'Razor' (1926), a police officer finds himself getting a shave from a man he once persecuted, the refugee barber now able to take an exquisite revenge as his oppressor sits in illusory comfort.

Nabokov's early short stories are not only exceptional in themselves but are the laboratory for later styles, configurations and themes. In 'The Return of Chorb' (1925), Nabokov uses the Orpheus myth to structure the tale, exploring loss and identity with a droll melancholy that anticipates *Transparent Things* (1972) half a century later, real worlds and other worlds colliding amid screams and dreams. In its complex, non-linear narrative, 'Chorb' also looks forward to many of Nabokov's later novels, most especially *Pale Fire* (1962).

Unpleasant figures populate all Nabokov's fiction, and this is not least the case in his stories. In 'The Aurelian' (1930), an unkind elderly German shopkeeper has dreamed of butterflies since he was a boy and suddenly departs for Spain, leaving his wife a curt note, before destiny intervenes and the worlds of his fantasy and reality abruptly interact. 'Torpid Smoke' (1935) features a disagreeable young Russian émigré, fond of reading and writing – he even has a copy of Nabokov's *Despair* (1934) on his bookshelves – who is able to find solace in art; he will shortly be reborn more attractively as Fyodor in *The Gift* (1938).

More sinister types inform many of the stories of the 1930s and '40s, as they do the murky illusory world of *Invitation to a Beheading* (1936). 'The Leonardo' (1933), 'Tyrants Destroyed' (1938), 'Lik' (1939) and 'The Assistant Producer' (1943) all feature artistic individuals pestered or persecuted by thuggish sorts, bullies and blockheads representative of the dark era in which they were created. In 'Cloud, Castle, Lake' (1937), a sensitive Russian émigré wins a trip in the lottery only to be hounded on the subsequent train journey by a German tour group, their mockery turning to inventive nastiness: corkscrews, belts and sticks are cleverly put to cruel use.

More ambiguous suffering is explored in two masterly stories from this period. In the fragile pearl 'Spring in Fialta' (1936), memory, doubles and the enduring pain of loss are surveyed through those familiar Nabokovian techniques of an out-of-sequence chronology and an untrustworthy, erratic narrator. Another delicate gem, 'A Russian Beauty' (1934), is a startling evaluation of despair and self-deception, wherein an attractive woman's appearance seems to represent the fading desirability of Russia herself.

'Ultima Thule' (1940) – originally the first chapter of an unfinished novel – develops Nabokov's great themes of borders, exile and the unknown. 'Ultima Thule' was the classical term for the northernmost boundary of the world, its farthest limit, and in this story a widower tries to communicate with his dead wife via a letter which structures the story. The narrator tells how his former tutor, Adam Falter, apparently discovered the mystery of life and death, crying out in agony when he did so. Falter disclosed this perilous, destructive knowledge to his psychiatrist, and the doctor promptly died of a heart attack. Falter is forthwith evasive about his secret and takes it with him to his grave.

The enigma persists, however. An obscure Nordic poet ('Swede or Dane – or Icelander, for all I know') commissions the narrator, an artist, to illustrate his epic poem *Ultima Thule*, whose inexplicable verses tell of political intrigues in a distant polar island kingdom. The poet vanishes, but the narrator continues to work on the poem, hoping it will help him reach his wife in the otherworld. This undertaking attracts the narrator as the 'home of my least expressible thoughts', an island realm 'born in the desolate, gray sea of my heartache for you' and located somewhere between grief, insanity, reality, art and imagination.

'Ultima Thule' has a companion piece: 'Solus Rex' (1940), which was to have been the second chapter of the unfinished novel. Here the narrator has become king of the strange and remote northern land, reunited with his queen. How 'real' is his account now? How 'real' was it before, in 'Ultima Thule'? Have misery and sorrow fermented to manic invention? Both stories, along with some elements of 'The Return of Chorb', contain the embryonic material for perhaps Nabokov's supreme achievement in the novel form: *Pale Fire*, his impeccably realized study of fantasy, invention and bereavement.

By the time he came to write 'Ultima Thule' and 'Solus Rex', Nabokov was already writing a novel in English, *The Real Life of Sebastian Knight* (1941), though he would compose only a handful of short stories in this new literary language. To a certain extent, his stories and the

Russian language went together: they proved an essential part of his development as a writer as he refined his work to exquisite levels of sophistication. In some measure, too, by the time he came to write in English, he had the supreme gifts as a creator of complex fictional worlds to be able to do so easily (and necessarily) on a larger scale.

After his move to English, however, between *Bend Sinister* (1947) and *Lolita* (1955), Nabokov produced two short stories of immense potency and poignant genius that stand comparison with the greatest of his novels: 'Signs and Symbols' (1948) and 'The Vane Sisters' (1951).

'Signs and Symbols' (1948)

There is more kindness, humanity and compressed sadness in this muted six-page wonder than in many a novel a hundred times its size. It flickers dimly in the dark, smouldering with inscrutability, inviting us to explain its mystery while also making us shudder at its power and poignancy. It is a silent tragedy, its quiet pain resounding indefinitely. But if this represents our species at its most sorrowful, it is also humankind at its most noble and dignified.

An ageing Russian Jewish couple living in America try to pay a visit to their only child on his birthday in order to give him his present. They are unable to see him, return home, have supper and go to bed. So much, so straightforward. But their boy is sick, deranged in his mind. He has tried to kill himself again, which is why they were turned away at the sanatorium where he is detained. They suffer mishaps on the way home, and a persistent wrong number disrupts their evening. We learn of other unhappy events and relentless troubles (both private and world changing) which this pair have quietly endured over the decades: revolution, emigration, genocide, destitution, psychosis.

The boy's own medical diagnosis, 'referential mania' (imagining 'everything happening around him [to be] a veiled reference to his personality and his existence'), makes us question our own reading of every detail of the story – something short stories in general, and Nabokov's in particular, always compel us to do. In short stories, as we have seen, every tiny feature seems substantial, alive with denotive suggestion and possibility. The parents' train briefly breaks down in a tunnel. A half-dead bird twitches in a puddle. A girl cries on a bus. The husband forgets he has given his wife the keys and has to wait outside their flat while she fetches supper. If these forlorn details mean something, as our training in reading short stories tell us they must (even if this might make us guilty of a manic referencing akin to the son's illness), then the story's final unknowable detail seems almost unbearably enigmatic, screaming wordlessly into infinity.

But there is one other detail from the story that allows its compassion, as well as its giddy metaphysics, to glow: the boy's birthday present. It has been carefully chosen because of his illness – ten miniature fruit jellies. We imagine their bright colours and delectable, scrumptious flavours, a sensory overload quite out of character with the subdued hues and muffled atmosphere of the story. Those ten little jars exude care and hope.

Nabokov's art, and never more particularly than in 'Signs and Symbols', is a quest to overcome the hapless, luckless nature of human existence. It is a private war against suffering, cruelty and misfortune, celebrating life's oddness and vitality, as well as the supremacy of love, while simultaneously rebuffing the convenient escape routes of sentimentality or despair.

'The Vane Sisters' (1951)

If 'Signs and Symbols' begs for the answers of an afterlife to reveal the patterns that might explain the pain, 'The Vane Sisters' seems to respond to that story's anxieties and open-endedness with the jubilant prospect that that most dynamic of Nabokovian components – human consciousness – outlasts death. The story is told in an unnerving first person, as *Lolita* will be, with subtle textual shifts that gently alert us to the narrator's possible unreliability – or rather, inadequacy. Inner, outer and otherworlds combine and overlap, obscuring, then illuminating, each other. Things are gained, then compromised; lost, then found.

A professor of French from a small women's college tells us about a dazzling icy afternoon, marked by scintillating icicles and then, later, the peculiar tinted shadow cast by a parking meter. That evening he happens upon a colleague, brazen Professor D., who once had an affair with a student, Sybil Vane, who killed herself when he ended it. It seems her sister, Cynthia, has just died.

This encounter activates the narrator's memories of the siblings, and we discover his self-importance, snobbery and cruel attention to the details of a person's anatomy and appearance (elements which link him, like his occupation, occasionally but not entirely to the impending Humbert

Humbert). He remembers Cynthia's paintings fondly but sneers at her spiritualist theories of ciphered signals from the post-mortem world, ideas which acquire for him a certain dread now that she is dead and he is home alone at night. He fears anything that might substantiate her conjecture. He has blurry dreams and writes them down. The story then concludes with a neat Nabokovian trick, carefully smuggling its resolution past the unseeing eyes of its own narrator.

The story is eerie, in many ways almost entirely encoded, but the narrator, for all his remarkable gifts of observation, cannot see the very signs he himself presents. His coldness and insensitivity – his lack of (artistic) imagination – deny him access to the tenderness, the secrets, the literal otherworldliness at the heart of an authentic existence beneath the shallow surveillances he is so pleased with. The particular vanity of the narrator (of the deceptively misnamed 'Vane Sisters', who are anything but 'vain') is his belief in his own brilliant faculty of vision, and it is this which ultimately dupes him (and us, if we're not careful).

Solipsists of varying degrees of menace and mental stability have been Nabokovian trademarks since (among others) Lev Glebovich Ganin in *Mary*, Martin Edelweiss in *Glory*, Hermann Hermann in *Despair*, the couple's son in 'Signs and Symbols', and thereafter Humbert Humbert (*Lolita*), Charles Kinbote (*Pale Fire*) and Hugh Person (*Transparent Things*). This self-absorbed insanity, where everything signifies the self, is a peril Nabokov relentlessly warns us about throughout his works.

'The Vane Sisters' argues against paranoia, pride, lunacy, superficiality, and the simple human tendency towards self-pity and gloom, when we close our eyes to the splendours of the cosmos and emblems of its perpetuity in the frontier-defying dignity of art. But it goes further than this: it is an unsettling work of fiction that confronts, and explodes, its own aesthetic boundaries as an imagined creation in human history.

This story's text is vulnerable not just to readers' missing the point but to their not taking the point far enough. The story's devious resolution, sneaked past even its own narrator, has understandably been missed by many readers. But those who have been aware of the closing trick – the acrostic contained in the final paragraph which reveals the sisters' otherworldly influence on the story – have sometimes also insisted on interpreting the story as a mere parable for art, not seeing that this itself confines art to a place within real-world dimensions rather than the boundary-flouting mystical and metaphysical spaces Nabokov asserts for it.

* * *

These two short stories, 'Signs and Symbols' and 'The Vane Sisters', encapsulate much of Nabokov's art. Both are painstakingly constructed and are necessarily precise in their use of language. Both understand what makes fiction work and therefore how it can be expanded or collapsed for an author's particular purposes. Both have secret signals and spinning, disorientating connotations associated with them.

Yet these 'secrets' are not simply riddles which merely attempt to bamboozle or annoy. They are part of the texture and meaning of the art. There is an oddity to Nabokov, an exhilarating abnormality to his work, which, combined with the difficulties his art presents, gauges our facility for intellectual and imaginative escapades. But his style – like Lewis Carroll's or James Joyce's in their vertiginous texts – is kind enough and engaging enough to do much of the magical work of discovery for us.

22

Poems, Plays, Eugene Onegin

Poems

Like many aspirant writers, the young Nabokov began his literary career as a poet, writing innumerable verses before his first novel, *Mary*, was published in 1926. The vast majority of his poems are in Russian, apart from a handful written in English during his undergraduate years at Cambridge from 1919 to 1922 and during his time in America in the 1940s and '50s. Given Nabokov's immense stature as a novelist and writer of short stories, his prose has always overshadowed his poetry, which has received only intermittent publication or translation into English. In the decades since his death, however, interest has steadily increased, with articles and editions trying to place Nabokov's poetry within the context of his other achievements.

Nabokov's own judgement on his early poetry, before he began to direct his lyrical instinct into some of the finest poetic prose of the twentieth century, has a certain reserved tenderness. He was astounded by the sheer bulk of juvenile verse he generated – poems probably numbering in the thousands, even allowing for some embellishment on Nabokov's part, and certainly far more than the five hundred or so that are now known to have survived. He was also fond of the subjects so many of his early verses took. In them he developed Byzantine imagery or crafted cynical reflections on the Revolution, as well as tackling the more recognizable Nabokovian themes: exile, memory, first love, butterflies, literature, the otherworld.

There is a straightforwardness to Nabokov's versification, not only in his early poems but throughout – something which is likely to disorientate (perhaps to the point of scepticism) a reader coming to his poetry from his very sophisticated novels and short stories. If not quite naive, Nabokov's poetic oeuvre is ardent, frank, forthright and undemanding, full of candid outcries and almost artlessly innocent pronouncements, and makes relatively conservative use of forms. The situations, subjects and settings tend to be somewhat hereditary, received directly from Romanticism: lonely lovers, moonlit nights, open fields, gloomy forests.

But there is more to it than this. If there is a limpid simplicity to the surface, there are darker depths and other, more familiar Nabokovian traits. Clever wordplay ('the ABC of the abyss'); original, often startling, imagery ('The rain has flown and burnt up in flight'); mysterious proto-Pnin or Humbert figures; and the usual wily jokes that flirt dangerously between wisdom, cunning and discourtesy.

We can gambol across the pages filled with these recognizable Nabokovian characteristics, allowing them to mingle, merge and rebound with the fiction we know well, relishing the young writer flexing his verbal muscles and licking his literary lips. We can question their apparent modesty, interrogate their innocence, asking ourselves – and Nabokov – what might lie beyond or behind such exteriors. Often, of course, the simplicity is just that, no more or less, but these are Nabokovian handiworks, and we can never quite be sure. Moreover, if he recycles familiar Romantic landscapes and images, he also reclaims them, salvaging their potency and meaning to be recast into his own time, idiom and identity.

We should not, moreover, overstate the plainness or orthodoxy of Nabokov's poetry. His forms and subjects can and do vary a great deal, especially in the relatively short collections most readers are likely to encounter. His infrequent divergences from nineteenth-century models are markedly conspicuous against the backdrop of his more conventional poetry – and few of the Romantic poets wrote verses honouring grapefruit or exploring the mysteries of the refrigerator …

A devastating cluster of poems, written around the time of his transition from Russian to English, probe the painful practicalities of this distressing shift. They explore the fun and bewilderment of new phrases and sayings, as well as the way language interacts with gesture and custom, confusing, enticing or breaking the heart. Nabokov probes how basic words can be potent or deficient, vessels of memory but only that: mere containers, seemingly inadequate to the monumental tasks of resurrection or survival. Leaving his Russian behind, all that is left are the phantoms of a slain language, forlornly reprimanding their executioner: not quite dead, but insufficiently alive to brandish their particular enchantment.

Several of Nabokov's novels feature poets and poems. Indeed, the climax of his career as a Russian novelist,

The Gift (1938), is a narrative about the birth and development of a writer, and the text features many of this character's youthful verses. A poem and a poet are even more central to what is perhaps the pinnacle of all Nabokov's art: *Pale Fire* (1962). Structured entirely around a 999-line poem by the fictitious New England poet John Shade, together with a surrounding foreword, commentary and index, the novel is a menacing and mercurial examination of literary criticism, friendship, madness, invention and loss. Veering routinely into dangerous, meticulous parody, it surveys the creative processes of poetry with scrupulous care – and the hazards of its interpretation with explosive curiosity.

The poem itself, also called 'Pale Fire', has attracted significant attention from those interested in Nabokov as a poet and indeed has been recently published separately from the novel. There can be no doubting the brilliance of the poem within the framework of the book *Pale Fire*, as well as its indisputable merits on its own terms, not least as a playful, endearing spoof of certain poetic forms and poets. However, the very intricacy of the poem and its uniqueness to its context – characterizing both old-fashioned John Shade and by association his unhinged commentator Charles Kinbote – limit its potential to be considered along with the rest of Nabokov's poetic output.

That being said, 'Pale Fire' is Nabokov's single greatest poetic achievement: a lyrical, charming work of affectionate parody, its undulating iambic pentameter and harmonious rhyming couplets belying (as Nabokov intended) its depths and its sophisticated consideration of its themes. If the poetic voice is not Nabokov's, it is nevertheless a perfect demonstration of his ability to create voices within voices, reflecting, echoing and distorting his own as part of his sumptuous world of playful profundity. 'Pale Fire' challenges the dimensions of time and space, just as *Pale Fire* confronts the form of the novel. Both assert the porous boundaries between Nabokov the novelist and Nabokov the poet.

One of the personal tragedies of his life, Nabokov felt, was that he never became a great Russian poet, a frustrated ambition which endured well into his adulthood, causing him anguish and disappointment which has often been overlooked. For all the charm and interest of his stand-alone Russian poems, they certainly seem to want for the essential genius and inimitable timbre of his other accomplishments. Yet 'Pale Fire', caught within the context of Nabokovian English prose, does stand as a substantial and durable poetic achievement, a work of playful parody and lasting beauty.

Plays

Many people are surprised to learn that Nabokov was also a playwright. Naturally, his exceptional talents as a novelist and short story writer have tended to eclipse his dramatic achievements – which are, with one notable exception, relatively slight. As a writer for the theatre, it often feels as though Nabokov is chasing butterflies with a hole in his net: sometimes he's successful, catching the odd specimen, but it is more luck than skill.

The complexity, force and fluidity of his novels and stories is not there. The dynamic subtlety of his prose style in fiction, the way he manipulates narrative structures, voices and dimensions, the provocative control of reader expectation, the need to read and reread his texts: all these struggle to find a place in his dramas. Ironically, the way we talk of Nabokov's fiction often seems to borrow a theatrical vernacular: the way he stage-manages his plots; the structural trapdoors he so ruthlessly springs open; the manner by which so many of his narrators soliloquize, drawing us into their confidence before whipping off the disguise and putting on a new costume, fleeing to the wings – or out of the theatre altogether.

All his plays were originally written in Russian, clustering first around his émigré years in Berlin during the early to mid-1920s, and then in Berlin and Paris towards the end of the 1930s. They range from a number of small-scale closet verse dramas to larger five-act prose plays. Some of them have only recently been published, and only in Russian, while others have now been translated into English. Shortly after his father's death, Dmitri Nabokov translated several of them, which were eventually published under the title *The Man from the USSR and Other Plays* (1984). Of those that are currently available, one stands out as approaching the depth and dexterity of some of his novels: *The Tragedy of Mister Morn* (1924).

The Tragedy of Mister Morn – Nabokov's first major work in any category – is a five-act verse play written in unrhymed iambic pentameter and first translated into English in 2012 in a compelling version by Anastasia Tolstoy and Thomas Karshan. The play tells of a masked king who rules his unspecified European country incognito and has re-established peace and prosperity after a bloody revolution. He falls in love with the wife of an expelled insurgent, and from here the inevitable tragedy of the title ensues as the dissident husband returns, provoking a reversion to chaos.

Morn is a seedbed, a place for Nabokov to unearth and cultivate many of the subjects to which he would return again and again in his novels: exile, memory, duplicity, thwarted love (and illicit lust). Subtler themes also emerge, especially the disorientating play between invention and reality, truth and falsity, work and games, as well as the role of the artist in society. In *Morn*, Nabokov forged a poignant study of inaccessible bliss and deluded fantasy, topics which key novels like *Despair* (1934), *Lolita* (1955) and *Pale Fire* (1962) would so mercilessly and powerfully explore.

After several unsuccessful attempts at Pushkinesque dramas in his early twenties, with *The Tragedy of Mister Morn* Nabokov unambiguously targeted Shakespeare, in both matter and method. To a degree, he succeeded, realizing much of the atmosphere and rhythm of Shakespeare's plays. Nabokov does this in part by means of the verse metre chosen but also through the opaque metaphorical language the characters regularly speak. In particular, *Morn* is full of Shakespearean motifs relating to kingship, authority and deceit, as well as classic exploratory images connecting throne and theatre, crown and art, power and poetry which Shakespeare's great cycle of history plays examined centuries earlier.

Both Shakespeare and Nabokov revel in turbulence and extravagance, intricacy and inscrutability, defying the limits of form and the proprieties of reason. But they both know, too, that artists, like kings, must perform the responsibilities of the power they wield: order and organization. In *Morn*, Nabokov created a playfully neo-Shakespearean drama of impeccably well-thought-out chaos and rational vivacity which anticipates the creative anarchy and imaginative reordering to come in his novels.

Eugene Onegin

Among Nabokov's works, only *Lolita* (1955) has caused more controversy than his annotated translation of Pushkin's *Eugene Onegin* (1964). His pugnaciously literal rendition, including an enormous commentary, appeared in four hefty volumes after more than a decade of intermittent toil and disputation. It was met with bruises and abuse, as well as thorny, abstruse debates about the philosophy of language and the geopolitics of philology. Certainly, by stubbornly refusing to accept all forms and standards of translation which he (at the time) found disagreeable, Nabokov alienated vast swaths of the literary and academic community, confirming for many his reputation as a self-aggrandizing elitist, belligerent and either blind or ignorant to the possibilities beyond his own preferred methodology.

The debates aroused by Nabokov's *Onegin* rumble on, as they should – since, for all the quarrelsome conceit from Nabokov, the considerations are important, helping us deliberate both what language is and what it does. Why, though, should general readers of Nabokov be concerned with this erudite but time-consuming behemoth?

If Pushkin is both the summit and the centre of Russian literature, as well as the equal of Shakespeare, Milton or Dante, it was largely Nabokov's contentious translation that conveyed to English-language readers why, making his *Eugene Onegin* a work that anyone interested in literature should be compelled to explore. Other translations, of course, had existed before; indeed, a rhymed version by Walter Arndt had appeared not long prior to Nabokov's and had won several prizes. Nabokov himself publicly condemned not only the infidelities obliged by Arndt's rhyme, but the misunderstandings of Russian lexicon and metre, as well as the apparent obliviousness to the literary and historical backgrounds that enrich Pushkin's world. Nabokov's version (actually completed some years before, but publishing wrangles meant it appeared only after Arndt's) was to be a vindication of Pushkin and his work, his sensibility and his style, whatever the consequences to, as he put it, 'elegance, euphony, clarity, good taste, modern usage, and even grammar'.

Nabokov's *Eugene Onegin* gives unequalled entry for non-Russian speakers into Russia's greatest work of literature, but it is not trouble-free access. We have to fumble with a multitude of keys, patiently reinserting them into a lock that at times seems to belong to not only the wrong door but the wrong house in the wrong hamlet. We might well wonder what is wrong with lyrical free translations, which surely can preserve enough literal accuracy within their verse harmony to be sufficient.

Unfortunately, such renderings tend to severely crush or distort Pushkin's meticulous meanings (along with the elegant sparseness of his style and the frugal music therein). On their own terms, as *English* poems, they may well be graceful and melodious. But the grace and melodies are not Pushkin's, and such translations further lack the subtlety and accuracy of his original. Of course, as Nabokov knew, his translation had its own clumsiness and occasional obscurity. But he also knew that while a translation could not hope to match Pushkin's own music, it could accurately match his meaning.

Nabokov demonstrates a discordant, often uncomfortable devotion to his subject, but this is a faithfulness that bears fruit, even if it accordingly needs more work and commitment than the tuneful flings and fragrant one-night stands of uninhibited free translations.

Nabokov's *Eugene Onegin*, fortunately, comes with a marriage guidance manual in the form of its thousand-plus pages of commentary and index. The commentary is huge and often very unscholarly, with a mischievous tone and teasing approach to the task in hand, traits familiar to fans of Nabokov's fiction. Its insights are useful, unusual and often quite unexpected. The research is unequivocally painstaking and unconditionally passionate, offering unparalleled access to the contexts and minutiae of the poem. Its opinions are routinely confrontational and wildly pejorative, making nitpicking and hair-splitting into Olympic events. It is, in short, absolutely outrageous and totally unmissable. And yet, understandably, it is likely to be studied only by an ardent minority.

Beyond the elephantine commentary, if it can be separated from the translation, Nabokov's *Onegin* is one that angers and alienates. It is not – ironically – great poetry; indeed, it is barely even poetry. But, paradoxically, it is astonishingly close to Pushkin's sense and meaning, exploring and elucidating with a novelist's eye – rather than a poet's ear – the detail and personality of the text, its distinctive and inimitable status.

23
Letters, Chess, Lepidoptery

Letters

As befits a prolific, oft-exiled author before the age of email or instant messaging, Nabokov wrote a staggering number of letters. For a writer so keen that his finished product (the carefully crafted literary artefact; the prudently edited public image) be the only one on display, his letters present a priceless opportunity to see Nabokov with his guard slightly down, away from the charade of fame and masks of art.

Three sets of correspondence are particularly valuable: those between Nabokov and Edmund Wilson, the American novelist and critic he befriended soon after arriving in the United States in 1940; those between Nabokov and his younger sister Elena; and those between Nabokov and Véra Evseevna Slonim, his wife, editor and enduring confidante – and the devoted first reader of his works.

The Nabokov-Wilson letters form a dynamic, sometimes tumultuous, sub-narrative to Nabokov's nineteen or so years living in America. We see the recent immigrant, anxious for work and the opportunity to start a second literary career in middle age; we perceive, for a time, the frailty and insecurity behind the self-assured persona, as his acquaintance with Wilson encouraged Nabokov to reveal his situation.

It was, nevertheless, a curious liaison. Wilson habitually utilizes Nabokov as a handy Russian tutor, while at the same time pointing out anomalies in the émigré's English. This proved a volatile, lopsided and ultimately detrimental master-pupil relationship. Wilson likes to show Teacher how good his (very wobbly) Russian has become and how much facility this gives him with the great Russian writers – something which would eventually come to destroy their association as they squabbled, then brawled, over Nabokov's translation of *Eugene Onegin*.

From their letters, we garner often amusing insights into Nabokov's new reading experiences. He was grateful for the Jane Austen tip-off but surly at Wilson's recommendation of Henry James, the latter coming in for Nabokov's unrelenting and scathing ire across multiple correspondences. We do not gain many direct insights into Nabokov's own work. What we do get are fascinating pen portraits of people Nabokov came across, on campus or when away hunting butterflies. Detailed, charming, forbidding: we observe Nabokov filing away their résumés for possible employment in future fictions.

If the Nabokov-Wilson letters are tense and combative, the two writers endlessly embroiled in a game of epistolary one-upmanship, those between Nabokov and his sister Elena are touching, egalitarian, compassionate. She shared not only a childhood with Nabokov but a love for, and knowledge of, Russia and Russian literature that

Wilson – as the American well knew – could only dream of. The siblings did not see each other for over twenty years, parted first by a war and then by an ocean, but their separation offered as recompense a precious and loving correspondence providing insights into Nabokov the writer, scientist, husband and father. Sharp, smart and altruistic, Elena was a vital spiritual, intellectual and emotional link to his family, Europe and Russia during his American years, and their letters reveal a side to Nabokov often overlooked, but one at the heart of his work. He is direct, honest, confessional, vulnerable and kind, delighting in the details of routine family news, and is fascinated by and interested in the lives of other people – not as novel fodder, but as human beings close to his heart.

Alongside the Nabokov-Elena letters can be placed those between Nabokov and Véra, his wife of over fifty years. They reveal a zealous and determined but also insecure and self-effacing writer, and the early letters from the 1920s show the usual misunderstandings, raptures and worries of any relationship in its embryonic and then burgeoning years, as each partner gets to know the other a little better (and a little worse). We gain insights into some of Nabokov's daily routines and activities as the nascent couple spend time together, then apart, Vladimir telling her of his passions and disappointments and describing his writing and tutoring, swimming and sunbathing.

Although Nabokov would claim his marriage 'cloudless' and their letters glow with love and tenderness, there were troubles. Nabokov's intense, reckless affair with Irina Guadanini in 1937 was a crisis for their marriage; health and financial concerns persisted; the ascent of Hitler further dented their already battered view of Germany. We see, in the 1930s, Nabokov frantically trying to provide for his family as well as sustain his growing reputation. Work trips around Europe generated letters which are full of fondness, as well as signs of the difficulties they faced, internally and externally.

While the rate of their correspondence drops off after the 1930s – increasing economic, domestic and political security meant they were simply together more – the passion and mutual affection is never dimmed, nor is Nabokov's ecstasy at receiving a letter from his wife. Their letters are a fascinating document of a marriage and a compelling insight into the fluctuating contexts of Nabokov's life as he progressed from desperation to success, anonymity to eminence. We have only one side of the correspondence – none of Véra's letters to Vladimir survive – yet theirs was truly a partnership, and the emotional, administrative and intellectual backing Véra gave her husband allowed him to endure, then thrive. His letters to her are a loving testament of that lifelong support and fierce devotion, which was never subservient but always reciprocal.

A considerable but disparate group of professional letters – to editors, publishers and so forth – helps provide insight into Nabokov's fiction. Nabokov was notoriously rebarbative and frequently defensive regarding his work, yet his communications with his editors and publishers give us otherwise forbidden access to his own thoughts on his output and some of the creative processes that spawned them. Occasional synopses and clarifications allow us to glimpse at his meanings and methodologies.

These letters also allow us to observe a quibbling salesman-agent-lawyer, eager to negotiate while also being a suspicious custodian of his own financial and legal rights. Cold, precise letters issuing threats over copyright violation must have terrified their recipients, their lethal fluency and icy civility producing as delicious a fright as one of his novels' lucid lunatics.

Nabokov takes an obsessive interest in the cover art for his books – unsurprising from a writer of such visual insight and aesthetic perspicacity. For Nabokov, the designs were an interpretative as well as commercial concern. And if his domineering supervision exasperated his publishers, it also allowed them (and us) to see his vision more clearly.

Taken as a whole, Nabokov's vast and varied correspondence shows a deeply committed and unusually versatile writer, thinker and human being. The letters exhibit both his flaws and his qualities, his blemishes and his genius, as well as providing powerful, immediate and unabridged insights into the everyday existence of a man who created art for eternity.

Chess

Nabokov was a lifelong setter of chess puzzles and problems, those teasing conundrums in which acquaintance with chess rules and pieces is used to solve a chess-related problem. Such puzzles can also run counter to the way the game is usually played – for instance, compelling one's adversary to help checkmate one's own king – and are more often than not designed for aesthetic satisfaction rather than any potential strategic benefit in a match.

Chess occurs frequently in Nabokov's novels and stories. *The Luzhin Defense* (1929) is named for a chess move of its titular prodigy, who becomes a grandmaster; *Invitation to a Beheading* (1936) features nightmarish games between a condemned prisoner and his duplicitous executioner; Fyodor, poet-hero of *The Gift* (1938), also composes chess problems; in *The Real Life of Sebastian Knight* (1941) the eponymous hero, as well as two heroines (Clare Bishop and the mysterious Nina Toorovetz), are named for chess pieces (*toora/tura* is the Russian word for rook); Humbert, Pnin and Kinbote (*Lolita*, 1955; *Pnin*, 1957; and *Pale Fire*, 1962) all play chess at certain junctures of their novels.

Across these texts, the game's cerebral orderliness torments the ferocious, often sensual maladies contained in the narratives. In these books, chess and chess patterns are seductively analogous, their representations and correspondences as tempting, deceptive and catastrophic for us as readers as their characters. Nabokov lures us into formulating and utilizing chess analogies, tricking us into relying on comfort in convenient signs and symbols. The ruthless rationality of chess helps distort reality and generate obsession and hysteria, ultimately collapsing sense and sanity.

More subtly, novels like *The Gift*, *Pale Fire* and *Bend Sinister* (1947) seem to model their whole narratives on chess problems, with maniacal final moves. Nabokov compared his inspiration for *Lolita* to an idea for a chess puzzle and often maintained that all his works could each be regarded as being a kind of problem of literary chess. The devilish setter establishes distinctive, never-to-be-repeated rules in a form of eloquent insanity, with outlandish complications and terrifying acuity.

A world as entire and self-contained as a madman's mind, as enticing as the sixty-four hypnotic squares of the chessboard, is created for a one-off game. The setter might turn the rules upside down, play them back to front or inside out, order the game to occur in three (or eight or eighty) dimensions. These chess-plots might also have two queens – or half a king – vanishing bishops, false knights, all played on a liquefying surface, white and black running into a splurge of vibrant greys.

Elsewhere, the tidy monochrome of the board might burst into a detonation of coloured quadrilaterals, a disco kaleidoscope, as chess pieces disintegrate and restructure the rainbow game – and self-replicating pawns don a regal pose.

Lepidoptery

Butterflies were a constant companion to Nabokov's life and its many vicissitudes, his interest developing from his father's own massive collection. From boyhood books studied on an uncle's knee to adolescent hunting excursions in exile, his mind consumed by love and poetry as he chased down words and wings, it was an all-consuming passion. Later, chauffeured by the ever-faithful Véra (Nabokov himself never learned to drive), the great landscapes of America – Arizona, Colorado, Wyoming, Montana – became the location for the further chasing of magical discoveries: researching and composing *Lolita*, the novel taking shape on hundreds of index cards, the specimens accumulating in the trunk. Nabokov would travel farther, and get to know America better, than Steinbeck or Kerouac, the pursuit of butterflies leading him, his wife and his writing to vast new places, both earthly and imaginative.

Nabokov's final years, back in Europe, were dominated by expeditions to pursue his infatuation – in the Alps or islands of the Mediterranean. Butterflies, too, directed his last literary thoughts: plans for a technical study of butterflies in art and a complete catalogue of European Lepidoptera – for Nabokov was no mere amateur enthusiast but a first-class, if not major, professional scientist, and his work informed and extended the subject he cared so much about.

To this day, Nabokov remains a notable, if often highly controversial, figure in lepidoptery, splitting scientific opinions as much as literary ones, especially regarding his doubt of aspects of Darwin's theories, as well as his provocative views on mimicry and genetics. Here – as he sometimes conceded – the writer's desire for patterns, subtlety, enchantment and trickery often overrode his strictly scientific sensibility. If some of his views seem, especially today, a touch preposterous, we should remember not only that Darwin is questioned far more than he used to be, but that science, like art, is a field for experimentation and investigation, where absolutes can be interrogated. As Darwin himself knew better than anyone, nothing is fixed, and change is not just inevitable but inherent – to life and the processes of scholarship.

Despite Nabokov's occasional isolation from contemporary scientific thought, hundreds of specialist and non-specialist books and articles now devote themselves to the legacy and significance of his occupation with butterflies, helping to unravel some of the mysteries of his life, science and art. Many showcase his exquisite scientific drawings. An immensely skilled illustrator, Nabokov created over a thousand painstakingly precise studies of the microscopic structures inside butterflies, as well as analyses of their wing colours and patterning, his understanding of construction, texture and design as exceptional as if he had invented butterflies himself.

Butterflies, like chess, colour Nabokov's books. Images, parallels, ciphers: they flush and layer the text, tinting it, intensifying it, containing elusive, ingenious puns or even fainter connotations available only to accomplished lepidopterists. As ever with Nabokov, wonder and erudition are in playful harmony, ready to excite, enthral and perplex. Some entomological evocations, however, elude even the scientists and textual hunters, their true meaning forever hidden in private delight between Nabokov and his wife, Véra.

Over five hundred references to butterflies flicker and flutter through Nabokov's fiction, all of which have been catalogued and indexed by Dieter E. Zimmer's stupendous *A Guide to Nabokov's Butterflies and Moths* (2001). Butterflies mattered to Nabokov, and they should matter to his readers as much as his other contexts: chess, painting, Pushkin, the cinema; Russia, Germany, America and Switzerland.

Nabokov is careful not to impose his passion and profession on indifferent readers, a vigilance to human sensibility which has often allowed his lepidopterological allusions to flurry by either unseen or actively overlooked, even by his most astute devotees. Yet butterflies are a fundamental aspect to understanding many of the depths of his work. So, to close this book, we might briefly observe examples from his fiction.

Butterflies are a necessary part not only to the plot, characterization and provenance of *The Gift* (1938), the novel's shimmering esoterica fulfilling many of Nabokov's unrealized ambitions for hunting Asian butterflies. They also influence its tone and texture, the meaning of its metaphysical and recounted journeys, the pathos of its generational communions, and the subtleties of its aesthetic pursuits.

Similarly, the tender, troubling allure of *Pale Fire* (1962) is increased by its repeated associations of butterflies (and birds) with family, mortality, eternity and the unknown. No mere stock images for poetic colour or thematic connectivity, Nabokov's literary portraits of butterflies have a realism and commitment to accuracy which heighten their poignant power in this dazzling novel so replete with insanity, deception and despair. One tantalizing instance will have to suffice.

A minute before poet John Shade's murder, a *Vanessa*, or red admiral, butterfly (hitherto associated both with his wife, Sybil, and, by association, with the daughter he lost to suicide, Hazel) lands on his arm. Is it a warning of danger ahead from his wife – or perhaps a compassionate gesture from his dead daughter from beyond the grave, as they prepare to meet again? It is a rapturous, lyrical and profoundly moving passage, one perhaps unmatched in all Nabokov's work, his prose finding new heights (and depths) as love, death and butterflies dissolve and intermingle on the page. It is a fitting climax to his greatest novel.[10]

---

10 The section in question is Kinbote's note to lines 993–995 of 'Pale Fire'.

FURTHER READING

Vladimir Nabokov: The Russian Years
Vladimir Nabokov: The American Years

Brian Boyd

The first, and still the only, major critical biography of Nabokov, Boyd's stunning two volumes give us unparalleled insight into this very private writer – not least because Boyd himself was granted several audiences with Nabokov's widow, Véra, and other family members, as well as access to a number of important archives in Switzerland and America. He is able to forensically investigate the many environments Nabokov inhabited, especially with regard to his aristocratic Russian upbringing and the alien, ostentatious world of academic America. The way this elusive, often aloof writer engaged with and reacted to his changing domains is sympathetically, but by no means uncritically, examined. Few people understand Nabokov's output – its complexities, traps and pleasures – as well as Boyd, and he is a commanding, faithful guide, prudently connecting work and world, negotiating the life and the art with an ideal mixture of interrogation and respect. Boyd's *Nabokov* is enthusiastic without being a hagiography and is likely to remain unsurpassed for some time to come. Essential.

The Garland Companion to Vladimir Nabokov

ed. Vladimir E. Alexandrov

A treasure trove of over seventy essays on a multitude of Nabokovian subjects. Not only his specific works (novels, stories and so on) but topics such as his language, humour, style and translations are explored. Nabokov's relationships with some twenty writers – including Pushkin, Poe, Bely, Joyce, Flaubert and Updike – are given individual treatment and help widen our understanding of Nabokov's influences and influence.

The Cambridge Companion to Nabokov

ed. Julian W. Connolly

An excellent collection of academic essays covering many components of Nabokov's broad career, including some helpful wide-angle lenses, such as Nabokov and cinema.

Vladimir Nabokov in Context

ed. David M. Bethea & Siggy Frank

This collection of over thirty relatively short essays takes Nabokov out of his preferred isolation and positions him within the numerous environments – both physical and intellectual – he occupied or has come to inhabit. A vital and valuable addition to contemporary Nabokov studies.

Nabokov: The Mystery of Literary Structures

Leona Toker

Focusing mainly on the first, Russian, half of Nabokov's writing career, but bookended by *Pnin* and *Lolita*, this monograph is a profound, fearless and beautifully written consideration of Nabokov's art, rigorously connecting his metaphysics and aesthetics.

Nabokov's Women: The Silent Sisterhood of Textual Nomads

ed. Elena Rakhimova-Sommers

An enthralling and very welcome contribution to Nabokov studies that, via an excellent group of contemporary scholars, explores the subtleties and paradoxes of his extraordinary heroines. We come to understand their elusive, often hidden, but powerful voices in innovative and endlessly captivating new ways. A brilliant and indispensable book, with an especially fascinating chapter on *Pale Fire* by Matthew Roth.

Vladimir Nabokov and the Art of Play

Thomas Karshan

Taking play as his theme, Karshan elegantly and meticulously shows how this thread runs imaginatively through all of Nabokov's work. Superbly methodical, rich in detail, and full of absorbing ideas.

Reading Lolita in Tehran: A Memoir in Books

Azar Nafisi

Rightly a bestseller, this tale of defiance and enchantment is not only a mesmerizing expansion of *Lolita*'s metaphors but also shows us the fundamental importance of literature – individually and collectively.

That Other World: Nabokov and the Puzzle of Exile

Azar Nafisi

The precursor to her international blockbuster, now finally available in English, Nafisi's academic study takes one of Nabokov's key themes – exile – and magnifies its meaning to enfold all aspects of his art. An exhilarating, perceptive voyage of discovery.

Véra (Mrs Vladimir Nabokov)

Stacy Schiff

A wonderful examination of a love story, a marriage – and a crucial literary partnership. Nabokov's wife committed her life to her husband's work (especially as editor and first reader) and he returned the devotion by dedicating all his books to her. This intriguing, important book restores the key position of Véra – too often overlooked – in Nabokov's life and art.

Nabokov's Pale Fire: The Magic of Artistic Discovery

Brian Boyd

A priceless and scrupulous guide on how to read (and reread and re-reread) Nabokov's greatest work. Marvellously organized and full of perfectly pitched excitement. Boyd's theses on *Pale Fire* have inevitably shifted over time – his approach here is different from his argument in *Vladimir Nabokov: The American Years* – but this is part of the mystery and magnificence of the novel as an ever-changing, elusive masterpiece.

Find What the Sailor Has Hidden: Vladimir Nabokov's Pale Fire

Priscilla Meyer

A book that is as eccentric and idiosyncratic as Charles Kinbote himself, but nonetheless hugely entertaining and full of fascinating ideas – chiefly, that *Pale Fire* is an amalgamation of Anglo-American culture. Not recommended for *Pale Fire* first-timers, but an engaging, if sometimes exasperating, work for those more familiar with the text and its critical history.

Anatomy of a Short Story: Nabokov's Puzzles, Codes, 'Signs and Symbols'

ed. Yuri Leving

This four-hundred-page book contains thirty-three essays exploring every possible facet of Nabokov's astonishing six-page short story 'Signs and Symbols' (1948). Everything from its structure, themes and contexts to its characters and objects is explored (including, mouth-wateringly, three essays on the story's ten fruit jars alone). A delightful indulgence and a wonderful work of collaborative scholarship.

Keys to The Gift:
A Guide to Vladimir Nabokov's Novel

Yuri Leving

A vast and painstaking examination of Nabokov's last, longest and greatest Russian novel. *The Gift* (1938) is a densely allusive work, rich in Russian literature, and Leving carefully reveals many of the precious subtleties hidden within the luxuriant prose.

Lolita in the Afterlife:
On Beauty, Risk, and Reckoning with the Most Indelible and Shocking Novel of the Twentieth Century

ed. Jenny Minton Quigley

As its humorously extended subtitle indicates, this is a vivacious collection of incisive contemporary essays (including one entitled '*Lolita* in Lockdown') exploring how *Lolita* has fixed its place in our culture, for good or ill. Like the novel itself, it is by turns funny, poignant and insightful, and this is a valuable modern assortment from a great range of minds, with an intriguing introductory essay by the book's editor (who is also the daughter of *Lolita*'s original American publisher).

Nabokov at the Movies: Film Perspectives in Fiction

Barbara Wyllie

Nabokov's Cinematic Afterlife

Ewa Mazierska

Two valuable, fascinating books exploring the influence of film on Nabokov's fiction and the way his work has been interpreted in cinema.

Nabokov's Theatrical Imagination

Siggy Frank

An absorbing and very original book investigating how notions of the theatre, theatricality and performance stage their way through both Nabokov's life and art.

Nabokov and the Art of Painting

Gerard de Vries & D. Barton Johnson

Nabokov was fascinated by painting, even training to become a painter at one point. Art and artists, colour and light, are vital components of his novels, and these essays explore in wonderful detail their importance within his fictional worlds, their dialogues and depth.

Fine Lines:
Vladimir Nabokov's Scientific Art

ed. Stephen H. Blackwell & Kurt Johnson

A gorgeous and captivating book exploring Nabokov's delectable and tremendously detailed lepidoptery drawings, with some terrific accompanying essays.

Letters to Véra

trans. & ed. Olga Voronina & Brian Boyd

An intimate portrait of the long marriage between Véra and Vladimir Nabokov, this huge book presents dozens of his tender letters across the decades. Mischievous, adoring, laconic, excitable: we see Nabokov constantly spellbound by both the world around him and his recipient.

Lectures on Literature
Lectures on Russian Literature

ed. Fredson Bowers

These two collections, a selection of Nabokov's university lectures from the 1940s and '50s, give fascinating insights not only into his views on the giants of literature – Austen, Chekhov, Dickens, Flaubert, Gogol, Kafka, Joyce, Proust – but also his concept of literature more generally. Replete with facsimiles of Nabokov's annotations to his teaching copies, as well as some of his famous maps and diagrams, this is an intriguing and invaluable journey through a great novelist's mind.

Strong Opinions

Vladimir Nabokov

'I think like a genius, I write like a distinguished author, and I speak like a child' – so begins this voluble, haughty, shrewd and unmissable assortment of interviews from the 1960s and early 1970s. The range of topics is extraordinary: from the premiere of Kubrick's film of *Lolita* to why that novel was its author's favourite, from lepidoptery to judgements on other writers and some rare insights into his working relationship with his beloved wife, Véra.

Think, Write, Speak:
Uncollected Essays, Reviews, Interviews and Letters to the Editor

ed. Brian Boyd & Anastasia Tolstoy

A huge, perhaps final, gathering of material from across Nabokov's career: student essays at Cambridge University, letters to editors, lectures, occasional pieces, and interviews given at the end of his life.

ACKNOWLEDGEMENTS

I would like to thank Steve Lally for his enthusiastic response to an early chapter. A late convert to Nabokov, he now evangelizes with the true zeal of the born-again.

Stephen Johnson, the great music writer and broadcaster, has been a wonderful and insightful correspondent regarding Russian literature: thank you, Stephen.

Erik Eklund, fast becoming an exceptionally gifted Nabokovian, has been a kind supporter of my book. Erik's work, especially on the more esoteric religious aspects of Nabokov's output, has been a fascinating – and vital – recent contribution to scholarship. Do hope I can buy you those owed pints in Scotland soon, my friend.

My editor, Elyse Lyon, has been, as always, infinitely patient with the changes I have wanted to make to the book, as well as being alert to my clumsy errors, missed points and frequent slip-ups. As ever, she sees what I cannot and always knows what I am trying to say. She is a writer's dream. Any errors are, of course, my own.

My wife's family – Dianne, Kitt, Jim and Miriam – were a patient audience as I prattled on about the book during a recent visit from the States. My grandmother-in-law's interrogations on *Lolita* as we strolled the Edinburgh streets were a terrifying treasure. Thank you, *team Bret Harte*, for your love and many kindnesses: so glad we will be meeting up again in Arizona so soon after this book is published.

Most of this book was written in Istanbul. I would like to thank the fine people of this diverse, invigorating city for some of the initial inspiration behind this work. My wife, to whom this book is dedicated, also knows how special this city is to us.

Finally, at the risk of indulgence and absurdity, thank you, Vladimir Vladimirovich Nabokov. The inexhaustible riches of your worlds are a constant source of inspiration, consolation and delight. I hope this book will lead people back again and again to your extraordinary art.

Milton Keynes UK
Ingram Content Group UK Ltd.
UKHW012113100124
435815UK00003B/25